The Book of the
SOUTHERN MOGULS

Part One: N, N1 Classes

Ian Sixsmith

Richard Derry

Irwell Press Ltd.

First published in the United Kingdom in 2018.
by Irwell Press Limited, 59A, High Street, Clophill,
Bedfordshire MK45 4BE
Printed by Akcent Media, UK

Contents

Locomotives in these books, for clarity and ease of reference, have always been presented in their BR number sequence. This doesn't quite work so well for the Maunsell Moguls, for the Southern was somewhat cavalier with numbering and the lists pre-Bulleid have a promiscuous look to them. The Ns and N1s are arranged in The Record as below.

Acknowledgements

Allan C. Baker, Eric Youldon, Mike King, Peter Groom; Gavin Glenister, Leslie Tibble and Mark Arscott for the drawings; all helped to rescue the project! For which, many thanks.

The original N, 810, in the austere SECR grey livery, at Bricklayers Arms, from where it worked for its first decade or so. Large white number, SE&CR plate on cabside, snifting valves on smokebox, piston tail rod, four lamp irons, 'stirrup' step hung from the motion bracket instead of a front footstep. transporttreasury

829 in the Maunsell lined green about 1930, equipped with extra lamp irons for the Southern six disc route codes. The train is the up Atlantic Coast Express, in turn new Maunsell stock. The location is the double track section near Pill Bridge, a mile or so to the south of Barnstaple Junction. On the buffer beam is the elaborate serif 'No' with a dash and a point under the little 'o', followed by the number, in this case that of Exmouth Junction's 829, a 'Woolworth'.

Introductory Notes

It is sobering to reflect that the N Class originated *over a century* ago... Maunsell was appointed Chief Mechanical Engineer to the South Eastern and Chatham Railway in 1913 at a difficult time, the transfer of its works from Longhedge in south London to Ashford having left the railway in some difficulties with respect to locomotive provision. Maunsell has been described as a manager rather than a locomotive designer. On his appointment he found drawings of Wainwright's new 4-4-0, later the L Class, of which Beyer Peacock were only able to undertake ten. He accordingly arranged for Borsig in Germany to build twelve – the inevitably-named 'Germans'. From his appointment to the Grouping in 1923 he was responsible for the introduction of three new types; the N 2-6-0 with 5ft 6in wheels, the K 2-6-4T (more or less the same but with 6ft wheels) and the N1 2-6-0, similar to the N but with three cylinders. During the same period much of his time was spent on Government work, managing and organising both here and in France. Belgian rolling stock had been 'evacuated' to France out of reach of the Germans but all drawings, patterns, stores and the rest had been left behind. Ashford 'stepped into the breach in no uncertain manner' (C.S. Cocks, *History of Southern Locomotives to 1938*, *Proceedings* of the Institution of Locomotive Engineers, 1948) and Maunsell at Ashford oversaw Ashford's role as a depot 'for all details necessary for repair'. This required new drawings, patterns and templates being made from returned worn parts to keep up the supply of spares. He was also a member of the Association of Railway Engineers (ARLE) working on a range of 'national' standard locos for British companies.

For its day the first N was a modern-looking locomotive; numbered 810, it was completed at Ashford in July 1917. Design work, begun as far back as 1914, had been much delayed by war-related activities. 810 had a taper boiler though this, oddly, is not so apparent as on a GW or Stanier loco. The N was also remarkable in a small way, being designed for easy servicing. Below the running plate, the new mogul looked like one of the contemporary 2-8-0s recently issued from Derby; big cylinders and Walschaerts valve gear to an arrangement still appearing on BR Standards more than forty years later.

The new engine had a single slidebar and a new type of superheater, devised by Maunsell: *In this header the saturated and superheated steam are carried in chambers along the full length of the header and not as the usual type in alternate chambers. The dividing wall between the two chambers is enlarged at intervals to accommodate the element fastening bolts. The saturated steam chamber is enlarged to take the steam pipe connection to the boiler and the superheat steam chamber is enlarged to take the main steam pipe to the cylinder flange. The headers are fitted with anti-vacuum or header relief valves.*

The leading truck was Cartazzi type with the slide enclosed in an oilbath. The taper boiler was similar in most respects to the GW model. It carried a dome used only for the feed water – it did not house a regulator – the water passing over a series of trays. The regulator, as in GW practice was in the smokebox combined with the superheater header. C.S. Cocks declared the N to be 'Probably the first engine in this country to have a combination of high superheat with long travel valves'. Peter Swift (*Maunsell Moguls*, Ian Allan, 2012) notes that the N combined 'the most advanced features of the GWR 4300 2-6-0 and the S&DJ 2-8-0, having a high superheat taper boiler and long travel valves driven by outside Walschaerts valve gear'. H.C. Casserley once made the same point: 'It is not therefore too far fetched to suggest that No.810 was in fact a Midlandised version of the GWR 43XX class'.

810 was finished in the wartime SECR grey livery and Maunsell had 810 tried and tested in short measure. Trials were run between Ashford and Tonbridge and deemed successful. It was then allocated to Bricklayers Arms shed in London, where it was used on the heavy

The same location with 857 in the early 1930s; same livery as 829. The curious cab windows are clear in this view, an oval and a circular window each side. There was a mass influx of new Ns to the West in 1925; in numbers, with an ample margin of power over all the existing 0-6-0s and 4-4-0s, this was sufficient to transform the workings.

Richborough goods, at the time normally double headed by a pair of class C 0-6-0s. So a modest mixed traffic mogul it may have looked to us in later years, but at the time it was a large, powerful and modern locomotive.

Fifteen further Ns were built at Ashford, ordered months after 810's appearance in September 1917 and these were turned out as SECR 811-821 from June 1920-October 1922. The final 'SECR' three, 823-825, appeared in 1923, by which time the SECR had been absorbed in the new Southern Railway. The last was actually in SR livery and numbered A825.

The Association of Railway Engineers (ARLE) as already mentioned, was engaged in preparing a design of standard locomotive to be used by all British companies. A 2-8-0 and a 2-6-0 were worked up at Ashford but interest waned once the Great War ended and Grouping, not Nationalisation, was in prospect. The ARLE decided on a mixed traffic 2-6-0 as a priority but only the larger companies (though Maunsell's SECR was a comparative minnow) such as the MR, GW and so on seem to have been really interested. Holcroft (*Locomotive Adventure*) records the demise of the *grand idée: Though an acceptable scheme for a 2-6-0 was in the making, the method of design by committee, circulation of its draft and approved minutes and drawings was so slow that the war was over long before any working drawings could be available.*

Here the Government intervened. It had conceived a plan that the prospective standard 2-6-0 should be built at Woolwich Arsenal after the War, to ease the employment effects of munitions manufacture coming to an end there. Apparently the Arsenal was advised of this as early as 1915. Come the Armistice, no such standard loco was in prospect so the Government ordered instead that Woolwich would build a hundred of Maunsell's Ns. It was of course a good choice technically; after all, as Phil Atkins has written in *The Railway Magazine*, the N '…could justifiably claim to be the most advanced mixed traffic engine in the country, with its taper boiler, high superheat, and long travel piston valves'. Ashford duly supplied the drawings and specimen components. It was a strange episode and an almost classic Government intervention disaster; Woolwich could build the locos but had no expertise in boiler construction (or any other locomotive parts for that matter) so a hundred of these and ten spares had to be sub-contracted to private contractors, the great part to North British and the rest to Kitson and Robert Stephenson.

The ARLE pontifications showed that no company would want a hundred Ns; a handful of what would be entirely non-standard locos would be just as unattractive. Time passed, costs rose; the Irish took some 'kits' of parts to build locos at knock-down prices and the Metropolitan took a few to build into 2-6-4Ts.

The natural home for the Ns, in any number, was of course the Southern which duly picked up fifty for half the cost of building them itself. Fifty were purchased in 1924 though many were incomplete, and there was much work still to do at Ashford. These became A826-A875, the last assembled in September 1925. The first to be observed at work had been 'A20' in 1923. Apparently two, 'A20' and 'A35' 'were loaned to the SR by the Arsenal authorities for trial running'. How it was that Ashford would need to 'trial' what were in effect its own engines is unclear. Presumably it had to be confirmed that Woolwich had made no unwanted alterations. A20 worked from Ashford in April-May 1923 and A35 for a couple of weeks in May on London-Ashford trains after which both engines were returned to Woolwich. There was no renumbering of the engines carrying the same numbers at that time in the SR Eastern Section list. It was not until mid-May 1924 that the first two of the Woolwich engines purchased by the SR were hauled dead from Woolwich to Ashford and the first six were placed in service towards the end of the month. A825, built at Ashford and completed in November 1923, began work on or about 1 December or roughly six months before the Woolwich batch. According to the surviving Works records the first six of the above entered service thus:- 826 3/6/24; 827 31/5/24; 828 2/6/24; 829 15/7/24; 830 13/6/24; 831 26/6/24. Such Ns were from thereon nicknamed 'Woolworths'; not in a simple mangling of 'Woolwich' but apparently a nod to the novel cheap department stores then spreading across the land. More followed, with an order for fifteen Ns in 1930, all built at Ashford and delivered 1932-34, numbered 1400-1414. There were (inevitably) modifications…

New N A830 waits to leave the old Exeter Queen Street station upon arrival with a train from Ilfracombe, 9 May 1930.

A very dirty A861 with only traces showing of the lined green. Most original features still there; of all the 'later' details only front steps and extra lamp irons have appeared. transporttreasury

Southern A870 at Ashford works about 1930; tender of L1 4-4-0 787 in the distance. transporttreasury

A871 (showing where the lamps were stowed) in original condition, amid the maze of tracks and blackened buildings that made up the rambling Bricklayers Arms shed in south London. It would have been built with the extra 'middle' pair of lamp irons. Snifting valves lively, long piston tail rod and no front steps, tapered buffer shanks (later they were parallel). To the right is the so-called 'St Patricks Shed' with the monstrous water tank behind; the empty space beyond was later filled by a water softener tank and associated structures. transporttreasury

8

Devil in the Detail
Given their numbers and longevity, it is hardly surprising that 'modifications' abounded in the N Class...

Smoke Deflectors
These were the most obvious 'deviation from the norm' but appeared so long ago that all Southern moguls (bar one, for a while) within living memory have had them. The moguls, with their high chimneys, might seem unlikely candidates for smoke deflectors. Low smoke obstructing the view forward had been solved in the 1930s by the fitting of smoke deflectors and they duly appeared on big 4-6-0s, Schools and all the moguls. The process began with the King Arthurs and was extended to the 2-6-0s in the middle 1930s. There were variations in the disposition of grab irons and hand holds, best illustrated by photographs. An 'Overall Survey' of Mogul smoke deflectors; N, N1, U and U1, follows in Volume Two.

Piston Tail Rods
Prominent piston tail rods were very obvious features early on. They were commonly provided in the belief that they reduced piston wear but their use was discontinued and most seem to have disappeared by the mid-1930s. The 1400-1414 series Ns of 1932-34 never had them to start off with.

Slidebars
810 had a single slidebar and so did subsequent engines; those built later by the Southern had double slidebars and some earlier engines also acquired them.

Footsteps
There was always a conventional set of footsteps for the cab but not at the front, behind the buffer beam; its presence after all complicated the drawing out of the piston at the front which in any case required the dismantling of part of the buffer beam. Instead an inadequate 'stirrup' attached to the motion bracket was provided. From about 1930 a proper step was provided at the front instead, in at least some cases prior to the fitting of smoke deflectors. The later 1400 series did not have the early 'stirrup' but had the front step from the first.

Chimneys
Chimney style is somewhat in the eye of the beholder and some see differences that others do not. The Ns at first had smallish chimneys, distinctly tapering up from the base with a prominent rim and capuchon. The Ns continued to appear with this chimney until a wider, more parallel chimney originally fashioned for the first three cylinder N1 began to be substituted, as and when a new chimney was required. An unexpected circumstance was the fitting BR Standard Class 4 2-6-0 chimneys, associated with frame replacements in the late 1950s-early 1960s. See, at end of this section, *New Frames for Old*.

There were also four briefly fitted with stovepipe chimneys in an effort to investigate the steaming, as follows (after Swift, *Maunsell Moguls*):

812	1/21-9/23
817	1/22-5/23
818	8/22-9/22
819	5/22-12/24

Lamp Irons
The Ns had the usual three along the buffer beam and one more at the top of the smokebox. Grouping saw two more added, low down on the

Another original, A862 (a Stewarts Lane engine) at Nine Elms in the 1920s. The dodgy-looking 'stirrup' footstep hangs by a thread it almost seems from the motion bracket. Behind is the curious coal stage, the lengthiest in the country, possibly, and certainly the longest length of roofing, complete with dormers! The little upright bottle-like item on the running plate by the smokebox saddle holds oil in connection with the lubrication of the pony truck slides. There was one on the other side too (see A871) but they disappeared after a few years.

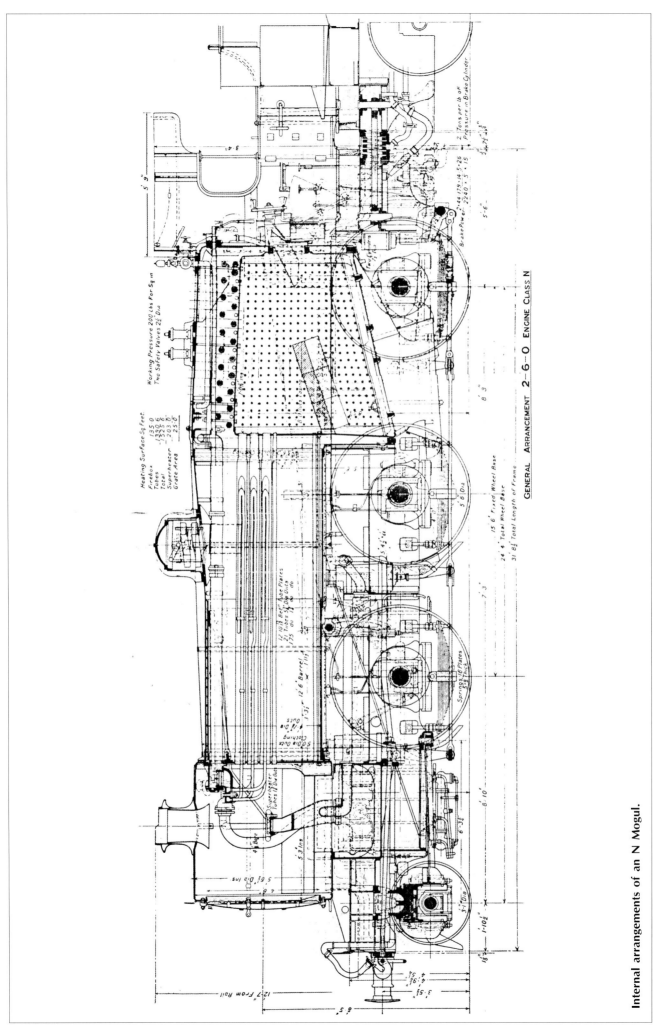

GENERAL ARRANGEMENT 2—6—0 ENGINE CLASS N

Internal arrangements of an N Mogul.

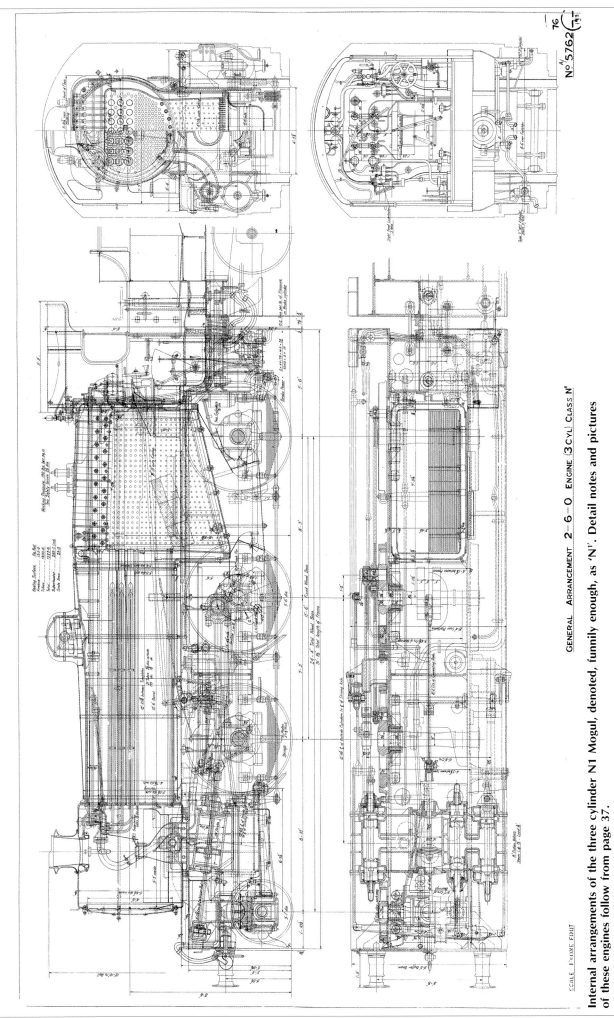

GENERAL ARRANGEMENT 2–6–0 ENGINE (3 CYL) CLASS N'

No 5762

SCALE 1=ONE FOOT

Internal arrangements of the three cylinder N1 Mogul, denoted, funnily enough, as 'N1'. Detail notes and pictures of these engines follow from page 37.

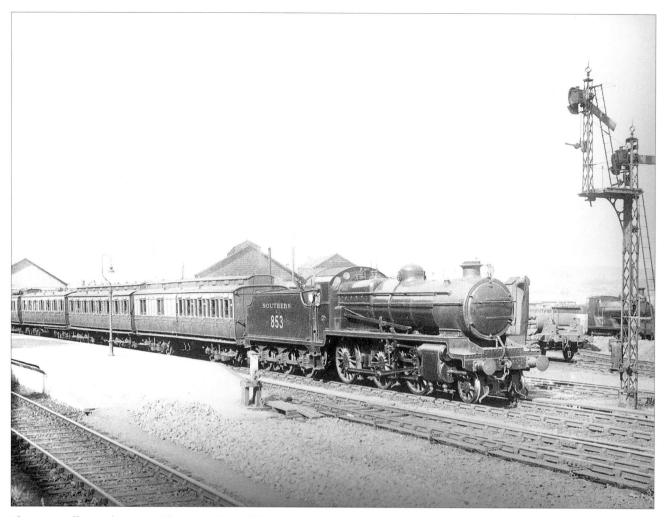

The Maunsell moguls were with us into the middle 1960s along with the later products of Bulleid, Stanier and Riddles but in truth they came from another age – take A853 with a train of clerestory stock at Barnstaple bound for Exeter about 1926, the mogul having newly arrived to serve on the Exmouth Junction allocation for its first decade.

A838 in 1924; the turntable (manually operated, though electric operation had been available for some years) is the one at the new Ashford shed; projecting beyond is a balloon tank, with wooden roof. The loco has a mechanical lubricator (later removed) sited above the cylinder; this one also has a pipe running along the boiler above the hand rail, possibly a steam supply to the sight feed lubricator in the cab. The A prefix, which denoted the 'home' works of a loco, not its area of operation, was abandoned from 1931 but was not expunged until the loco's next works visit, when 1000 was added to the former 'A' engines, A838 becoming 1831. transporttreasury

Charming period piece at Braunton; it may even be 1925, when Barnstaple stalwart (it stayed there well into the 1930s) A857 was brand new, in 1925. The picture is interesting in that it shows how the number was put in serif style on the rear buffer beam at this period. The new mogul is serving on one of Barnstaple's perennial jobs, banking north to Mortehoe in the distance. It sits in one of the engine spurs provided for stabling between jobs.

A857 now blows off impatiently in its banking engine spur at Braunton. It was kept immaculate by its delighted new owners at Barnstaple. The lined green stands out well, even from the bridge over the adjacent River Caen. The cabside plate is also clear; now an oval with a third plate on the tender rear.

smokebox front, so that the engines could carry the six-disc Southern route codes. Existing engines had them added, subsequent engines were built with them. The top lamp had been fixed at the beginning to the smokebox rim, above the door, but in the 1930s this was moved to the door itself.

Washout Plugs
There was a line of five washout plugs on the left-hand side of the firebox and four on the right. There were at least four more, two almost at the boiler top and two more a little lower down, towards the smokebox. These ones are visible only really in later photographs, presumably when the covers which rendered them invisible in such photographs were no longer replaced so assiduously.

Snifting Valves
'Snifting valves' were prominent either side of the chimney, just as in other Southern classes with the Maunsell superheater. From 1946 they were deemed not to warrant the maintenance time and money involved and their general removal from Southern engines was decreed.

Left-Hand Drive
1407-1414 were built with left-hand drive; the outward manifestation of this was that the vacuum ejector (the wide pipe running from cab to smokebox)

and the reversing lever were on the left-hand side of 1407-1414, whereas on all the others they were on the right-hand side. The terms 'right' and 'left' here apply looking forward from the cab, as a driver or fireman would. The change came about because the SR decided upon standardising left-hand drive in 1932, the decision disrupting in a small way the delivery of the engines.

Domes
Sometimes it seems, a works would alter the look of something just because it could. Early domes were rounded, later ones were much flatter on the top. After a while, as boilers were exchanged, any loco might carry either type.

Sanding
Sand was delivered to the front of the leading and intermediate coupled wheels, an early 'wet-sand' system (*The Maunsell Moguls*, Peter Rowledge, Oakwood Press, 1976) soon giving way to conventional gravity sanding. The sandboxes on the Ns were invisible to the observer, tucked behind the frames – tidied away in typically British fashion – and the fireman was required to crouch down on the running plate to fill them.

Lubrication
The first N, 810, had a visible mechanical lubricator on the left-hand running

plate, removed after a few years. They were also fitted to one or two others; A837 and A847 had one pre-War, and A852 for much of its life – see individual photographs. Two were also equipped with mechanical lubricators in BR days, 31857 and 31870.

All the 2-6-0s (and the tanks) apart from the first two, had sight feed lubricators in the cab for valves and pistons with wick feeds for everything else.

AWS
It was presumably intended that all the moguls should get the Automatic Warning System but time was running out and quite a few never got it. Some fittings are not recorded in the Record, in other instances it is called ATC – Automatic Train Control. The battery box together with air reservoir was on the driver's side on the running plate.

Power Classification
The Southern Region started to show the 'BR' power classification of its locomotives on the cabside in May 1954. The Ns were 4P5FB, though in the very early days it was just 4P5F (or 4P/5F). The Southern was unique in sub-dividing two power classes, 2 and 5 into A (higher) and B (lower) and displaying the results (stencilled at first) on the cabside. At operating level clearly no one knew anything of the distinction and no notice was taken of it. See *Flamin' Bad*

Changes afoot, with A839 renumbered 1839 (from January 1933) and now with conventionally robust front footstep behind buffer beam, though it still has the piston tail rods. The snifting valve, or superheater release valves, are prominent still on the smokebox top. They were removed and replaced by anti-vacuum valves. On firebox top are the safety valves and behind them the whistle, together with the piping for the steam take-off for the manifold in the cab. The location is unrecorded but it almost certainly Exmouth Junction, where the loco was based for virtually all its forty year life – it is displaying the Exeter Central-Exmouth Junction disc code. The only time it did not work in the West was during a wartime spell of a year or so at Bricklayers Arms. ColourRail

1860 after renumbering (still serif on the buffer, with the dash and 'dropped dot') and with front steps and smoke deflectors, running light up the incline at Exeter from St David's (visible in the right background) to Central and, probably, Exmouth Junction shed. Cabside cast plates proved a nuisance on any Grouped railway apart from the GW, which enjoyed a unique continuity. The LMS wisely abandoned the (admittedly lovely) LNW plates but the Southern had replacements made for the mogul SE&CR plates, which read SOUTHERN RAILWAY with the 'A' number. With the 'A' prefix gone, another set of plates were required, minus of course the confounded 'A'. Plates finally disappeared once Bulleid turned his attention to liveries. ColourRail

815, still more or less an SECR loco, though it has just acquired the necessary SR extra lamp irons – the year is thus assumed to be 1923. The location is recorded as Sandwich station. transporttreasury

One of the final Ns of the 1400 series, 1406 in Maunsell lined green at Exmouth Junction shed shortly after arriving there new from Ashford in 1933. It is 'as built' with no piston tail rods but conventional front steps, more muscular chimney, lamp irons. Note how the running plate of the new 4,000 gallon tender is raised up ('joggled' if you like) to meet the line of the cab base. The sides 'lean in' at the top. The oil delivery pipes on the moguls ran down from the cab and were contained along the side of the firebox in a distinctively shaped length of channelling. Needless to say this saw some variations over the years. This was the final right-hand drive mogul built. ColourRail

Fellow Exmouth Junction N, also new at the shed, 1848 in 1933. On this right-hand side, it can be seen that the oil delivery pipes are run through a tube rather than box channelling. The differences in the tender sides, 3,500 gallon compared to the version of the 4,000 gallon one behind 1406, determined the positioning of the number and SOUTHERN and can be compared in these two. The one obvious 'modern' feature lacking in the moguls was outside steam pipes and when some did get them later they were hidden behind the smoke deflectors; 31848 was an exception for a while – see its individual entry. ColourRail

Mogul transition on a turntable; two Ns at Dover Marine; the first, 1875, is more or less 'as built' the second has the new smoke deflectors, lined green at first but later painted black. 1875 has the long piston tail rods (almost obscured by the turntable hand rail) and no front steps while 1825 has acquired the front steps and lost the tail rod. The deflectors have vertical grab irons and a circular handhold cut-out. Variations occurred inevitably, illustrated as we come across them in the book. Beyond is the vast Lord Warden Hotel – where in the world was a better view of an engine shed? Bombed, shelled, machine gunned in the Second World War, requisitioned by the Admiralty and neglected for years it is now a listed building, and serves as an office block. Dover shed hardly fared any better and attacks became so frequent that engines were withdrawn 'up country' for a period. The loco has double slidebars, the first N so fitted from new. transporttreasury

1826 at Plymouth Friary on 5 August 1938. Smoke deflectors, with upright grab iron below and simple hole cut-out hand-hold above; recently lined, they are now black. Top lamp iron still on smokebox, serif buffer beam number and so on. Apart from the left-hand drive series 1404-1414 the vacuum ejector pipe to the smokebox and the reverser were on the right-hand side, as here. transporttreasury

and Flamin' Awful: Peter Groom Wonders for the long and short of all this in *British Railways Illustrated* Vol.11 No.4, January 2002. It is a marvel of engine picking.

New Frames for Old
The following notes derive in the main from *Modified Maunsell Moguls* by E.S. Youldon in *British Railways Illustrated* Vol.17 No.5, February 2008. With some N and Us starting to show their age (frames in particular) in the 1950s a programme was embarked upon for replacement frames together with new cylinders incorporating snifting valves (see above) on top, outside steam pipes and in many cases BR Class 4 blastpipes and chimneys. After a while, complete frame replacements were not always necessary so renewal was confined to the front half where appropriate. Whether full or part frame renewal was undertaken the appearance of the finished product was the same.

The new frames were identified by the curved top profile ahead of the smokebox and they were 4½ inches longer, perhaps to create more platform for char shovellers. A total of fifty N and U moguls were dealt with and such a round figure suggests either this was the number authorised or else that when the fiftieth had been modified (31858 in June 1961) a realistic assessment of future needs showed that further expenditure was not warranted.

The first locomotive taken in hand was U class 31621 in February 1955 and the second was sister engine 31634 in April 1955. These were followed by N 31848 turned out without smoke deflectors in October 1955 giving a clear view of the new external steam delivery pipes; deflectors returned to this one in February 1957. Some conversions retained Maunsell chimneys but others were equipped with BR4 chimneys which, it was generally agreed, ruined the engines' appearance. Progress per year was:-

YEAR	CHIMNEY	
	MAUNSELL	BR
1955	5	-
1956	2	-
1957	4	7
1958	-	7
1959	1	5
1960	2	12
1961	-	5

The conversions were excellent steamers although these two cylinder moguls (N and U) were competent machines in any event. The three cylinder classes N1 and U1 were not seriously beset with frame problems so were not involved in these changes. In parallel with the conversions, thirty-seven other Ns and Us were given BR blastpipes and chimneys but were not otherwise altered. A table of the fifty conversions

follows on p20 together with date when ex-works under the chimney pattern involved. The heading 'new frames' indicates either full or front half only. All were turned out at Ashford Works.

There were just two instances where an engine retained a Maunsell chimney to start with but later progressed to a BR version. These were, as shown, 31614 and 31624. Where a locomotive retained its Maunsell chimney the latter was fitted with an internal sleeve in order to create an inside profile to match a BR chimney and blastpipe.

The 37 engines, already mentioned, that received BR blastpipes and chimneys but not otherwise altered were 31402, 31410, 31412, 31414, 31611, 31612, 31618, 31629, 31632, 31639, 31793, 31799, 31800, 31804, 31805, 31807, 31814, 31815, 31817, 31818, 31825, 31826, 31828, 31834, 31836, 31839, 31841, 31847, 31851, 31863, 31865, 31866, 31867, 31870, 31872, 31873 and 31875.

The remaining N and U locomotives not quoted anywhere in this survey retained Maunsell cylinders, frames and chimneys to the end. A modified mogul was capable of being driven harder and this in turn demanded a rate of feedwater beyond the existing injector limit and so a replacement injector producing an enhanced feed was fitted.

1867 with proud driver at Dover, 30 September 1938. The prominent pipe under the cab is for the exhaust steam injector, from the grease separator which would be between the frames. This later gave way to a much more unobtrusive arrangement. The live steam injector is on the other side of the cab. 1867 has acquired the front steps but has yet to lose the piston tail rod. transporttreasury

Left-hand drive 1412 with reverser and ejector accordingly on the (left-hand) driver's side. Differences from, say 1867 include shape of dome, rounded on the latter, flat on this loco. The new 4,000 gallon tender tapered in at the top with SOUTHERN very close to the 'boundary' of the 'rave' with the straight sides; the number has had to be moved lower down than on tenders like that of 1826, say. The 1400 series of Ns had twin slidebars, as here. transporttreasury

DATES OF CONVERSIONS

LOCO	NEW FRAMES		LOCO	NEW FRAMES	
	MAUNSELL CHIMNEY	BR CHIMNEY		MAUNSELL CHIMNEY	BR CHIMNEY
31400		1/58	31806		11/57
31405	3/57		31809		9/60
31406		1/60	31829	10/60	
31408		4/57	31830	11/55	
31413		5/60	31831		8/60
31613		3/58	31833		6/59
31614	2/57	12/61	31835		5/57
31615		6/60	31837		2/61
31617		1/61	31838		6/57
31621	2/55		31840	2/57	
31622		11/60	31842		12/57
31623	3/56		31843		8/58
31624	5/56	6/61	31845		3/60
31625		1/59	31846	5/59	
31628	1/57		31848	10/55	
31631	10/60		31853		7/60
31633		9/60	31854		8/57
31634	4/55		31855	12/55	
31635		1/59	31858		6/61
31637		10/59	31862		4/60
31791		4/60	31864		1/59
31792		10/58	31868		12/60
31795		2/58	31869		2/58
31796		1/61	31871		3/61
31802		1/58	31874		5/57

Engines numbered between 31613 and 31809 were U class and all others N class.

Experiments and Asides
Simply Bizarre

The Ns served as suitable 'vehicles' for a number of 'experiments'. Perhaps the one that resulted in the most outlandish alterations in appearance was the 'recycled steam' system carried by A816 for several years in the 1930s. As well as pumps and piping there were tanks on the running plate which housed cooler and compressor; the steam was accordingly cooled and compressed to then be returned to the boiler. There was no steam exhaust and draughting was accomplished using a fan. Literally topping off this monstrosity was, for a time at least, a *square* chimney...

In 1930 A816 was taken out of normal service and fitted with the steam conversion equipment which, incidentally, had been invented by a draughtsman employed in a marine engineering works in Glasgow. It was a way to improve the efficiency of the steam locomotive in the way exhaust steam was dealt with. It was to be applied to the marine world and a private company had the condensing set fixed to their generator along with a cooling tower and it duly produced the savings predicted. Maunsell and Holcroft visited the generating station in 1927 and must have been intrigued by what they saw.

An N was chosen because of its low axle loading with adequate room alongside the boiler above the running plate to take the equipment. The conversion took over a year which is mildly astounding and involved extensive alterations to A816. Les Elsey comments: *The main exhaust from the cylinders was led through the side of the smokebox into the condenser tank, with a non return valve to prevent the water entering the cylinders. It was suggested that the experiment failed owing to poor draughting arrangements and back pressure set up by the condensing system which made it impossible to give a standard N performance.* Problems with the fan could not in the end be overcome, '...an illustration of the manner in which the additional complication associated with most departures from the basic Stephensonian form easily proves their undoing'.

In between trials 1816 spent a good deal of time back in Eastleigh Works undergoing alterations and

A newish left-hand drive 1411 in lined green. Note double slidebar and tender running plate angled up to match the bottom of the cab. The system of piping on the smokebox side appears to be a form of steam supply for a tube cleaning lance. Parallel buffer shanks from the first. ColourRail

Combinations of lettering/numbering could be found in the first two years of BR; 1825 is a corker at Brighton in 1948, with 's' prefix and **BRITISH RAILWAYS** in 'sunshine'; even the front buffer beam number was in this style, though it can't be seen. Sniffing valves gone, with the faint outline of a circular blanking plate just visible on the smokebox – on the original print at least. Retains twin slidebars it had when new. R.C. Riley, transporttreasury

31816 at New Cross Gate in 1949; BR Gill sans front number, Bulleid 'sunshine' SOUTHERN and BR cab number in same style. When a loco was turned out like this it usually indicated it had been renumbered but not repainted. Horizontal grab iron on lower part of smoke deflector and oval cut-out hand-hold at the front edge. transporttreasury

The only oil burning N, 1831 at Eastleigh during its year so fitted, September 1947 to September 1948.

modifications with no trial runs at all reported in 1934. A glance at the Record is instructive! The final series of trials began in spring 1935 when the locomotive spent a few weeks out of use at Basingstoke shed; it was converted back to a conventional class N 27/5/35-3/8/35 at Eastleigh having run, it appears, just 14,383 miles since conversion in 1930. Full details of this experiment can be found in *Leader and Southern Experimental Steam* by Kevin Robertson, published in 1990. As BR 31816, when withdrawn on 9/1/66 it was the last surviving pre-Grouping locomotive on the Southern Region in service apart from the O2 tanks on the Isle of Wight.

Feedwater Heating
A number of lines examined feedwater heating before the War and wherever this was employed it always involved further sprouting pipework, this time on A819 in the 1920s. Such systems never found great favour in the British Isles and were much more commonly found abroad. The coal saving was marginal and was more than cancelled out by the maintenance required to keep the feed water apparatus working. The worst problem was scaling up and in areas of very hard water this might mean *daily* examination. The 'experiment' was curiously protracted, from 1922 to 1929; you'd suspect that for some or even much of that time the feed equipment was not actually functioning.

Marshall Gear
There was obviously something about an Ns that lent itself to experimentation

and in 1933-34 1850 was fitted with the curious Marshall valve gear, designed to look like it wouldn't work. Among other wonders it employed two sets of reversing gear which in turn required a forward extension to the cab. It suffered a bad failure and was promptly abandoned.

The Irish Connection
Twelve N 'kits' were purchased from Woolwich by the Midland Great Western Railway of Ireland at £2,000 each. They were shipped to Ireland and assembled at the Broadstone Works; the first one completed was No.49. The Great Southern Railway of Ireland absorbed the MGWR and 49 became 410. The GSR then purchased fifteen more sets of parts and 410 became 372. All the Irish locomotives of course were assembled to run on the 5ft 3in gauge of the Emerald Isle. The last six of the GSR order were erected at Inchicore Works between 1927 and 1930; they had 6ft driving wheels instead of 5ft 6in and were classified Class K1A and numbered 393-398. The earlier batch numbered 372 to 391 were classified K1 and from the batch of the GSR fifteen one set was kept as spares for the rest. It is said that in Ireland they were called 'Woolwiches' (more accurately with respect to provenance it must be said) rather than 'Woolworths'. Perhaps the US budget department store had not made its debut in Ireland. Interestingly, the Irish versions never bore smoke deflectors.

Ns on the Met
The Metropolitan Railway acquired six sets of parts from Woolwich and

converted them into 2-6-4Ts, a handsome design similar to the ill-fated K River class tanks. These six locomotives were needed to handle the increase in traffic and were adapted for the Metropolitan Railway by Armstrong Whitworth & Co. of Newcastle with boilers supplied in 1925 by Robert Stephenson & Co. Darlington. Classified K and numbered 111 to 116 they were painted in Crimson Lake. In the 1930s they spent most of their time on goods trains on the Aylesbury line sometimes, it is said, rescuing the odd broken down electric. In 1937 the LNER took over most of the steam operations of the Metropolitan part of London Transport. Thus 111-116 were transferred to LNER stock, reclassified L2 and renumbered 6158-6163, repainted black and based at Neasden (GC) shed. When pressed into occasional passenger service to Aylesbury they proved perfectly capable. They were all withdrawn by 1948.

Oil Firing
After World War Two came the great oil fuel debacle, at the instigation of the Government. 'The Men at the Ministry' were not finished with the N class! The SR responded with some considerable enthusiasm, with an initial target of 110 locomotives. In the event only thirty conversions took place and of the planned 29 Ns just one was so fitted, 1831 which according to its record card was dealt with 3/6/47-18/9/47 during an A class service at Ashford Works having run 105,303 miles since its last General Repair. Running in trials took place after which 1831 was based at Fratton where

Gill sans **BRITISH RAILWAYS** on the tender of 31833 at Devonport, 27 April 1954. A.Lathey, transporttreasury

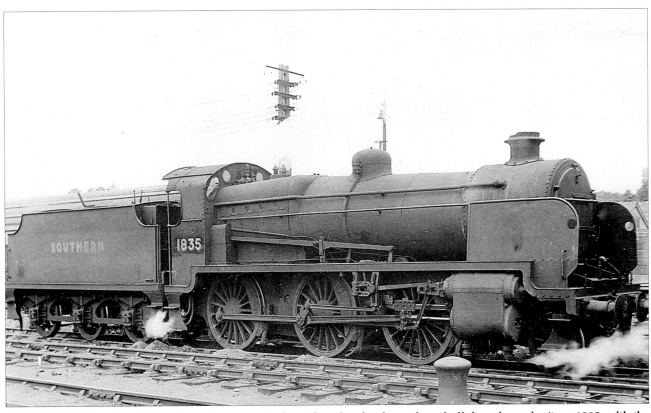

Bulleid black livery (though it's only really apparent where the grime has been cleared off the cab number!) on 1835, with the Great Man's shaded 'sunshine' lettering and number. J.H. Aston.

31853 at Wadebridge shed, 15 March 1950; consider the more expansive style of the numbering, compared to say 31837 below. Renumbering was always and only a works task and the larger 10in figures were possible here because the cab lining was 'well-spaced' out, unlike on 31837 with its 'set-in' panel necessitating 8in numbers. Tender bare as yet in the absence of suitable transfers. Note how the old thin lining follows closely the outline of the cab. A.E. West, courtesy Mike King.

31837 at Tresmeer on 2 May 1961 with an all stations to Okehampton. Note simple water gauge fitted at the front of the tender on the fireman's side, 4P5FB power classification, small second emblem, water 'slacker' pipe hanging through hand rail GW-style. Chalked on 31837's cabside in a patch wiped of grime is what looks like DON'T TAKE. TOOLS ALL READY FOR 5.12am FRI. The white (actually yellow) spot below the number is not part of the chalking but an indication that the loco has been equipped for water treatment, in the form of briquettes dropped in the tender tank, initiated by the Southern in the mid-1950s. It's worth noting that the BR cab lining did not follow the cab outline but was cut off just short of the running plate though not always; see 31864 at Reading, later in the book for instance. R.C. Riley, transporttreasury

31858 at Redhill with tender paint spoilt, it looks like, by ash being shovelled out off the footplate. This engine too has the cabside spot indicating water treatment. It was later replaced by a triangle (the spot was said to have been confused with the WR route code) but presumably not on every loco concerned. RailOnline

That fine BR black on 31401 at Ashford in the 1950s; small first tender emblem. RailOnline

31850 arrayed in full Gill sans style, at Stewarts Lane in early 1949.

an oil fuel plant was established carrying out local duties including work to Eastleigh and back. Having run 30,034 miles 1831 was back in Ashford Works for conversion back to a coal burner 8/11/48-4/12/48. There were other Ns in Ashford at one time awaiting conversion to oil firing, 1830 and 1859 but they re-entered service still as coal burners.

S Prefix

With Nationalisation all SR steam locomotives were renumbered but before the proper renumbering took place eight Ns carried the S prefix. The list below shows the works visits when the S was added and when they received their proper BR running numbers.

Tenders

The first N, 810, had a tender of a new simple, symmetrical design, neat and flat-sided; like other aspects of the design, there were echoes of Derby practice. The new tender carried 3,500 gallons and 5 tons of coal.

There was a minor variation in the buffer beam ends; on 810 and the Woolwich-built 826-875 they were square, but on 811-826 were angled to match the footstep. Minor variations crept in, as ever; there were straight and tapered buffers, and grab rails differed at the front. Some interchange was inevitable, with some locos getting types that were not original to their particular 'batch'. Some River 2-6-4Ts found themselves with N tenders when rebuilt to U 2-6-0s while some Ns got 3,500 gallon tenders originally earmarked for the new Us.

A new standard came in 1928. Ten King Arthurs, soon substituted by Lord Nelsons, were assigned six wheel 4,000 gallon straight sided tenders, suitable for use on the Eastern Section. This was not how it turned out and only two Lord Nelsons got the new tenders and then only for a short while. This new pattern tender was used for the new U moguls and the later N series 1400-1414. They had curved edges at the rear; those on

the Us, U1s and Ns sloped inwards at the top, those on the N1 were flat-sided.

The 4,000 gallon six wheelers were designed to Western Section specification. When paired with an Eastern Section loco such as a mogul the front end framing had to be raised to match the loco connection. Outwardly the tender framing had to be stepped up as seen in photographs.

MAUNSELL MOGUL LIVERIES
Note by Eric Youldon

The Maunsell Moguls generally all followed the same path with liveries. The SECR in the Great War adopted a most austere livery of unlined slate grey with a large plain white number on tenders and tanks. A small cabside or bunkerside plate read SE&CR. This style persisted after the 1918 Armistice into early Southern days. As far as Moguls were concerned 810 to 821, 823 and 824 were the Ns affected, plus N1 822 and 2-6-4T 790 which in the fullness of time became U class A790. The last N of the SECR order, 825, entered service in December 1923 in SR green (often referred to as Maunsell green, a dark shade with black and white lining) and numbered A825. The Southern Railway added an 'A' for Ashford, to former and future Eastern Section locomotives of Ashford design until 1931 from when 1000 was added and the A prefix discarded.

No.	Works/Mileage	No.	Works/Mileage
S1405	21/1/48-19/2/48 68,400 A	31405	21/10/49-15/11/49 44,629 LI
S1813	9/1/48-13/2/48 109,747 A	31813	24/5/50-23/6/50 55,322 HC*
S1814	13/2/48-10/3/48 no mileage D	31814	13/5/49-15/6/49 46,007 HI
S1825	28/1/48-2/3/48 96,774 A	31825	14/2/51-16/3/51 68,373 GO
S1832	20/1/48-26/2/48 92,975 A	31832	2/6/49-9/7/49 41,345 HI
S1838	2/1/48-7/2/48 101,392 A	31838	16/11/49-16/12/49 59,430 A
S1858	19/1/48-26/2/48 93,553 A	31858	30/5/50-23/6/50 59,979 HI
S1871	29/1/48-3/3/48 83,914 A	31871	3/6/48-11/6/48 3,598 D

*Brighton, all others Ashford

'Sunshine' 31827 still with SOUTHERN on the tender in October 1948 (renumbered but not repainted – common enough) bears its new number on the 'wrong' part of the buffer beam, and offset to the right to boot. A little later it got a proper Gill sans smokebox plate but retained the painted one too for a while. ColourRail

There were four further forward washout plugs, on the boiler top, visible really only in later years. Presumably they had covers until relatively late on. They are certainly obvious now on 31865 at London Bridge about 1962. Also visible are the clips holding the boiler sheeting together on the firebox top and one of the sand box fillers. B.W.L. Brooksbank, Initial Photographics.

Valve and piston exam on AWS-fitted 31861 in the open at Redhill MPD, 3 June 1962. It would be considered strange in some other railway circles to leave the motion up. Both curved dropped portion of running plate and lower part of smoke deflector (leaving the grab iron dangling) have had to be removed. J.H. Aston.

Above. 31862 at Ashford works, possibly during its Light Casual of 1961. With driving wheelsets still in place what's going on appears little more than a shed valve and piston exam. AWS conduit runs up the top edge of the right-hand main frame, then proceeds behind the deflector to emerge through the valence, above the cylinder. After looping over the snifting valve it is further routed along the platform valence to the cab. ColourRail

Left. Disposition of AWS and associated conduit at the front of 31830 at Norwood Junction MPD, 1963. The function of the 'protector plate' was of course to protect the relatively delicate pick-up gear from the swinging screw coupling, though hooks were provided (the sides varied) to stow it out of the way in any event. The front lamp iron has long been sited on the smokebox door, and 31830 has lost its Brighton shed plate. A sharp eye will discern a hole drilled at the top edge of the buffer beam each end. This was to give the valve spindle clearance when the valve was withdrawn from the front. RailOnline

Above. 31401 in mid gear at Ashford on 8 July 1950 – the 1400-1414 series all had double slidebars though as already noted they were not positioned either side of the crosshead. The coupling rod knuckle joint is ahead of the crank pin and is hidden therefore in this view by the connecting rod. A.E. West, courtesy Mike King.

Left. Single slidebar arrangement on 31852, at Redhill on 23 April 1961; three holes in crosshead to help in reducing the weight of the reciprocating parts, sandboxes still invisible behind frames even at this close 'eye-balling' level. What is a revelation is the massive sheet steel splasher arrangement over the leading wheel, a feature invisible in all conventional photographs. John Eyers, South Western Circle.

Ns broken up at Eastleigh. First date is withdrawal and the second the week ending it was scrapped.

31402:	w/d 8/63;	cut up w/e 7/3/64
31403:	w/d 6/7/63;	cut up w/e 12/10/63
31404:	w/d 7/12/63;	cut up w/e 4/1/64
31409:	w/d 17/11/62;	cut up w/e 29/2/64
31414:	w/d 24/11/62;	cut up w/e 2/3/63
31813:	w/d 26/10/63;	cut up w/e 14/12/63
31815:	w/d 1/6/63;	cut up w/e 27/7/63
31817:	w/d 18/1/64;	cut up w/e 8/2/64
31818:	w/d 7/9/63;	cut up w/e 28/9/63
31820:	w/d 24/8/63;	cut up w/e 2/12/63
31823:	w/d 21/9/63;	cut up w/e 25/164
31824:	w/d 26/10/63;	cut up w/e 18/1/64
31825:	w/d 2/8/63;	cut up w/e 28/12/63
31826:	w/d 25/8/63;	cut up w/e 11/1/64
31829:	w/d 5/1/64;	cut up w/e 2/5/64
31830:	w/d 5/1/64;	cut up w/e 11/4/64
31832:	w/d 1/5/64;	cut up w/e 11/4/64
31833:	w/d 23/2/64;	cut up w/e 25/4/64
31836:	w/d 12/1963;	cut up w/e 18/4/64
31838:	w/d 2/1964;	cut up w/e 21/3/64
31839:	w/d 12/1963;	cut up w/e 18/4/64
31844:	w/d 12/1963;	cut up w/e 18/4/64
31847:	w/d 5/10/63;	cut up w/e 16/11/63
31848:	w/d 15/2/64;	cut up w/e 15/2/64
31852:	w/d 21/9/63;	cut up w/e 14/12/63
31857:	w/d 5/1/64;	cut up w/e 22/2/64
31860:	w/d 2/11/63;	cut up w/e 18/1/64
31861:	w/d 11/5/63;	cut up w/e 29/6/63
31863:	w/d 7/7/63;	cut up w/e 7/3/64
31865:	w/d 25/8/63;	cut up w/e 21/3/64
31867:	w/d 7/7/63;	cut up w/e 22/2/64
31871:	w/d 7/12/63;	cut up w/e 1/2/64
31872:	w/d 1/6/63;	cut up w/e 10/8/63

31852, at Redhill again. Position of the radius rod and die-block mid-way in the slotted, curved expansion link, indicates the engine is in mid-gear. Reversing lever above, working on the motion bracket. John Eyers, South Western Circle.

The fifty Woolwich built, or partly built, Ns, A826 to A875 entered service in Maunsell livery with a few short-lived exceptions; some were seen in goods black and one, A832 was observed in grey. All future Moguls and related River tanks were Maunsell liveried when new. When smoke deflectors came along, they too were lined green until early 1938 from when on they were black. The first Bulleid livery for Moguls was unlined dark green with Maunsell style lettering; this was applied to fifteen engines from September 1939. Starting in January 1940 unlined dark green with Bulleid lettering was applied to 63 Moguls. March 1941 marked the introduction of plain black with 'sunshine' lettering which was the order of the day to the end of the SR's existence with two colourful exceptions in 1946. These were 1817 and 1854 which were turned out in Malachite green with black smoke deflectors. Lining was black edged in yellow. The reason behind this exercise was to provide Brighton with 'prestige' Ns to work the shed's principal Victoria trains via Uckfield.

From late March 1948 BR numbers were applied as locomotives passed through workshops. Renumbering was accompanied by a wide variety of interim styles often after a change of engine – through a hot box and so on – such as lettering and figures in 'sunshine', Gill sans, BR number but tender retaining SOUTHERN to quote examples.

(Continued on page 37).

Application of BR lined black livery

31400 9/53	31818 5/54	31842 6/50	31866 1/49
31401 3/51	31819 3/53	31843 5/50	31867 12/48
31402 1/54	31820 5/50	31844 3/59	31868 11/48
31403 6/49	31821 12/48	31845 9/51	31869 7/55
31404 10/50		31846 7/50	31870 3/50
31405 3/57	31823 1/49	31847 7/49	31871 3/53
31406 9/51	31824 9/49	31848 3/49**	31872 7/49
31407 8/49	31825 3/51	31849 8/49	31873 5/54
31408 7/49	31826 12/48	31850 12/48	31874 7/53
31409 1/49	31827 1/51	31851 7/49	31875 9/50
31410 5/52	31828 8/49	31852 7/52	
31411 10/48	31829 4/50	31853 3/49	31822 2/51
31412 12/49	31830 5/50	31854 8/50*	
31413 7/55	31831 6/52	31855 3/49	31876 3/54
31414 4/50	31832 2/53	31856 6/49	31877 6/49
	31833 11/48	31857 11/52	31878 11/54
31810 12/52	31834 1/49	31858 1/53	31879 1/49
31811 12/49	31835 5/50	31859 2/52**	31880 9/49
31812 1/49	31836 2/53	31860 5/50	
31813 5/53	31837 11/49	31861 4/50	
31814 5/51	31838 12/49	31862 4/51	
31815 10/51	31839 10/52	31863 1/50	
31816 6/50	31840 10/50	31864 2/50	
31817 4/49*	31841 10/50	31865 11/50	

* malachite: 31817 8/46; 31854 8/46
**period recorded; no works visit shown on card

Detail of middle tender SE&CR axlebox on 31852 at Redhill. Vacuum cylinder behind. John Eyers, South Western Circle.

1854 in for attention at Ashford works on 8 May 1948, its tender already renumbered and lettered for BR service. The curious Bulleid malachite green (black deflectors) was a consequence of two Ns (the other was 1817) at Brighton being assigned to the prestigious Victoria trains via Uckfield. J.H. Aston.

4,000 gallon tender behind 31401 at Ashford, 8 July 1950; BRITISH RAILWAYS newly applied. The frames of the 4,000 gallon tenders were not so deep as the 3,500 gallon predecessors, and were continuous; that is they did not have the rather pleasingly curved slots. Note also that they were wider than the loco cab. A.E. West, courtesy Mike King.

Left. 31852 at Redhill. There were differences in the lockers/toolboxes on the tenders. The 3,500 gallon straight sided ones had these three in a line; on the similar-looking 4,000 gallon straight-sided tenders for the N1s for instance the lockers came up to the tender side. The later series 1400-1414 had the rather different 4,000 gallon tenders with inward-curved 'raves' and these had two lockers/toolboxes. John Eyers, South Western Circle.

Return crank, middle drivers, on 31852 at Redhill. John Eyers, South Western Circle.

Still poking around under 31852 at Redhill. This is the live steam injector with the two pipes; one live steam and the other delivery. The large pipe above is the vacuum ejector pipe winding its way from the engine to the tender coupling. The circular valve behind the injector is one of the vacuum train pipe drain valves. These are held closed when vacuum is created, but when it is destroyed during a brake application, they open and allow any water condensate to drain away. There would be another at the front of the engine and at least one on the tender. Maybe even another on the engine too, cleaned out on a 7-9 week exam! John Eyers, South Western Circle.

34

Contrast in 3,500 (31802, nearest, small second emblem) and 4,000 gallon tenders (31408, leading, large second emblem) about 1960 at Yeovil Town. 31408, being left-hand drive, has the AWS equipment on the left side as well as the vacuum ejector and reverser. The contrast in tender widths is highlighted.

31848 – see *New Frames For Old* – running with outside steam pipes from October 1955 to February 1957, when the deflectors were reinstated. The extended framing (with curved top) ahead of the cylinder can be discerned. ColourRail

Exquisite new coat of BR black applied to 31873, in 1959 it is tempting to suppose, after its General that year. The pipes under the cab this side are for the exhaust steam injector, this later version was a good deal less obvious than the one on, for instance 1867 illustrated earlier at Dover, in 1938. ColourRail

Ns under repair at Redhill MPD, 19 October 1963; 31412 to left, 31410 to right, both left-hand drive. The latter is the one with the somewhat irrelevant (you'd think) extra plates (thin and battered) fixed to the top edge of the smoke deflectors. The superheater and elements are partially dismantled and the blastpipe is carefully bagged to prevent any small but deadly item falling in to the cylinders with disastrous consequences. The chimney is bagged presumably because it is sitting with its front end in the open for a protracted period. The AWS conduit (on 31410) is seen to emerge above the cylinder to be clipped down to the AWS attached in turn presumably to the pony truck, in which case the final connection would need a flexible hose. Richard Vitler Collection.

In late 1948 lined black became the Mogul livery with at first BRITISH RAILWAYS in Gill sans. This was followed by unmarked tenders and finally the first BR emblem from August 1949. In a few cases the emblem was applied to an engine still in unlined black. In April 1957 the second BR emblem was introduced; after this no further livery change was made of any importance.

Richard Derry – It was a long time Ago
My Ian Allan *abcs* reveal that I saw 60 of the 80 N 2-6-0s. The missing ones were far away at Exmouth Junction and seldom ventured this side of Salisbury, let alone into our Sussex/Surrey orbit. Schoolboy finances precluded long trips. A good majority of my sightings were during visits to Guildford where from 1957 at least 32 of them were based at different times and of course some of the Redhill engines were noted on Reading trains. (More than thirty worked from Redhill post-1957.) One summer Sunday in 1961 a friend's father drove us from Weybridge to Reading where we easily infiltrated the two steam sheds and a few more Maunsell moguls were in the bag. The ones based in the South West had a fair old journey up to Ashford Works in Kent for overhaul – the longest single trip in their everyday working, almost certainly. Ashford closed to locomotive repairs on 16 June 1962 and final repairs were undertaken by Eastleigh until they were all withdrawn. The last steam locomotive repaired at Ashford indeed appears to have been an N, 31400 period 15/5/62-9/6/62 145,633 miles LI-HI with water treatment included.

A number of Ns were broken up at Eastleigh Works – see Table page 31. The remainder were broken up at private scrap yards and we await the publications by the *What Really Happened to Steam* group to confirm where any particular steam locomotive was cut up away from the BR Works. One definite 'known' is 31850, broken up (unusually) in the yard at its home shed, Redhill.

THREE CYLINDER N1
The biggest and most notable modification of course was the addition of a third cylinder to produce the N1 class. It almost seems that the attraction lay as much in the opportunity to explore Holcroft's ideas on conjugated valve gear as it owed to operational needs. He had been at Swindon with Churchward and had become Maunsell's Assistant in 1914. His ideas also influenced Gresley on the Great Northern. A three cylinder locomotive was accordingly prepared for the SECR principally, it would appear, because such a loco could be marginally narrower across the cylinders; for while three is obviously more than two, all three could be rather smaller, reducing width overall. There was the usual trade-off of course; a three cylinder engine was better balanced and smoother running with less wear but was more expensive to build and maintain. The main reason for such a loco it is said was to get it within the loading gauge of the notorious tunnels on the Tonbridge-Hastings line.

The first N1 was 822, which could not quite be called 'rebuilt' from an N so

much as 'diverted' for construction of the engine as an N was already underway at Ashford. It emerged with conjugated valve gear but the arrangement seems never to have lived up to hopes and expectations. It was replaced in 1931 by three sets of Walschaerts gear, of which more anon.

C.S. Cocks throws some near-contemporary light on the three cylinder N1 with conjugated valve gear, as designed by Holcroft, in his *Paper* to the Institution of Locomotive Engineers in 1948. The 16inx28in cylinders drove the middle driving wheels, the outside pair being horizontal and the inside one inclined at 1 in 8. The piston valves were above the outside cylinders, conventionally, and to the side of the inside cylinder. The left-hand and the middle cylinder were combined in one casting, the right-hand cylinder being bolted to this casting to form a single unit. Cocks described this further: *The frame arrangement is unusual in order to enable the cylinders which are constructed in one block to be dropped into the gap in the frame. The top of the frame is then tied across the gap by a spliced plate which is also bolted to the saddle. The front end therefore formed a very rigid type of structure.*

Five more N1s were ordered in 1928 and delivered in 1930 as A876-A880. The great difference from their progenitor A822 was the absence of conjugated valve gear; instead they emerged with three sets of Walschaerts gear. The Holcroft/Gresley conjugated arrangement, was plainly not satisfactory and the original, A822, was

The prototype N1 822 in its original manifestation with conjugated valve gear, at Ashford after completion in March 1923. It was a production N, chosen for the purpose; like the prototype N, it was finished in SECR grey but was very different in appearance, at the front end. Most marked was the curious elongated pair of rods across the cylinders; these connected the outside valve gears to the combination levers. The large front sand box was also a prominent difference.

soon altered to match the five 'production' engines, in 1931, being renumbered 1822 at the same time.

The conjugated 822 had suffered less wear and returned a coal consumption 10% less, though water was up 11%. Cocks in 1948 frankly expressed some doubts ('at this distance of time' as he put it) as to why the conjugated gear was abandoned in 1929: *The only reason which can now be discovered for its removal is the fact that there was some over-travel of the middle valve. The rigidity of the conjugated valve gears was not mechanically quite satisfactory, for it was found that, owing to back lash in the joints and springiness in the levers, and movement of the reversing shaft due to slackness of the clutch, the central valve over-ran its travel when the engine was running at high speed in full gear.* The valve head, under some conditions, was actually touching the valve chest cover.

The N as noted had been designed for ease of servicing, Maunsell making the parts accessible so that oiling by the driver could be accomplished at ground level without the need for a pit. He issued instructions that this advantage should not be lost in the three cylinder N1. Accordingly grease lubrication was used in certain parts of the motion 'especially with regard to the operation of the inside cylinders'. While this spared the driver a job, the grease had to be applied weekly by the fitters. Strict adherence to this could not of course

be guaranteed; moreover, the grease flowed out when heated up and subsequent unlooked-for wear became a problem.

The N1 boiler was higher and the running plate was straight all the way to the buffers to accommodate the cylinder casting. So, instead of the front sandboxes concealed behind the framing, they had large prominent square boxes on the running plate, of a sort you would not be surprised to find on an industrial saddletank!

The first N1 had a 3,500 gallon tender but the five subsequent ones had the larger 4,000 gallon one. Much of the detail observations made above apply to the N1s as much as the Ns; the first conjugated N1 engine had a 'stirrup' front footstep like the earlier Ns, the later five had the conventional front step from the first. Double slidebars had become the convention but because of the more evenly distributed forces, the three cylinder engines had a single slidebar. Other minor differences will be pointed out 'along the way'.

A Warning From History. There is no mention in the Engine Records of the work done on A822 to render it a three cylinder N1, the removal of its conjugated gear and so on. Not a peep!

The Record
Abbreviations for Southern Railway repairs:

A = General
B = Intermediate
C = Casual
D = Non-classified

The following codes were used for repairs under British Railways, based on LMS practice.
GO = General Overhaul
HC = Heavy Casual
HI = Heavy Intermediate
LC = Light Casual
LI = Light Intermediate
Int = Intermediate
NC = Non-classified
Some were upgraded as the work unfolded such as LI-HI but downgrading, as in LC-NC for instance, seldom occurred.

Right. **New N1 A879 in lined green finery in 1930, at the old New Cross Gate establishment (that's the three road 'Middle Shed' behind). Even the sandbox has its own lining. The old place lingered on, despite being bombed, into the early 1950s. transporttreasury**

There were only five 'production' N1s built, which hardly seems to have justified the experimental and exploratory work and it was also an odd outcome that the 'production' engines were based on a modified – failed if you like – version of the N1, with three sets of Walschaerts gear in place of the conjugated arrangement *before* the original, the ostensible prototype, had been so altered. N1s A876-A880 all appeared in 1930 with 'original' A822 altered the following year. This is A876, the first to be built, very soon after its introduction, at Eastbourne engine shed. The curious outline of the tender beyond belongs to U 2-6-0 A629, converted at this period to burn pulverised fuel – see next volume. That extraordinary structure is the hopper for dispensing the said fuel. transporttreasury

'Return' or 'Defect' indicates a return visit to works normally soon after a classified repair to rectify (on the LMS for instance it was called 'Rectification') a problem often found during running-in trials. The vast majority of repairs were carried out at Ashford until the latter closed in June 1962, so the last work on the moguls was done at Eastleigh.

CI indicates 'cast iron' in respect of new type firebars introduced late on.

One final tiny point concerns the odd term 'silencer'. This, it is thought, was the item more usually called a 'muffler', fitted on the end of the blowdown discharge pipe, it main purpose to break up the escaping water and thus prevent damage to the track. They also tended to reduce the noise of the discharge. Other railways, like the LMS, used automatic blowdowns which could annoy the Civil's even more until the discharge was diverted into the ashpan!

Left. N1 31877 at St Leonards MPD, 7 August 1956. An N1 looked much like an N of course at first glance; a closer look though, took in that high flat front, the cylinders angled inwards, the sandbox and the long casing along the running plate by the firebox. This casing (present both sides) covered the brackets attached to the top of the frame and the side of the firebox which together took the weight of the rear of the boiler and firebox assembly; provision was made for expansion. transporttreasury

Bottom left. A822 became an N1, then the rest of the class was built leaving it the odd man out among the N1s; it was officially converted to the same form as the others (that is, with three sets of Walschaerts gear) from October 1931 and renumbered 1822, still within the number series of the Ns. Apparently smoke deflectors appeared at the same time; if so, it would be amongst the earliest, if not the first so numbered and equipped. The star is a puzzle; the loco might well have been used on one of the VIP trains from Dover up to Victoria, which the Southern frequently had responsibility for.

Below. A BR N1, 31876 at Hither Green coal stage, 14 October 1956. The tender, with small first emblem, is the 4,000 gallon type attached to the 'series' N1s, A876-A880. They looked like the earlier 3,500 gallon tenders but had the 'stepped' front to the running plate to match the cab and different framing/axleboxes. A822 retained a straight sided 3,500 gallon example as running with the Ns. R.J. Buckley, Initial Photographics.

An N1 in typical period shape, 31877 at St Leonards in the summer of 1956; shabby in its 'BR grey' obscuring almost the entirety of the lined black underneath. Small first emblem. A perfect illustration of how the cliff line here was utilised for the shed water tanks, in turn feeding by gravity the columns below. W. Hermiston, transporttreasury

The Record

Some N differences, just in the later 1400-1414 series. 31402 (above) at Three Bridges in July 1963 has acquired a 3,500 gallon straight sided tender late in life while 31411 (at Salisbury on 3 April 1966 after a Special working) has the more usual 4,000 gallon type with sloping tops. It's chimney contrasts sharply with the BR one on 31402. Different deflector cut-outs and grab irons. 31402 is right-hand drive, 31411 left-hand. More Ns follow overleaf!

31400

To traffic as 1400 on 7/1932
Renumbered 31400 no date

Works
16/7/34	65 nuts renewed Set of new and large tubes
27/2/41	504 copper and 314 steel stays renewed 200 copper stays riveted over 173 new small tubes 'Talbot and Stead'
17/9/43	At Ashford shed 70 new small tubes. New steel'
28/5/52-13/6/52**HI**	
25/8/53-24/9/53**GO**	BR lined black livery
19/10/54-23/10/54**LC**	31,255
22/8/55-9/9/55**LI**	5
7/1/58-25/1/58**GO**	125,012 Front end conversion
1/3/60-26/3/60**LI-HI**	68,552 New type CI firebars AWS part fitted
15/5/62-9/6/62**LI-HI**	145,633 Water treatment
30/9/63-17/10/63**LC**	180,349 Eastleigh

Tender
No.3065 in BR days

Boilers
No.1015 16/7/34
No.1075 27/2/41

Allocations
7/1932	Ashford
3/3/53	Bricklayers Arms
20/7/53	Ashford
8/7/60	Guildford
8/12/61	Brighton
22/7/63	Redhill

Withdrawn 6/64

31400 on an unusual occasion on 11 August 1963 at Dorking Town. Trains from Reading/Guildford were terminating here due to bridge works further east, passengers proceeding by bus to Betchworth for the onward journey to Redhill. It got new frames in 1958, work that included a BR Standard Class 4 style of chimney. Derek Clayton.

1400 and its long transformation to 31400. Above, in lined green very early on at what is possibly Feltham and below, in final condition at Paddock Wood with a lengthy train, on 6 June 1960. ColourRail

31401

To traffic as 1401 on 8/1932
Renumbered 31401 no date

Works

8/10/41	201 copper and 624 steel stays renewed 150 copper stays riveted over 74 nuts renewed 301 holes bushed New copper firebox Set new small tubes Large new steel tubes with copper ends
2/10/48	445 copper and 130 steel stays renewed Set new small tubes 'Howell Co' Large tubes repaired, steel with copper ends
9/3/51	All small and large tubes renewed
30/6/53-22/7/53**HI**	75 copper stays riveted over 53 nuts renewed All small and large tubes renewed
29/6/55-15/7/55**GO**	114,509
4/9/57-21/9/57**LI**	65,122
17/9/59-23/10/59**LI**	129,482 New type Cast Iron firebars ATC Spark arrester Manganese liners
31/8/61-30/9/61**GO**	177,178 Water treatment

Tender
No.1920 in BR days

Boilers
No.1031	8/10/41
No.1070	2/10/48
No.1043	9/3/51

Allocations
8/1932	Ashford
8/7/60	Guildford
8/12/61	Brighton
6/1/64	Guildford

Withdrawn 18/7/65

31401 with small first emblem on 4,000 gallon tender, at Ashford MPD on 4 October 1952. Lining follows the outline of the cab rather than the more generally adopted form; that is, disappearing into the running plate. No power classification yet. The oil delivery pipes this side on the 31400 series were held in a length of channelling rather than a tube. The series had double slidebars and the big tenders required the running plate to be angled up to match that of the cab. As explained earlier, the 4,000 gallon tenders were essentially a Western Section design for the likes of Nelsons, Arthurs and Schools. When married to a mogul the framing at the front had to be raised to align with the loco drawgear, as demonstrated here. Initial Photographics.

Ashford's long-term N, 31401, well and truly in the Garden of England, near Chilham on the Ashford-Canterbury West line, 8 June 1957. D.C. Ovenden, ColourRail

AWS fitted 31401 at Guildford MPD, 21 August 1960.

31402

To traffic as 1402 on 8/1932
Renumbered 31402 no date

Works

26/9/38	447 copper stays renewed and 275 riveted over Copper tube 82 studs fitted Set new small tubes 'Tubes ltd' Set new large tubes steel with copper ends
14/5/41	456 steel stays replaced by copper Set new small tubes 'Jarrow Tube Co'
2/7/43	350 copper stays riveted over Copper Tube 47 studs fitted
13/5/44	Brighton 228 roof stays renewed 219 holes bushed New firebox Set new small tubes 'Howell Co'
20/7/44	250 copper stays riveted over Foundation Ring 2 rivets renewed
7/12/46	At Ashford shed Set new small tubes 'Talbot and Stead'
5/8/47	At Ashford shed All large tubes renewed
21/1/48	705 monel metal stays renewed New Firebox Set new small tubes 'Talbot and Stead' T2093
30/11/49	80 nuts renewed 5 small tubes repaired
13/11/50	18 large tubes expanded and refferuled
23/10/51	358 nuts renewed Internal tube 18 copper studs fitted
25/7/52-8/8/52**LC**	No boiler work
16/12/53-15/1/54**GO**	150,754 32 new small tubes 'Stewart and Lloyds'
13/12/55-14/1/56**LI-HI**	56,604 705 steel stays renewed 173 new small tubes 'Stewart and Lloyds'
12/2/58-1/3/58**GO**	170,244
20/4/60-14/5/60**LI-HI**	68,892 New type CI firebars AWS part fitted 18 large tubes expanded and refferuled
10/4/62-11/4/62**NC**	Bricklayers Arms

Tenders
No.3068 in BR days
Straight sided 3,500 gallon tender at the end, 7/63

Boilers

No.962	26/9/38
No.1040	14/5/41
No.845	13/5/44
No.1035	21/1/48
No.1080	15/1/54
No.1016	14/5/60

Allocations

8/1932	Ashford
10/2/61	Tonbridge
26/5/61	Guildford
8/12/61	Brighton

Withdrawn 8/63 Cut up at Eastleigh Works w/e 7/3/64

31402, AWS fitted, at Ashford MPD on 25 March 1961; it had gone there new in 1932 and did not leave for all but thirty years. Peter Groom.

31402 at Three Bridges MPD on 4 June 1963; cab disc to denote water treatment, washout plugs on boiler top prominent. We have here the rarely-spotted right-hand facing lion on the tender. These Ns had the same cab front as the earlier series of Ns. Peter Groom.

31403

To traffic as 1403 on 5/9/32
Renumbered 31403 3/6/49

Works

16/6/33-23/6/33**C**	19,759	Brighton Extension of mileage 5000
19/3/34-20/4/34**C**		
24/4/35-30/5/35**A**	72,512	51 Copper and 282 stays renewed, 50 copper renewed. 87 nuts renewed 173 new small tubes 'Talbot and Stead'
30/8/37-7/10/37**A**	63,437	
13/2/40-13/3/40**A**	61,973	Class plate fitted
2/12/42**D**		
10/5/43-9/6/43**A**	80,971	
30/6/44-22/7/44**C**	32,072	
26/2/45-26/3/45**C**		
6/7/45-28/7/45**B**	51,211	Ashford shed. Extension of mileage 10,000
17/11/45-26/11/45**C**	59,543	
24/1/46-5/2/46**D**	63,254	
18/7/46-20/8/46**C**	72,409	
23/5/47-20/6/47**A**	88,701	147 copper stays renewed and 50 riveted over 108 nuts renewed 173 new small tubes 'Talbot and Stead' 2 Foundation Ring rivets renewed
27/4/49-3/6/49**A**	46,964	57 copper stays renewed and 150 riveted over 173 new small tubes 'Howells'
9/1/51-2/2/51**LI**	50,141	175 nuts renewed Internal Tube 9 studs fitted 60 studs caulked 173 new small tubes 'Talbot and Stead'
10/9/52-26/9/52**GO**	91,269	New Firebox 173 new small tubes 'Tubes ltd'
3/1/55-27/1/55**LI**	57,885	32 new small tubes and 3 new superheater tubes
6/6/57-29/6/57**GO**	122,809	362 copper stays renewed and 86 riveted over 2 fusible plugs 173 new small tubes 'Talbot and Stead' electrically welded
31/10/57-9/11/57**return**	10,245	
5/11/59-28/11/59**LI**	67,523	377 copper stays riveted over New type CI firegrate fitted 32 new small tubes 'Stewart and Lloyds' electrically welded
5/7/61-6/7/61**NC**	114,016	Spark arrester

Tender
No.3069 from new

31403 at its Ashford home, strikingly clean after its General of 1952; low capuchon chimney, small first emblem. It was another N that did a thirty-year stint at the shed, from new. Initial Photographics.

Boilers
No.1073 from new
No.1044 30/5/35
No.849 7/10/37
No.1041 13/3/40
No.898 9/6/43
No.1077 20/6/47
No.1159 3/6/49
No.1078 26/9/52
No.890 29/6/57

Allocations
9/1932   Ashford
10/2/61 Tonbridge
26/5/61 Guildford
8/12/61 Brighton

Withdrawn 6/7/63 Cut up at Eastleigh Works w/e 12/10/63

31403 at Ashford MPD, 19 July 1959, now with power classification and disc indicating water treatment; large second emblem. Peter Groom.

Further descending into scruffiness in the early 1960s; 31403 is at its new shed Brighton, so the period is between the end of 1963 when it was transferred there and its withdrawal towards the end of 1963. ColourRail

31404

To traffic as 1404 on 1/10/32
Renumbered 31404 20/4/48

Works

30/3/33-3/4/33**D**	13,103	
23/8/34-25/9/34**C**	55,653	Extension of mileage 10,000 Large tubes expanded and referruled
13/6/35-16/7/35**A**	75,635	76 copper and 409 steel stays renewed 40 nuts renewed
5/1/37**D**		
30/4/37-16/6/37**C**	51,526	Extension of mileage 10,000
5/2/38-18/3/38**C**	67,766	Extension of mileage 10,000 Class plate fitted Copper tube 2 flange patches
16/11/38-14/12/38**C**	83,131	Ashford shed
25/5/39-21/6/39**A**	94,607	186 steel stays replaced by copper 173 new small tubes 'Howell and Co.'
2/1/43-30/1/43**A**	83,998	284 nuts renewed Copper tube 5 studs fitted 173 new small tubes 'Howell and Co.'
10/5/44-15/5/44**D**		
1/7/44-27/7/44**C**		Ashford shed 3 copper stays renewed
23/6/45-1/8/45**D**	61,306	
29/3/46-2/5/46**A**	80,276	130 steel stays replaced by copper 173 new small tubes 'Tubes Ltd'
26/3/47-27/3/47**D**	21,681	Fracture welded lhs of Casing Back Plate
16/9/47-5/11/47**C**	30,633	
1/4/48-20/4/48**D**	40,020	
4/6/48-24/8/48**C**	41,550	
25/9/50-20/10/50**GO**	89,281	
17/9/51-5/10/51**LC**	24,690	
25/6/52-3/7/52	43,369	Guildford
16/12/53-9/1/54**HI**	77,117	350 copper stays riveted over 173 new small tubes 'Stewart and Lloyds' 13 rivets in firehole
21/9/54-2/10/54**LC**	94,791	
30/12/55-21/1/56**GO**	129,641	
24/2/58-15/3/58**LI**	64,543	462 copper stays riveted over 2 fusible plugs 173 new small tubes 'Stewart and Lloyds' 3 Superheater tubes
7/9/60-21/10/60**GO**	135,613	AWS part fitted 705 nuts renewed 173 new small tubes 'Stewart and Lloyds'
1/10/61-3/10/61		Exmouth Jct Test 2260

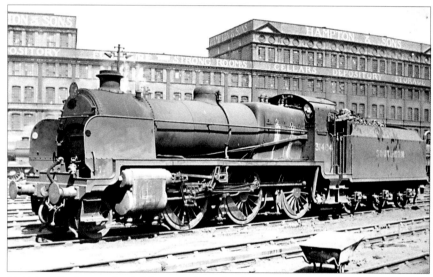

31404 with the unmistakable Depository backdrop at Stewarts Lane, on 10 June 1950. It's far too shabby for the 'sunshine' lettering to cheer it up at all and the '3' has just been awkwardly shoehorned in at the end. Snifting valves still in situ.

Tender
No.3070 from new

Boilers

No.1074	from new
No.1015	16/7/35
No.1030	21/6/39
No.1023	30/1/43
No.1030	2/5/46
No.867	20/10/50
No.969	21/1/56
No.1024	21/10/60

Allocations
10/1932 Ashford
10/2/61 Tonbridge
26/5/61 Salisbury
16/9/63 Guildford

Withdrawn 7/12/63 Cut up at Eastleigh Works w/e 4/1/64

31404 in first BR guise, with lining following outline of cabside and the little first emblem; 19 April 1954, snifting valves gone.

31405

To traffic as 1405 on 4/11/32
Renumbered 31405 15/10/49

Works

23/4/34-15/5/34**D**	47,132	
22/10/34-16/11/34**B**	61,565	Extension of mileage 10,000 50 copper stays riveted over 69 nuts renewed
18/9/35-18/10/35**A**	84,633	
19/4/37-25/5/37**D**	39,720	
8/12/37-11/1/38**C**	52,064	
24/10/38-25/11/38**A**	72,146	Class plate fitted
1/2/40-28/2/40**C**	30,598	Extension of mileage 10,000
19/2/42-1/4/42**A**	81,844	
4/10/44-4/11/44**A**	69,296	150 copper stays riveted over 462 nuts renewed 2 fusible plugs Set new small tubes 'Howell Co' New set large tubes with copper ends
27/3/47-26/4/47**B**	50,756	36 monel metal stays replaced by copper Set new small tubes 'Howell Co'
21/1/48-19/2/48**A**	68,400	336 nuts renewed Flanges caulked Set new small tubes 'Howell Co' Large tubes expanded and referruled
21/10/49-15/11/49**LI**	44,629	
28/2/51-22/3/51**HC**	76,188	
7/5/51**NC**		
25/7/51-3/8/51**LC**	85,522	No boiler work
9/9/52-26/9/52**LI**	114,098	34 new small tubes 'Tubes Ltd'
3/12/54-22/12/54**HI-LI**	174,525	
9/2/56-17/2/56**LC**	205,588	No boiler work
15/2/57-9/3/57**GO**	234,677	Front end conversion 2 x 9mm injectors fitted Lhs to Drg.A10317 120 nuts renewed 2 fusible plugs 173 new small tubes 'Universal'
31/3/59-25/4/59**LI-HI**	63,539	New CI fire bars 200 copper stays riveted over 32 new small tubes 'Tube Products' 3 new large tubes electrically welded
5/10/59-17/10/59**NC**	78,806	ATC
11/9/61-7/10/61**GO**	131,616	Spark Arrester 505 copper stays riveted over 2 fusible plugs 173 new small tubes 'Tube Products' electrically welded

Tender
No.3071 from new

Boilers

No.1075	from new
No.963	18/10/35
No.872	25/11/38
No.1029	1/4/42
No.992	4/11/44
No.845	19/2/48
No.973	22/3/51
No.1156	9/3/57
No.1021	7/10/61

Allocations

11/1932	Ashford
22/4/33	Salisbury
1/12/34	Ashford
12/7/47	Stewarts Lane
31/3/48	Ashford
10/2/61	Tonbridge
26/5/61	Weymouth
22/6/64	Redhill
18/1/65	Guildford

Withdrawn 5/6/66

31405, something of a throw-back at Hither Green MPD on 14 October 1956, with traces of BRITISH RAILWAYS still on the filthy tender. This would finally disappear in the course of a General repair the following year. R.J. Buckley, Initial Photographics.

31405 ready in the shed yard at Redhill, 14 March 1965. C.P. Stacey, Initial Photographics.

31406

To traffic as 1406 on 5/1/33
Renumbered 31406 15/10/49

Works

5/10/34-7/11/34**A**	98,032	56 copper and 693 steel stays renewed Copper Firehole 14 studs fitted Set new small tubes 'Talbot and Stead'
23/1/36-21/2/36**C**	61,004	Extension of mileage 5,000
8/12/36-15/1/37**A**	102,804	801 steel stays renewed 175 copper riveted over Set new small tubes 'Howell Co'
23/1/39-23/2/39**A**	94,905	Class plate fitted
29/7/40-30/9/40**C**	108,271	Exmouth Jct Extension of mileage 10,000
19/9/41-21/10/41**A**	68,272	
30/11/42-26/1/43**B**		Exmouth Jct Extension of mileage 5,000
15/7/43-27/8/43**C**		Exmouth Jct Extension of mileage 5,000
30/11/43-18/1/44**D**	63,880	
21/2/44-11/3/44**D**		
14/9/44-14/10/44**A**	79,370	823 copper stays renewed and 100 riveted over Copper Firehole ¾ new Set new small tubes 'Howell Co'
14/11/45-13/12/45**C**	43,826	
4/10/46-26/10/46**C**	63,958	Casing Covering left bottom corner on radius welded
3/12/47-8/1/48**A**	89,825	
23/9/49-15/10/49**HI**	46,975	
29/6/51-14/9/51**GO**	93,058	
2/9/53-19/9/53**HI**	55,422	60 copper stays riveted over 12 steel studs fitted and 12 caulked in laps 173 new small tubes
5/9/55-23/9/55**GO**	109,032	
1/6/56-19/6/56**LC**	20,052	
18/10/57-8/11/57**LI-HI**	61,129	
21/12/59-23/1/60**GO**	126,093	Full frame conversion Manganese liners New type CI (cast iron) firebars
21/2/61-18/3/61**LC**	32,905	AWS part fitted
2/7/62-4/8/62**HI**	65,602	Eastleigh 286 copper stays riveted over 86 seams and studs recaulked Foundation Ring 24 corner rivets caulked

Tenders

No.3072 from new
No.1966 14/9/51
No.3067 19/9/53

Boilers

No.1018	from new
No.1026	7/11/34
No.1079	15/1/37
No.963	23/2/39
No.869	21/10/41
No.962	14/10/44
No.894	8/1/48
No.968	14/9/51
No.830	23/9/55
No.865	23/1/60

Allocations

1/1933	Exmouth Jct
15/6/46	Brighton
10/8/47	Redhill
31/5/48	Stewarts Lane
4/2/50	Ashford
3/3/53	Hither Green
20/7/53	Ashford
10/2/61	Tonbridge
26/5/61	Weymouth
5/3/62	Exmouth Jct

Withdrawn 7/9/64 Sold to G. Cohen, Morriston, 14/10/64

1406 with green lined smoke deflectors at Exmouth Junction shed, where it had been allocated since new, in June 1938; snifting valves, top lamp iron still on smokebox top. transporttreasury

1406 took its leave of the West after the War, seldom if ever to return until the 1960s, first to Weymouth (newly a Southern Region MPD) and then finally Exmouth Junction. In between it worked from a number of sheds – here it is as 31406, an Ashford engine, at Hither Green on 8 July 1956. Ken Fairey, ColourRail

Waiting to leave Wadebridge with an up working, AWS fitted, probably in the summer of 1962. RailOnline

31407

To traffic as 1407 on 19/8/33
Renumbered 31407 20/8/49

Works

18/1/35-28/2/35**A**	76,990	216 steel stays renewed and 100 copper riveted over 173 new small tubes 'Howell Co'
18/3/36-25/3/36**D**	51,336	Eastleigh
24/11/36-6/1/37**A**	87,654	
23/9/37-27/9/37**D**	31,620	
25/11/37-11/1/38**C**	35,113	Eastleigh
7/5/38-3/6/38**C**	51,116	Exmouth Jct Extension of mileage 5,000
19/1/39-9/2/39**C**	74,857	Class plate fitted
13/10/39-8/11/39**A**	100,516	292 copper stays renewed and 181 nuts renewed Copper tube 26 studs fitted 173 new small tubes 'Talbot and Stead'
5/2/41-13/2/41**C**	65,897	Exmouth Jct Extension of mileage 10,000 Superheater ferrules renewed
9/7/41-30/7/41**A**	87,845	300 steel stays replaced by copper Large tubes repaired steel with copper ends
6/9/43-28/10/43**C**		Exmouth Jct Extension of mileage 20,000 48 second hand small tubes
11/4/44-13/5/44**A**	114,220	
15/7/46-31/8/46**A**	76,969	
7/11/46**D**		
12/5/47-20/5/47**C**	20,756	
5/7/49-20/8/49**A**	88,924	
13/6/51-13/7/51**LI**	62,207	
20/7/51**Defect**		
27/7/51-3/8/51**Defect**		
16/8/51-17/8/51**Defect**		
18/2/52-22/2/52**LC**		
10/4/52-9/5/52**HC**	79,614	
11/11/53-4/12/53**GO**	123,177	
10/12/53-18/12/53**Defect**		
13/1/55-22/1/55**LC**	30,829	
14/12/55-5/1/56**LI**	52,395	148 copper stays riveted over 78 nuts renewed 32 small tubes repaired, 141 rebeaded
11/5/56-25/5/56**NC**		60,799 Casing Back fracture welded
2/5/57-11/5/57**LC**	88,472	6 small tubes 'Stewart and Lloyds' electrically welded
26/11/57-14/12/57**LI-HI**	103,561	Inner Tube 7 studs fitted in laps 173 new small tubes 'Universal'
22/1/60-13/2/60**GO**		164,099 New type CI firebars
19/9/61-20/9/61**NC**		40,309 Spark arrester
28/2/63-1/3/63**NC**		59,735 Eastleigh

Tenders

No.3073	from new
No.3080	27/9/37

Boilers

No.1076	from new
No.1010	6/1/37
No.994	8/11/39
No.1078	30/7/41
No.828	13/5/44
No.857	31/8/46
No.1155	20/8/49
No.985	4/12/53
No.1154	13/2/60

Allocations

8/1932	Exmouth Jct
4/2/50	Stewarts Lane
5/2/51	Ashford
4/6/55	Dover
30/9/55	Ashford
10/2/61	Tonbridge
26/5/61	Weymouth

Withdrawn 7/7/63

1407 at Dover in the 1930s. Snifting valves of course but the old familiar circular hand-hold 'porthole' in the smoke deflector has gone, to be replaced by an oblong, while the bottom grab iron is horizontal not vertical. 1407 is the first of the left-hand drive Ns and the first mogul built with the four figure 1931 number.

31407 at Ashford MPD, 22 March 1956; reverser and ejector pipe are now on left-hand side for the driver standing on the left but the smoke deflector now has two oblong handholds and a vertical grab iron, though the holes for the preceding horizontal one are still there. Power classification squashed down above number. Peter Groom.

31408

To traffic as 1408 on 9/9/33
Renumbered 31408 22/7/49

Works

4/3/35-16/4/35**A**	80,780	
6/10/36-9/11/36**A**	79,437	100 copper stays riveted over 54 nuts renewed Set new small tubes 'Tubes Ltd'
22/9/37-23/9/37**D**	44,221	
9/6/38**D**		Exmouth Jct 2 steel stays renewed
5/10/38-10/11/38**A**	94,413	Class plate fitted 204 steel stays replaced by copper Set new small tubes 'Howell and Co'
13/11/39-1/12/39**D**	47,467	
1/10/40-6/11/40**A**	85,917	80 steel stays replaced by copper Set new small tubes 'Chesterfield Tube Co.'
1/4/42-29/4/42**C**	50,616	Extension of mileage 5,000
21/9/42-6/10/42**C**		Exmouth Jct Extension of mileage 5,000 12 nuts renewed 2 fusible plugs 165 new small tubes
9/11/43-15/12/43**A**	101,196	608 copper and 188 steel stays renewed 2 fusible plugs Large tubes repaired steel with copper ends
9/7/45-6/10/45**C**	56,162	Extension of mileage 5,000
24/10/46-16/11/46**A**	90,949	705 monel metal stays renewed New firebox
14/6/49-22/7/49**A**	89,509	Set new small tubes 'Howell and Co.'Large tubes new steel with copper ends
30/3/51-20/4/51**LI**	61,177	50 copper stays riveted over 2 fusible plugs
22/7/52-12/9/52**HI**	92,563	
24/9/52-26/9/52**Defect**		
22/9/53-25/9/53**LC**	121,850	
5/10/53-13/10/53**NC**		
10/11/54-26/11/54**GO**	152,881	New type 9mm injectors 766 copper stays renewed 173 new small tubes 'Howells and Co.'
28/12/55-12/2/56**LC**	32,848	Stewarts Lane Set new large tubes
28/2/57-18/4/57**GO**	64,741	Front end conversion New type 9mm injectors fitted to Drg.A10068 173 new small tubes 'Universal'
17/9/57-26/9/57**NC-LC**	17,447	
29/7/58-16/8/58**LC**	35,079	
24/12/59-7/1/60**NC**	67,083	ATC
26/8/60-23/9/60**LI-GO**	83,502	
8/6/61-24/6/61**LC**	18,731	
14/7/61-18/7/61**NC**	20,943	Spark arrester 173 new small tubes 'Stewart and Lloyds' electrically welded
7/10/63-9/11/63**LI**	63,070	Eastleigh Blowdown gear and silencer 492 copper stays riveted over 2 fusible plugs 173 new small tubes 'Tube Products'

Tenders

No.3074	from new
No.3081	23/9/37

Boilers

No.1079	from new
No.1010	16/4/35
No.1078	9/11/36
No.1076	10/11/38
No.1025	6/11/40
No.1074	15/12/43
No.1025	16/11/46
No.999	22/7/49
No.890	26/11/54
No.993	18/4/57
No.846	22/9/60

Allocations

9/1933	Exmouth Jct
4/2/50	Stewarts Lane
5/2/51	Ashford
3/3/53	Hither Green
1/10/53	Bricklayers Arms
8/2/55	Stewarts Lane
14/6/59	Ashford
9/11/61	Salisbury
16/9/63	Guildford

Withdrawn 5/6/66

1408 in pre-War Southern Railway livery; two cut-outs, vertical grab iron on smoke deflector.

Grimy and grey at its home shed Ashford, on 2 April 1960, AWS fitted. Behind is H tank 31512 and another mogul. David Idle, transporttreasury

31409

To traffic as 1409 on 4/10/33
Renumbered 31409 8/1/49

Works

1/4/35-10/5/35**A**	82,021	
27/12/35**D**		Eastleigh
28/10/36-4/12/36**A**	80,637	388 steel stays renewed and 100 copper riveted over
2/2/38-4/2/38**D**	54,475	
22/6/38-12/7/38**C**	74,110	Exmouth Jct Extension of mileage 10,000
5/1/39-8/2/39**A**	96,504	Class plate fitted 615 monel metal stays renewed Set new small tubes 'Howell and Co.'
30/1/41-5/3/41**A**	82,356	
23/7/41-13/10/41**C**	5,953	Eastleigh
15/10/42-9/11/42**C**		Exmouth Jct Extension of mileage 5,000
25/1/44-26/2/44**A**	94,136	
17/1/45-1/2/45**C**		Exmouth Jct
15/10/45-17/11/45**C**	55,504	Extension of mileage 5,000
28/2/46-2/5/46**A**	66,459	
14/12/47-21/1/48		Exmouth Jct
30/1/48**D**	55,142	Eastleigh Weighing only
1/12/48-8/1/49**A**	82,818	247 nuts renewed Steel Tube bottom flange repaired
30/1/50-17/2/50**LC**	31,902	No boiler work
12/2/52-21/3/52**GO**	81,085	New firebox 173 new small tubes 'Howells and Co.'
31/3/52-2/4/52**Defect**		
26/1/54-20/2/54**HI**	48,075	350 copper stays riveted over 173 new small tubes 'Stewart and Lloyds'
8/9/55-26/9/55**HI**	95,768	525 copper stays riveted over 2 fusible plugs 173 new small tubes 'Stewart and Lloyds' electrically welded
6/2/57-1/3/57**GO**	133,375	
3/6/57-13/6/57**LC**	6,038	
16/10/58-8/11/58**LI**	43,615	New CI (cast iron) firegrate fitted 462 copper stays riveted over 2 fusible plugs 173 new small tubes 'Stewart and Lloyds' electrically welded
19/4/60-14/5/60**LI-HI**	78,919	AWS part fitted 534 copper stays riveted over 2 fusible plugs 173 new small tubes 'Howells and Co.'
12/7/61-13/7/61**NC**	102,896	Spark arrester

Tenders

No.3075	from new
No.3082	4/2/38

Boilers

No.1019	from new
No.1079	10/5/35
No.1082	4/12/36
No.1024	8/2/39
No.894	5/3/41
No.973	26/2/44
No.957	2/5/46
No.1078	8/1/49
No.898	21/3/52
No.892	1/3/57

Allocations

10/1933	Exmouth Jct
4/2/50	Stewarts Lane
14/6/59	Ashford
9/11/61	Exmouth Jct

Withdrawn 17/11/62 Cut up at Eastleigh Works w/e 29/2/64

31409 with an up train from Dover/Folkestone on 29 January 1960. In the background the crane marks Ashford North Yard permanent way dump. D.C. Ovenden, ColourRail.

31410

To traffic as 1410 on 4/11/33
Renumbered 31410 15/12/49

Works

11/7/35-29/8/35**C**	52,083	Bricklayers Arms
27/7/36-10/9/36**A**	81,666	310 steel stays replaced by copper Set new small tubes 'Tubes Ltd'
28/1/38-2/2/38**D**	48,511	
12/7/38**D**		Bricklayers Arms Stays renewed
23/11/38-3/1/39**A**	73,779	150 nuts renewed Copper Tube 14 studs fitted Large tubes repaired steel with copper ends
14/5/41-18/6/41**A**	64,248	150 copper stays riveted over 290 nuts renewed Copper Tube 54 stays fitted Set new small tubes 'Tubes Ltd'
31/1/44-26/2/44**A**	72,172	
11/9/45-3/11/45**B**	47,902	Bricklayers Arms Extension of mileage 10,000
24/7/46-30/8/46**C**		Bricklayers Arms
10/11/47-12/12/47**A**	93,052	391 copper stays renewed and 300 riveted over Large tubes new steel with copper ends
25/7/49-5/8/49**LC**	36,216	Brighton
23/11/49-15/12/49**HI**	43,884	Inner Tube 38 studs fitted 84caulked Set new small tubes 'Tubes Ltd'
1/6/51-22/6/51**HC**	80,837	No boiler work
16/4/52-2/5/52**GO**	95,829	
18/5/53-4/7/53**LC**		No Boiler work
8/5/54-12/6/54**LC**		Stewarts Lane Set new small tubes
15/10/54-30/10/54**HI**	65,244	400 copper stays riveted over
4/1/56-21/1/56**GO**	95,651	173 new small tubes 'Stewart and Lloyds' electrically welded
15/3/57-23/3/57**LC**	32,051	173 new small tubes 'Universal'
16/1/58-7/2/58**LI**	52,830	45 copper stays riveted over 2 fusible plugs 173 new small tubes 'Stewart and Lloyds' electrically welded
10/9/59-3/10/59**LI-HI**	93,473	ATC New type CI firebars 475 copper stays riveted over 2 fusible plugs 173 new small tubes 'Tube Products' electrically welded
27/4/61-20/5/61**GO**		125,919
9/11/61-10/11/61**NC**		Bricklayers Arms

Tenders

No.3076	from new
No.3083	2/2/38
No.3034	5/8/49
No.3083	22/6/51
No.3041	7/12/63

Boilers

No.1080	from new
No.985	10/9/36
No.1078	3/1/39
No.1024	18/6/41
No.1033	26/2/44
No.1074	12/12/47
No.903	2/5/52
No.899	21/1/56
No.897	20/5/61

Allocations

11/1933	Bricklayers Arms
21/4/34	Eastleigh
1/12/34	Ashford
23/2/35	Bricklayers Arms
25/3/44	Stewarts Lane
27/1/45	Bricklayers Arms
20/4/46	Stewarts Lane
22/7/63	Norwood Jct
16/9/63	Redhill
6/1/64	Guildford

Withdrawn 1/11/64

Stewarts Lane's 31410, glisteningly fresh off a General at the adjacent works and probably in the first flush of steam, plays with some material wagons on the up main line at Ashford in May 1961. John Scrace.

In the same period – the same day maybe – 31410 takes coal at Ashford MPD. We now find the Ns with a single oblong handhold and horizontal grab iron on the smoke deflector. This was the one with the strange additional flimsy strip added to the top of the deflector.

31411

To traffic as 1411 on 13/11/33
Renumbered 31411 30/10/48

Works

Date	Mileage	Notes
2/9/34-4/10/34		Eastleigh
9/9/35-19/10/35**C**		Bricklayers Arms Extension of mileage 5,000
17/7/36-26/8/36**A**	80,114	377 steel stays and 42 nuts renewed Set new small tubes 'Tubes Ltd'
13/5/38-20/5/38**D**	55,891	Class plate fitted
11/10/38-11/11/38**C**	67,569	Extension of mileage 10,000
22/2/39-22/3/39**A**	72,744	150 copper stays riveted over 270 nuts renewed Set new small tubes 'Tubes Ltd' Large tubes repaired steel with copper ends
3/4/41-26/5/41**B**	52,839	Brighton Extension of mileage 10,000
15/3/42-1/5/42**C**		Bricklayers Arms Extension of mileage 10,000 3 second hand large tubes
17/8/42-19/9/42**B**	83,239	Extension of mileage 15,000
17/5/43-7/7/43**C**		Bricklayers Arms 20 steel stays replaced by copper
1/4/44-26/4/44**C**		Stewarts Lane
24/8/44-29/9/44**A**	135,323	859 copper stays renewed and 50 riveted over Set new small tubes 'Howells and Co'
18/12/46-17/1/47**B**	61,919	
6/7/47-14/7/47**C**		Stewarts Lane
15/8/47-11/9/47**C**		Stewarts Lane
27/9/48-30/10/48**A**	93,542	99 nuts renewed Set new small tubes 'Talbot and Stead'
19/12/50-19/1/51**HI**	60,713	
19/2/53-10/4/53**GO**		705 steel stays and 705 nuts renewed 173 new small tubes 'Universal'
16/3/55-1/4/55**LI-HI**	56,969	Inner Tube 52 studs fitted and 28 caulked 173 new small tubes 'Universal'
19/12/56-19/1/57**GO**	125,253	Inner Tube 32 studs fitted 2 fusible plugs 173 new small tubes 'Stewart and Lloyds'
1/10/58-18/10/58**LI-HI**	47,681	CI (cast iron) firebars 250 copper stays riveted over 173 new small tubes 'Stewart and Lloyds'
10/10/60-5/11/60**LI-HI**	90,422	240 copper stays riveted over 2 fusible plugs 173 new small tubes 'Tube Products'
27/7/61-28/7/61**NC**		
21/3/63-27/4/63**GO**	129,823	Eastleigh Blowdown gear and silencer Briquette tube feeder
24/10/63-2/11/63**LC**	13,341	Eastleigh
10/1/64-18/1/64**LC**	16,683	Eastleigh 173 new small tubes 'Tube Products'

Tenders

No.3077 from new
No.3085 20/5/38

Boilers

No.1081 from new
No.1077 26/8/36
No.1079 22/3/39
No.1078 29/9/44
No.1083 30/10/48
No.1156 10/4/53
No.987 19/1/57
No.1156 27/4/63

Allocations

11/1933	Bricklayers Arms
21/4/34	Eastleigh
19/5/34	Brighton
16/6/34	Eastleigh
1/12/34	Ashford
23/2/35	Bricklayers Arms
25/3/44	Stewarts Lane
27/1/45	Bricklayers Arms
20/4/46	Stewarts Lane
22/7/63	Redhill
18/1/65	Guildford

Withdrawn 24/4/66

31411 near St Mary Cray with an up Kent Coast train on 13 June 1959; like all the series 31407-31414, the loco has left-hand drive. This was the last Saturday of steam working on the North Kent line. Peter Groom.

31411 stayed on at Stewarts Lane after the Kent Coast electrification but was finally transferred away when the grand old London shed closed to steam in 1963. It had, unusually, undergone a General at Eastleigh earlier in the year (hence its relatively late withdrawal) and was briefly working back at Stewarts Lane again before transfer to Redhill in July 1963. Here we see it at its future home, Redhill (with 75D Stewarts Lane plate) on 8 June 1963. ColourRail

31412

To traffic as 1412 on 9/12/33
Renumbered 31412 17/12/48

Works

3/6/35-10/7/35**C**	52,853	Bricklayers Arms
4/3/36-24/4/36**A**	74,961	
13/10/37-12/11/37**B**	47,536	Extension of mileage 15,000
1/6/38-20/6/38**D**	66,216	Class plate fitted
6/2/39-10/3/39**A**	85,516	125 copper stays riveted over 187 nuts renewed Set new small tubes 'Howells and Co'
29/11/41-31/12/41**A**	72,490	
11/6/43-7/8/43**C**		Bricklayers Arms Extension of mileage 5,000
22/1/43-22/12/43**C**	61,142	
1/8/45-8/9/45**A**	102,992	
20/3/46-26/3/46**D**	17,259	
15/11/48-17/12/48**B**	63,437	
14/11/49-14/12/49**A**	86,894	97 copper and 1010 steel stays renewed Set new small tubes 'Howells and Co'
24/7/50-11/8/50**LC**	16,054	No boiler work
24/10/51-16/11/51**LI**	49,175	11 copper and 76 steel stays renewed 173 new small tubes 'Talbot and Stead'
8/5/53-12/6/53**GO**	83,067	744 copper stays renewed 173 new small tubes 'Howells and Co'
27/7/54-28/8/54**LC**	32,487	No boiler work
27/2/55-25/3/55**LC**		Bricklayers Arms 173 small tubes 'repaired'
27/3/56-14/5/56**LC-HI**	61,096	Brighton 432 copper stays riveted over 2 fusible plugs 173 new small tubes 'Stewart and Lloyds'
14/3/57-17/4/57**LC**	88,495	Stewarts Lane Inner Tube studs and seams, left side, caulked
6/12/57-4/1/58**GO**	108,819	
16/4/59-16/5/59**LC**	30,697	
2/11/60-2/12/60**LI-HI**	62,599	New type CI (cast iron) firebars
5/12/61**NC**		Bricklayers Arms

Tenders

No.3078 from new
No.3084 20/6/38

Boilers

No.1077	from new
No.1019	24/4/36
No.1082	10/3/39
No.1083	31/12/41
No.862	8/9/45
No.994	14/12/49
No.937	12/6/53
No.961	4/1/58

Allocations

12/1933	Bricklayers Arms
21/4/34	Eastleigh
19/5/34	Nine Elms
3/11/34	Eastleigh
1/12/34	Redhill
23/2/35	Bricklayers Arms
25/3/44	Stewarts Lane
27/1/45	Bricklayers Arms
20/4/46	Stewarts Lane
22/7/63	Norwood Jct
16/9/63	Redhill
6/1/64	Guildford

Withdrawn 9/8/64

31412 with a Sunday Special (carefully chalked on the smokebox door) of WR stock, at St Mary Cray Junction on 2 August 1959. D.C. Ovenden, ColourRail

At home at Stewarts Lane, 5 September 1961. One time Shedmaster at 'The Lane' Richard Hardy considered the Ns 'remarkably useful'. They were the main line freight engines on both Eastern and Central Sections during the week and, on busy weekends in the mid-1950s, were hurled into the fray to stand in for King Arthurs and West Countrys on the Ramsgates and for many of the trains to be worked forward from Willesden and Kensington to Kent and the South Coast resorts: *Our Chief Running Foreman, Fred Pankhurst, had to cover around 30 'West Country' duties and goodness knows how many 'King Arthur' turns on a Saturday or Sunday so the Ns came to be known as "Panky's bleedin' Pacifics". Some Ns were in good order, some very rough and usually one or two had flats on the tender wheels, gained while braking heavily on freight work. But they had to do the job.* Norman Preedy.

31413

To traffic as 1413 on 8/1/34
Renumbered 31413 24/9/49

Works

25/9/34**D**		
19/11/34-11/1/35**C**	31,803	Brighton
11/9/36-16/10/36**A**	74,077	47 copper and 445 steel stays renewed Set new small tubes 'Tubes Ltd'
26/1/38**D**		Salisbury 1 steel stay renewed
21/9/38-26/9/38**D**	62,128	Class plate fitted
22/11/38-24/12/38**C**	63,945	Brighton extension of mileage 10,000 Copper Tube 10 collar bolts Set new small tubes 'Chesterfield'
21/11/39-18/12/39**A**	85,839	All steel stays replaced by copper Set new small tubes 'Howells and Co'
3/1/42-24/2/42**C**		Guildford Extension of mileage 5,000 21 large tubes expanded
30/4/42-1/6/42**C**	63,481	
7/9/42-6/10/43**A**	103,372	
7/2/46-6/3/46**C**		Bricklayers Arms
20/6/46-13/7/46**A**	74,831	
1/3/48-20/3/48**B**	40,817	
19/7/48-26/7/48**C**	46,407	Stewarts Lane
22/8/49-24/9/49**LC**	66,188	
7/9/50-29/9/50**LC**	91,226	
9/3/51-30/3/51**HC**	100,947	50 roof stays renewed 168 holes bushed Set new small tubes 'Talbot and Stead'
13/7/53-7/8/53**HI**	158,541	450 copper stays riveted over 173 new small tubes 'Howells and Co'
21/4/54-8/5/54**HC-LC**	176,814	No boiler work
14/6/55-2/7/55**GO**	208,012	705 monel metal stays and 705 nuts renewed 173 new small tubes 'Universal'
5/10/56-17/11/56	37,480	Stewarts Lane
10/1/58-31/1/58**LI-HI**	65,401	117 copper stays riveted over 324 nuts renewed 173 new small tubes 'Stewart and Lloyds'
8/4/60-14/5/60**GO**	116,418	Full frame conversion New type CI firebars AWS part fitted
5/2/62-24/2/62**NC-LC**	31,479	Eastleigh
21/3/63-20/4/63**LC**		Guildford

Tenders

No.3079 from new
No.3086 26/9/38

Boilers

No.1082	from new
No.1080	16/10/36
No.989	18/12/39
No.891	6/10/43
No.961	13/7/46
No.940	30/3/51
No.990	3/7/55
No.885	14/5/60

Allocations

1/1934	Salisbury
21/4/34	Eastleigh
19/5/34	Salisbury
25/3/44	Stewarts Lane
27/1/45	Bricklayers Arms
20/4/46	Stewarts Lane
14/6/59	Dover
26/5/61	Eastleigh
16/9/63	Guildford

Withdrawn 14/6/64

31413 in the shed yard at Eastleigh on 25 May 1963 looking good after a Light Casual at the nearby works. BR chimney and modified frames acquired in 1960. Rob Tibbits, ColourRail

31414

To traffic as 1414 on 26/1/34
Renumbered 31414 28/4/50

Works

21/9/34-25/9/34		Eastleigh 36 stays repaired Foundation Ring corners caulked
10/5/35-27/6/35**C**	44,909	Extension of mileage 10,000 2 copper stays renewed
4/11/35-14/11/35**D**	54,613	Eastleigh
8/8/36-22/9/36**A**	79,253	615 steel stays renewed and 175 copper riveted over
11/1/38-22/3/38**C**		Salisbury 4 copper stays renewed
23/9/38-28/9/38**D**	58,423	Class plate fitted
26/10/38**D**		Eastleigh
15/11/38-20/12/38**C**	62,091	Salisbury
17/8/39-19/9/39**A**	76,607	246 steel stays replaced by copper Copper Tube 30 studs fitted Set new small tubes 'Howell and Co'
11/11/41-20/12/41**C**	60,216	Guildford 151 new small tubes
26/5/43-28/6/43**A**	102,813	
1/10/45-31/10/45**A**	72,511	
31/10/47-20/12/47		Brighton
24/3/50-28/4/50**A**	103,759	100 copper stays riveted over 409 nuts renewed 173 new small tubes 'Tubes Ltd'
28/9/51-19/10/51**LI**	37,044	278 monel metal nuts renewed Inner Tube laps copper welded Set new small tubes
21/10/52-14/11/52**GO**	63,514	588 copper stays renewed 173 new small tubes 'Tubes Ltd'
29/3/54-23/4/54**LC**		Stewarts Lane
5/8/55-31/8/55**HI**	67,260	205 copper stays renewed and 266 riveted over Internal wrapping 5 plugs fitted in weld 173 new small tubes 'Stewart and Lloyds' electrically welded New cylinders
14/1/57-1/2/57**GO**	103,827	753 copper stays renewed 2 fusible plugs Set new small tubes 'Stewart and Lloyds'
15/10/58-1/11/58**LI**	54,156	New CI firebars fitted 521 copper stays riveted over 2 fusible plugs Set new small tubes 'Stewart and Lloyds'
4/5/60-28/5/60**LI-HI**	91,616	AWS part fitted 16 copper stays renewed and 478 riveted over 2 fusible plugs 173 new small tubes 'Universal'
3/6/61-10/6/61**LC**		Guildford 167 small tubes rebeaded 6 new small tubes 12 second hand large tubes

Tenders

No.3066 from new
No.3087 28/9/38

Boilers

No.1078	from new
No.994	22/9/36
No.1015	19/9/39
No.820	28/6/43
No.1065	31/10/45
No.1160	28/4/50
No.863	14/11/52
No.869	1/2/57

Allocations

1/1934	Salisbury
21/4/34	Eastleigh
19/5/34	Nine Elms
1/8/34	Salisbury
25/3/44	Stewarts Lane
27/1/45	Bricklayers Arms
20/4/46	Stewarts Lane
14/6/59	Dover
17/1/61	Feltham
10/2/61	Guildford

Withdrawn 24/11/62 Cut up at Eastleigh Works w/e 2/3/63

31414 at that now-familiar viewpoint west of Ashford station with an up train from the coast on 26 February 1960; PW Yard in the distance (see page 63). D.C. Ovenden, ColourRail

31414 stopped at Feltham MPD in the early 1960, with dome top off, panel removed on firebox side; small old emblem. Richard Vitler Collection.

31810

To traffic as 810 on 4/8/17 with boiler no.821
Renumbered A810, 1810, no dates, 31810 10/48

Works

8/4/18-26/4/18**L**	22,196	
7/9/18-26/4/18**L**	41,975	
25/2/19-7/5/19**G**	55,567	
12/6/19**L**		
11/1/19-19/11/19**L**	21,873	
2/2/20-27/2/20**L**	30,040	
13/5/20-20/5/20**L**	33,915	
8/9/20-16/10/20**L**	44,912	
6/12/20-1/3/21**G**	49,912	
20/9/21-15/10/21**L**	16,343	
3/3/22-6/5/22**L**	28,099	
3/8/22-15/9/22**L**	34,328	
6/12/22-4/1/23**L**	42,635	
15/3/23-29/3/23**L**	48,963	
3/5/23-29/5/23**L**	50,131	
28/8/23-25/10/23**L**	57,110	
11/1924		Southern Railway green livery
24/2/37		13 copper and 18 steel stays renewed 100 copper riveted over 285 nuts renewed Copper Tubeplate "6 holes bushed 12 studs fitted" Set new small tubes 'Talbot and Stead' Large tubes repaired steel with copper ends
20/5/39		Stewarts Lane Set new small tubes
9/10/48		277 copper stays renewed 250 copper riveted over Copper Tubeplate 50 studs fitted Steel Tubeplate "level bottom flange repair" Firehole 26 rivets caulked Set new small tubes 'Howells and Co' Large tubes "new steel with copper ends"
14/2/49		Copper stays riveted over "in fire area" "Tubeplate seam and Barrel connecting seam caulked"
24/6/50		Copper stays riveted over "in fire area" 173 new small tubes 'Howells'
24/12/52		1 steel stay renewed 173 new small tubes 'Stewart and Lloyds' 13 rivets in Firehole Large tubes repaired steel with copper ends
11/6/54		Bricklayers Arms 60 nuts renewed 173 small tubes repaired 3 new large tubes 18 second hand expanded and referruled
28/4/55-13/5/55**LI-HI**	61,849	160 steel stays replaced by copper 140 nuts renewed Internal Tubeplate "6 studs fitted in laps" 2 fusible plugs 32 new small tubes 141 rebeaded All large tubes repaired Firehole 13 rivets caulked Foundation Ring 28 rivets caulked
12/3/56		Stewarts Lane 2 fusible plugs 173 new small tubes
19/9/57-12/10/57**GO**	125,165	260 copper and 704 steel stays renewed 705 nuts renewed 14 roof nuts renewed 243 holes bushed Internal tubeplate new 2 fusible plugs barrel scaled 173 new small tubes 'Tube Products' electrically welded
21/9/59-17/10/59**LI-HI**	49,524	Spark arrester ATC New type CI firebars 63 copper stays riveted over 271 nuts renewed Internal Tubeplate "36 flange 20 corner and 8 casing rivets caulked" 2 fusible plugs 173 new small tubes 'Tube Products' 3 new large tubes 18 second hand expanded and referruled
22/12/61-20/1/62**NC-LC**	87,594	Eastleigh 2 fusible plugs 173 new small tubes 'Stewart and Lloyds' 6 new large tubes 15 second hand 15 expanded 21 referruled

Tender
No.3000 no date

Boilers
No.996 24/2/37
No.846 OUT 23/8/48
No.937 9/10/48
No.964 24/12/52
No.1036 12/10/57

Allocations
From new Bricklayers Arms
5/11/32 New Cross Gate
2/11/35 Stewarts Lane
14/6/59 Dover
26/5/61 Eastleigh
16/9/63 Guildford

Withdrawn 3/64

The first N which, as befits a prototype, lived a lone existence for a few years and worked exclusively in the east until a late transfer to Eastleigh in 1961. These moguls were 4P, let it be remembered, so our old one-time A810 is doing very well with a train of this size so late on in life, the 10.26 Victoria-Ramsgate at Herne Bay, on 17 August 1958. B. Wadey, transporttreasury

31810 at Bournemouth (MPD behind, station away to right) on 6 August 1961. 31810 left its Kentish haunts at the last, seeing out its final years at Eastleigh and Bournemouth. During that time it paid what was probably its only visit to Eastleigh, for some relatively minor work. R. Broughton, ColourRail

31811

To traffic as 811 on 29/6/20
Renumbered A811 no date, 1811 20/2/32; 31811 29/12/49

Works

20/3/21-9/4/21**L**	23,408	
24/8/21-1/10/21**L**	33,960	
14/10/22-24/10/22**L**	67,216	
3/1/23-9/3/23**G**	72,858	
9/9/23-12/10/23**L**	10,748	
21/2/24-9/4/24**C**	19,586	
8/8/24-16/8/24**D**		
19/2/25-1/5/25**D**	44,091	
15/7/25-16/10/25**A**	48,319	Southern Railway green livery
2/9/26-11/9/26**D**		
16/11/26-27/1/27**B**	28,661	Extension of mileage 15,000
6/10/27-24/11/27**B**	48,508	
12/7/28-3/8/28**B**	66,192	Extension of mileage 15,000
27/6/29-15/8/29**A**	93,631	
22/1/31-25/2/31**C**		Bricklayers Arms
17/2/32-20/2/32**A**	63,240	
7/9/33-19/10/33**B**	40,834	Extension of mileage 5,000
10/4/34-15/6/34**C**	48,081	
29/12/34-8/2/35**A**	60,926	
21/2/36**D**		
6/7/36-14/8/36**C**	34,959	Extension of mileage 5,000
30/1/37-26/2/37**C**	46,246	Stewarts Lane
2/4/37-15/4/37**C**	47,992	Stewarts Lane
27/6/38-12/8/38**A**	75,204	Class plate fitted 743 copper stays renewed 342 holes bushed Copper Tubeplate new Throat Plate two patches Firehole rivets renewed Set new small tubes 'Tubes Ltd' Large tubes repaired steel with copper ends [5 roller expanders]
25/9/40-18/12/40**C**		50,425 Brighton Extension of mileage 5,000
23/5/41-28/6/41**C**	57,190	Brighton 5 copper stays renewed 535 copper riveted over Copper Tubeplate 20 studs fitted Set new small tubes 'Talbot and Stead' "5 roller expanders" Large tubes expanded
29/8/42-6/10/42**A**	89,545	
4/11/42-2/12/42**B**		
28/3/44-1/6/44**C**		Stewarts Lane
10/2/45-10/3/45**C**	52,982	Extension of mileage 5,000
11/5/45-8/6/45**C**	56,267	
21/9/45-7/2/46**A**	61,389	
8/7/47-26/7/47**B**	23,397	
19/3/48-14/4/48**C**	35,913	Stewarts Lane
23/11/49-29/12/49**A**	75,916	525 copper and 705 steel stays renewed 228 roof stays renewed Internal Tubeplate new Smokebox Tubeplate new Set new small tubes 'Howells' Large tubes repaired steel with copper ends
18/3/52-4/4/52**LI**	61,900	125 copper stays riveted over 149 nuts renewed Internal Firehole Plate 13 rivets caulked 173 new small tubes 'Tubes Ltd' 21 second hand tubes expanded and referruled
11/9/53-3/10/53**HI**	98,302	6 copper and 3 steel stays renewed 75 copper riveted over 159 nuts renewed Internal Tubeplate "13 studs fitted in Tubeplate lap" 173 new small tubes 'Howells'
7/10/53-16/10/53**defect**		
18/5/55-3/6/55**GO**	140,564	30 copper and 50 monel metal stays renewed 278 steel replaced by copper 93 nuts renewed Internal Tubeplate "Fit 34 studs" 2 fusible plugs Smokebox Tubeplate bottom flange repaired Barrel scaled 173 new small tubes 'Howells' Firehole 13 new rivets
2/8/56-18/8/56**LC**	31,007	394 copper stays riveted over 59 nuts renewed 173 new small tubes 'Stewart and Lloyds' electrically welded 3 new large tubes 18 second hand expanded and referruled Foundation Ring 12 corner rivets caulked
26/3/57-13/4/57**LI**	45,501	390 copper stays riveted over 20 nuts renewed Internal Tubeplate 7 studs fitted and 19 studs caulked 2 fusible plugs 32 new small tubes 'Universal' 141 rebeaded 15 new large tubes 6 second hand expanded and referruled Firehole 13 rivets caulked Foundation Ring 12 corner rivets caulked

2/10/58-25/10/58**LI-HI**	88,618	135 copper stays renewed 270 copper riveted over 82 nuts renewed "Firehole laps and flanges caulked flanges and 20 corner rivets caulked" 2 fusible plugs 2 mud door holes welded 173 new small tubes 'Stewart and Lloyds' electrically welded 3 new large tubes 18 second hand expanded and referruled Firehole 15 new rivets 2 brick arch studs
9/5/60-4/6/60**GO**	126,311	Water treatment New type CI (cast iron) firebars AWS part fitted
20/10/61**NC**		Bricklayers Arms
1/3/63-13/4/63**LI**	63,642	Eastleigh

Tenders
No.3001 27/1/27
No.3034 12/8/38
No.3027 4/6/60
No.1891 15/8/64

Boilers
No.828 16/10/25
No.893 15/8/29
No.901 20/2/32
No.880 8/2/35
No.935 12/8/38
No.906 6/10/42
No.874 7/2/46
No.1034 29/12/49
No.1024 3/6/55
No.872 4/6/60

Allocations
From new Tonbridge
25/1/25 Bricklayers Arms
2/11/35 Stewarts Lane
14/6/59 Guildford

Withdrawn 4/7/65

31811 was one of many engines, not just moguls, transferred wholesale westwards when the Kent Coast Electrification was completed. It was active on the Kent Coast service till June 1959 – the last days of steam on the line. Here it is in similarly pleasant surrounds to its former Kent Coast haunts, in May 1963. Transfer to Guildford sees it on the line to Redhill, at Betchworth; moreover, it is looking very bright, even at this distance, due to a recent Light Intermediate at Eastleigh.

31811 at its new home, Guildford, on 24 June 1961. The view is particularly interesting as it shows the 'business' side of the Guildford coal stage. Out of the ordinary in that the shed building itself was on the other side of a road bridge in the distance, it was highly unusual (for such a lofty building) in that there was no stage as such, but an arrangement of electric cranes which hoisted buckets of coal up into tenders.

31812

To traffic as 812 on 21/8/20
Renumbered A812, 1812 no dates; 31812 29/1/49

Works

Date	Mileage	Notes
28/4/21-30/4/21**L**	20,195	Copper stays [Bottom rows] riveted over
9/6/21-18/6/21**L**		
24/8/21-8/10/21**L**	28,001	
24/8/22-11/10/22**L**	55,323	402 copper stays riveted over
5/9/23-13/12/23**G**	80,624	Southern Railway green livery 559 copper stays renewed 220 copper riveted over 8 roof nuts renewed Firehole rivets renewed Set new small tubes 'Stewart and Lloyds' Large tubes expanded and rebeaded
19/8/24-28/8/24**D**		
9/3/25-15/5/25**B**	32,098	400 copper stays riveted over
8/6/25-16/7/25**D**	32,597	21 new large tube
1/12/26-19/3/27**A**	61,873	
15/7/27-29/7/27**D**	9,731	
21/6/29-10/8/29**A**	61,752	707 steel stays in fire area
21/8/29-24/8/29**D**	436	
26/1/32-3/3/32**A**	59,676	
23/2/34-23/3/34**B**	48,664	Extension of mileage 5,000
5/10/34-7/11/34**C**	63,455	
14/12/34-25/1/35**A**	63,867	
2/3/36-6/3/36**D**	25,544	
10/1/38-1/3/38**A**	66,270	
18/8/38-21/9/38**C**	9,338	Brighton
7/1/41-7/3/41**C**	64,384	Stewarts Lane
1/5/42-12/6/42**A**	93,773	
29/8/43-29/10/43**C**		Stewarts Lane
21/3/4-21/4/45**A**	73,918	
8/5/47-6/6/47**B**	49,026	
21/6/47-3/7/47**D**	49,453	
9/12/48-29/1/49**A**	80,501	171 copper and 663 monel metal stays renewed 303 holes bushed Copper Tubeplate new Firehole all rivets renewed Set new small tubes 'Talbot and Stead' Large tubes new steel with copper ends
8/3/51-6/4/51**LI**	54,807	6 copper stays renewed 75 riveted over 200 nuts renewed Internal Tubeplate 4 laps caulked 2 fusible plugs Set new small tubes 'Tubes Ltd' Large tubes referruled
14/1/53-6/3/53**HI**	99,237	10 copper stays renewed 279 riveted over 100 roof stays and 100 roof nuts renewed Internal Tubeplate 49 studs fitted and 41 caulked in laps 173 new small tubes 'Howells'
19/10/53-3/11/53**LC**		No Boiler work
9/12/54-31/12/54**GO**	145,779	612 copper stays renewed 100 riveted over 213 roof stays and 213 roof nuts renewed 272 holes bushed Internal Tubeplate new Smokebox Tubeplate new Barrel scaled Set new small tubes 'Howells' Set new large tubes
4/4/56-13/4/56**LC**	34,587	1 copper stays renewed 350 copper riveted over Internal Tubeplate 20 rivets and laps caulked 173 new small tubes 'Stewart and Lloyds' electrically welded
22/8/56**NC**	45,187	No Boiler work
26/8/57-14/9/57**LI-HI**	71,606	185 copper stays renewed 235 riveted over Internal Tubeplate 24 studs fitted and roof fracture welded 2 fusible plugs 173 new small tubes 'Tube Products' electrically welded Firehole 15 new rivets Foundation Ring 21 rivets caulked
19/1/60-13/2/60**GO**	117,964	New type CI firebars
29/2/60-19/3/60**defect**		
19/3/62-7/4/62**LI**	47,902	AWS complete [minus batteries] Water treatment Spark arrester 'Overhead live wire notices'
5/9/62-8/9/62**LC**	53,784	Eastleigh

Tenders

No.3002 10/8/29
No.3005 12/6/42
No.3002 6/3/53

Boilers

No.812 21/8/20
No.829 19/3/27
No.999 10/8/29
No.960 3/3/32
No.883 25/1/35
No.910 1/3/38
No.970 12/6/42
No.832 21/4/45
No.1013 29/1/49
No.877 31/12/54
No.843 13/2/60

Allocations

From new Tonbridge
25/1/25 Ashford
5/11/32 New Cross Gate
2/11/35 Stewarts Lane
14/6/59 Guildford
31/8/63 Exmouth Jct

Withdrawn 8/8/64 Sold to Birds, Morriston 4/9/64

31812 in the unmistakable confines of Stewarts Lane MPD, 5 May 1956. It had been based here since 1935. transporttreasury

AWS fitted 31812 at Reading MPD, the vast bulk of the GWR signalbox in the background, 9 June 1963. Another one redundant from Kent Coast workings, 31812 had been working from Guildford since June 1959. The washout plug holes on the top of the boiler, forward of the dome, are for once clear to see. The oil delivery pipes once they leave the tube restraining them this side, begin to acquire various directions of travel. The AWS conduit is clipped to the running plate valence, disappearing inside above the cylinder and re-emerging just by the right-hand framing at the front. Peter Groom.

31813

To traffic as 813 on 27/9/20
Renumbered A813 no date; 1813 12/12/31; 31831 23/6/50

Works

8/7/21-31/8/21**L**	27,237	
1/12/22-21/2/23**G**	67,170	
28/5/23-29/5/23 'Not to count'		
23/11/23-1/2/24**C**	24,456	
13/3/24**D**		
16/10/24-17/10/24**D**		
18/9/25-6/1/26**A**	58,643	Southern Railway green livery
10/6/27-26/7/27**C**	39,331	Extension of mileage 10,000
21/9/28-12/12/28**A**	72,323	332 copper stays renewed 225 copper riveted over Copper Tubeplate 36 studs fitted Firehole rivets hammered Set new small tubes 'Howell and Co' Large tubes welded
17/7/29-23/7/29**D**	14,591	Extension of mileage 5,000
1/1/31**C**		Brighton
13/11/31-12/12/31**A**	70,773	22 copper and 614 steel stays renewed 300 copper riveted over Copper Tubeplate 3 studs fitted Firehole rivets hammered Set new small tubes 'Howell and Co' Second hand large tubes with copper ends
21/8/33-6/10/33**B**	49,652	Extension of mileage 10,000 2 copper stays and 106 nuts renewed Copper Tubeplate 2 angle patches 4 studs fitted "8 bottom rows of small tubes expanded and rebeaded 1 large ferule renewed
11/12/34		Bricklayers Arms 4 steel stays replaced by copper
2/1/35-11/2/35**A**	80,138	
20/4/36-14/5/36**D**	27,100	
9/4/37-11/6/37**C**	46,488	Brighton Extension of mileage 5,000
5/5/38-8/6/38**C**	66,473	Class plate fitted Extension of mileage 15,000
14/10/38-9/11/38**B**	73,895	
22/2/40-3/4/40**A**	98,458	
26/1/42-25/2/42**C**	44,476	
23/6/42-5/8/42**C**	53,339	Extension of mileage 5,000
10/2/43-10/3/43**A**	63,279	351 copper stays renewed 350 copper riveted over Copper Tubeplate 69 studs fitted 2 fusible plugs Firehole 13 new rivets Set new small tubes 'Howell and co' Set new large tubes steel with copper ends
9/8/44		New Cross Gate
4/2/46-9/3/46**B**	73,583	Extension of mileage 10,000 "Clackbox seating and Butt joint caulked" 123 new small tubes 'Talbot and Stead' other small tubes expanded and rebeaded Large tubes expanded and referruled
9/1/48-13/2/48**A**	109,747	
24/5/50-23/6/50**HC**	55,322	125 copper stays riveted over 368 nuts renewed Internal Tubeplate 32 corner rivets and 4 seams caulked Barrel scaled Set new tubes 'Talbot and Stead' Set new large tubes steel with copper ends
1/10/51-26/10/51**HI**	89,606	100 copper stays riveted over 370 nuts renewed Internal Tubeplate 96 steel studs fitted in laps 173 new small tubes 'Tubes Ltd' 21 second hand large tubes expanded and referruled Firehole 15 new rivets
13/11/51-14/12/51**return**		
26/3/53-16/5/53**GO**		Brighton 705 nuts renewed 67 holes bushed Internal Tubeplate and Internal Firehole plate new 173 new small tubes
8/7/55-13/8/55**LI-HI**	59,164	New type 9mm injectors fitted rhs 42 copper stays riveted over 219 nuts renewed 2 fusible plugs 173 new small tubes 'Stewart and Lloyds' electrically welded Set new large tubes
1/10/57-19/10/57**GO**	110,539	834 copper stays renewed 156 holes bushed Internal Tubeplate new 2 fusible plugs Barrel scaled 173 new small tubes 'Universal' Set new large tubes
8/5/59-23/5/59**LC**	44,824	1 mud door welded 173 new small tubes 'Tube Products' electrically welded 3 new large tubes 18 second hand expanded and referruled
2/12/59-2/1/60**LI**	57,273	"New cast iron firegrate' 465 copper stays riveted over "Firehole lap and flanges caulked 42 flanges and 20 corner rivets caulked" 2 fusible plugs 32 new small tubes 'Tube Products' electrically welded 141 rebeaded Set new large tubes Firehole 15 rivets caulked
29/3/62-7/4/62**NC**	108,535	Eastleigh AWS
26/6/62-28/6/62**NC**		Exmouth Jct
13/12/62-12/1/63**LC**		Salisbury

Tenders
No.3003 26/7/27
No.3058 10/3/43

Boilers
No.874 6/1/26
No.831 12/12/28
No.962 12/12/31
No.911 11/2/35
No.912 9/11/38
No.870 3/4/40
No.935 10/3/43
No.1154 13/2/48
No.969 23/6/50
No.1016 16/5/53
No.898 19/10/57

Allocations

1/1925	Bricklayers Arms
2/11/35	Eastbourne
28/12/35	Eastleigh
16/5/36	Bricklayers Arms
20/6/36	Eastbourne
1/7/40	Norwood Jct
21/4/45	Stewarts Lane
1/10/53	Salisbury
16/9/63	Guildford

Withdrawn 26/10/63 Cut up at Eastleigh Works w/e 14/12/63

Left. Salisbury's 31813 in Fratton goods yard on 27 April 1960.

Below. 31813, with large second emblem on the tender, at Salisbury MPD on 3 June 1960. The bolts on the (Maunsell) chimney indicate a BR Class 4 blastpipe fitted inside the smokebox. Peter Groom.

31814

To traffic as 814 on 11/11/20
Renumbered A814 no date; 1814 24/11/34; 31814 15/6/49

Works

2/7/21-3/9/21**L**	20,169	300 copper stays riveted over
20/1/22-1/2/22**L**	31,737	250 copper stays riveted over
24/8/22-7/10/22**L**	50,080	406 copper stays riveted over
4/1/23-9/1/23**L**		
22/2/23-9/3/23**L**	62,156	550 copper stays riveted over
17/5/23-3/8/23**G**	66,819	505 copper stays renewed 250 riveted over Set new small tubes 'Howell and Co' Large tubes expanded and rebeaded
29/10/23		Set new large tubes
16/2/25-26/2/25**D**	40,504	
7/4/25-17/4/25**C**		450 copper stays riveted over
24/8/25-27/11/25**A**	51,582	571 copper stays renewed 175 copper riveted over Copper Tubeplate 6 studs in flanges Firehole 16 new rivets Set new small tubes 'Howell and Co'
23/5/27-15/7/27**B**	42,427	Extension of mileage 15,000 450 copper stays riveted over
14/7/28-5/10/28**A**	72,384	
6/5/29-29/5/29**D**	15,377	Whistle seating caulked
3/7/29-18/7/29**D**	17,749	Casing seating caulked
3/9/29-18/9/29**D**	21,611	Seating and firebox casing caulked
25/11/29-18/12/29**C**		Stewarts Lane
7/3/30-8/4/30**D**	29,041	Combination seating and seam caulked
28/8/30-3/9/30**D**	39,060	
13/6/31-17/7/31**A**	56,415	All steel stays renewed 100 copper riveted over Firehole rivets hammered Set new small tubes 'Howell and Co' Large tubes expanded and rebeaded
3/5/32-7/6/32**C**	21,650	
11/4/33-23/5/33**B**	55,599	Extension of mileage 10,000 Small tubes expanded and referruled Large tubes repaired steel with copper ends
11/1/34-21/2/34**C**		Bricklayers Arms ["Retubed at B'Arms"]
16/10/34-24/11/34**A**	82,938	
24/3/36-25/3/36**D**	36,100	
9/7/37-17/8/37**B**	64,806	Extension of mileage 10,000
21/9/38-1/11/38**A**	86,291	Class plate fitted 250 copper, 615 and 90 steel stays renewed 100 copper riveted over 358 holes bushed Copper Tubeplate new Set new small tubes 'Tubes Ltd' Large tubes repaired steel with copper ends "Tubes rolled with 5 roller expanders"
24/5/41-23/6/41**B**	56,355	Extension of mileage 10,000 2 copper stays renewed
20/4/42-14/5/42**C**		Norwood Jct Extension of mileage 10,000 2 copper stays renewed 30 nuts renewed 151 second hand small tubes
17/12/43-18/1/44**A**	108,793	
10/8/44-4/9/44**B**	20,454	
29/11/44-14/12/44**D**	26,666	
1/10/45-30/10/45**C**	47,206	Extension of mileage 5,000
10/12/45-14/12/45**C**	48,418	
15/11/46-28/11/46**D**	73,139	
30/4/47-7/6/47**A**	88,371	
13/2/48-10/3/48**D**		Brighton
13/5/49-15/6/49**HI**	46,007	
25/4/51-25/5/51**GO**	97,384	
12/1/53-27/2/53**HI**		
14/4/53-1/5/53**LC**		
2/6/55-23/6/55**GO**	53,789	55 copper and 705 monel metal stays renewed 70 copper riveted over Internal Tubeplate 48 studs fitted and seams caulked 2 fusible plugs Barrel scaled 173 new small tubes 'Howells' Firehole 13 rivets caulked
1/7/57-3/8/57**HI**	58,764	285 copper stays riveted over 292 nuts renewed "Firehole laps and fractures in roof of crown welded 17 studs fitted 20 studs and laps caulked" 2 fusible plugs 173 new small tubes 'Tube Products' electrically welded Firehole 15 rivets caulked Large tubes new steel
4/3/59-3/4/59**GO**	100,381	New type CI (cast iron) firebars
3/5/61-27/5/61**LI-HI**	52,667	Water treatment 'Overhead live wire notices'
29/11/61-9/12/61**NC**	64,944	AWS Spark arrester

Tender
No.1891 5/10/28

Boilers
No.831 from new
No.936 5/10/28
No.998 17/7/31
No.889 24/11/34
No.969 1/11/38
No.854 18/1/44
No.852 7/6/47
No.1070 25/5/51
No.967 23/6/55
No.878 3/4/59

Allocations
25/1/25   Bricklayers Arms
2/11/35   Eastbourne
28/12/35   Eastleigh
16/5/36   Bricklayers Arms
20/6/36   Eastbourne
1/7/40   Norwood Jct
30/1/43   Redhill
30/11/47   Norwood Jct
31/3/48   Stewarts Lane
1/10/53   Salisbury
16/9/63   Guildford

Withdrawn 26/7/64

Left. 31814 at Norwood Junction MPD, 17 September 1960. As a Salisbury engine, it is out of its normal haunts. Small emblem, flat dome.

Below. 31814 an up train at Salisbury in June 1962. In the background is East signal box with its wartime flat roof. To the left is the Market House siding junction. transporttreasury

31815

To traffic as 815 on 10/12/20
Renumbered A815 no date; 1815 21/6/32; 31815 4/3/49

Works

6/9/21-17/9/21**L**	25,844	
3/12/21-28/2/22**L**	32,666	
10/5/22-2/6/22**L**	38,956	
26/8/22-30/8/22**L**		
9/1/23-19/1/23**L**		
31/5/23-5/9/23**G**	70,918	
30/6/24-10/9/24**B**	22,314	
14/11/24-24/12/24**D**	26,096	
2/3/25-3/3/25**D**		
9/12/25-27/2/26**A**	52,208	Southern Railway green livery
4/11/27-4/1/28**B**	42,704	Extension of mileage 10,000
1/6/28-26/9/28**C**	51,817	
9/8/29-27/9/29**A**	72,784	
8/10/31-4/11/31**C**		Brighton Extension of mileage 10,000
9/5/32-21/6/32**A**	62,099	
13/1/34-21/2/34**C**		Bricklayers Arms Extension of mileage 5,000
29/4/35-7/6/35**A**	76,298	768 copper stays renewed 100 riveted over [All steel stays replaced by copper] 228 roof stays renewed Copper Tubeplate new Firehole rivets renewed 173 new small tubes 'Talbot and Stead' Large tubes repaired steel with copper ends
17/3/36-19/3/36**D**	20,518	
28/7/38-5/9/38**A**	72,619	Class plate fitted
15/9/39-25/10/39**C**	24,620	Extension of mileage 5,000
13/9/41-11/11/41**B**	57,256	Extension of mileage 5,000
6/10/42-12/10/42**C**		New Cross Gate
7/6/43-7/7/43**A**	87,123	
21/6/44-24/7/44**C**		Bricklayers Arms
7/4/45-17/5/45**C**	49,882	
23/6/45-28/6/45**C**	52,473	
18/1/47-15/2/47**A**	94,442	54 copper stays renewed 50 copper riveted over 216 nuts renewed [140 monel metal stays replaced by copper] Copper Tubeplate 70 stays fitted Firehole 11 new rivets 12 new small tubes 'Talbot and Stead' 21 new large tubes steel with copper ends
24/6/47-4/7/47**D**	9,256	Copper Tubeplate studs and flanges caulked Casing Back Plate 'fracture LH side welded'
23/8/47-3/9/47**D**	11,684	4 copper stays renewed 'Casing plate welded between stays LH side of Back Plate'
14/1/49-4/3/49**HI**	46,728	2 copper and 102 monel metal stays renewed 150 copper riveted over 146 nuts renewed Internal Tubeplate 33 studs fitted 101 rivets caulked Foundation Ring corners caulked Set new small tubes 'Howell and Co' 12 large tubes expanded and rebeaded 9 repaired studs with copper ends
2/9/49-26/10/49**LC**		Stewarts Lane 21 copper,11 monel metal and 11 steel stays renewed
28/7/50-8/9/50**LC**		
3/9/51-10/10/51**GO**	100,759	
7/4/52-17/4/52**LC**		
24/2/53-13/3/53**LC**	26,435	
30/6/54-17/7/54**LI-HI**	51,686	
12/10/55-29/10/55**GO**	71,924	388 copper and 74 monel metal stays renewed 350 nuts renewed Internal Tubeplate new Internal Firehole plate seams caulked and 20 studs fitted 2 fusible plugs Barrel scaled Firehole rivets repaired 173 new small tubes 'Howells' electrically welded Foundation Ring 48 new rivets
18/10/56-9/11/56**LC**	17,377	173 new small tubes 'Stewart and Lloyds' electrically welded Set new large tubes
27/2/58-20/3/58**LI-HI**	42,681	1 copper stays renewed 418 copper riveted over 88 nuts renewed Internal Tubeplate 48 flanges and 20 corner rivets caulked 2 fusible plugs 3 mud door holes welded 173 new small tubes 'Stewart and Lloyds' electrically welded Firehole 15 rivets caulked Set new large tubes
23/10/59-21/11/59**GO**	79,216	Manganese liners New type CI (cast iron) firebars 235 copper and 705 monel metal stays renewed 290 copper riveted over 705 nuts renewed 195 holes bushed Internal Tubeplate new 2 fusible plugs '2 mud holes welded' Barrel scaled 173 new small tubes 'Stewart and Lloyds' electrically welded Set new large tubes
30/12/59-13/1/60**return**	985	1 copper stay renewed
14/3/61-7/4/61**LC**	31,343	'Overhead live wire notices' AWS part fitted
17/5/61-3/6/61**LC**		Guildford

Tenders
No.3005 27/9/29
No.3034 21/6/32
No.3001 5/9/38
No.3100 21/11/59

Boilers
No.830 27/2/26
No.849 27/9/29
No.893 21/6/32
No.962 7/6/35
No.964 5/9/38
No.991 7/7/42
No.993 15/2/47
No.866 10/10/51
No.1011 29/10/55
No.1015 21/11/59

Allocations

25/1/25	Stewarts Lane
2/11/35	Eastbourne
28/12/35	Eastleigh
16/5/36	New Cross Gate
20/6/36	Eastbourne
1/7/40	Norwood Jct
30/1/43	Redhill
31/3/48	Stewarts Lane
6/12/51	Gillingham
1/10/53	Stewarts Lane
13/5/54	Gillingham
30/5/59	Hither Green
14/6/59	Guildford

Withdrawn 1/6/63 Cut up at Eastleigh Works w/e 27/7/63

Left. Displaced by the Kent Coast scheme 31815 was one of several moguls finding their way to Guildford, in June 1959. Here it is a little later, on 16 January 1960, at Hither Green, in one of the fogs that were so familiar then. The holes at the top of each end of the buffer beam are clearly seen (see page 29) in spite of the fog.

Below. 31815 now AWS equipped, at Eastleigh MPD on 1 June 1963; BR Class 4 chimney. Peter Groom.

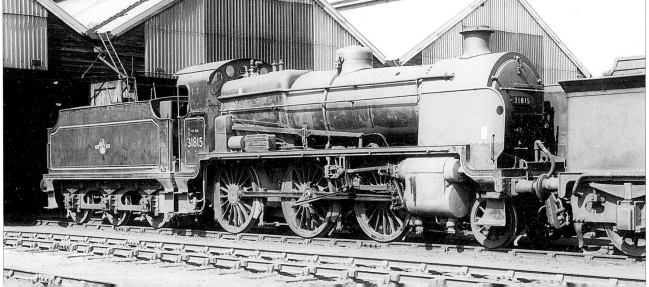

31816

To traffic as 816 on 29/12/21
Renumbered A816 no date; 1816 no date; 31816 19/1/49

Works

Date	Mileage	Notes
28/1/24-17/4/24**A**	61,581	Southern Railway green livery 258 copper and 37 steel stays renewed and 100 copper riveted over 311 nuts renewed 4 roof nuts renewed Firehole rivets hammered Set new small tubes 'Howell and Co' Large tubes expanded and rebeaded
19/7/24-22/7/24**D**		
8/2/26-19/5/26**A**	51,356	
29/12/26-17/8/27**D**	16,290	
10/8/27-17/8/27**C**	33,743	
12/1/28-23/3/28**B**	43,432	Extension of mileage 15,000
27/8/29-17/10/29**A**	81,096	
22/1/30-5/2/30**D**	3,863	

Engine at Eastleigh for Heat Conversion from 12/7/30

Date	Mileage	Notes
23/6/30-31/12/31**B**		Eastleigh
15/1/32-8/4/32**D**		Eastleigh
19/4/32-30/4/32**D**		Eastleigh
20/5/32-8/7/32**D**		Eastleigh
11/7/32-7/10/32**D**		Eastleigh
10/10/32-23/1/33**D**		Eastleigh
26/1/33-12/10/33**D**		Eastleigh
20/10/33-26/6/34**D**		Eastleigh
29/6/34-25/5/35**D**		Eastleigh
27/5/35-3/8/35**A**		Eastleigh Conversion to standard N
7/7/36-8/7/36**D**	31,559	
24/2/37-16/4/37	49,898	Bricklayers Arms
29/3/38-23/5/38**A**	71,422	Class plate fitted
28/5/41-25/6/41**A**	71,105	200 copper and 387 steel stays renewed 125 copper riveted over [306 steel stays replaced by copper] 228 roof nuts renewed 6 holes bushed Copper Tubeplate new Firehole all rivets renewed Foundation Ring 70 rivets renewed 173 new small tubes 91 by 'Chesterfield Tube Co' 82 by 'Tubes Ltd' Large tubes repaired with copper ends
20/3/44-22/4/44**A**	73,904	
3/2/45-9/3/45**B**	27,860	
3/5/46-24/5/46**C**	58,894	
12/8/46-14/9/46**C**		Redhill
16/6/47-19/7/47**A**	88,673	
13/12/48-19/1/49**B**	41,274	
12/5/50-16/6/50**GO**	76,576	
21/1/52-7/3/52**HI**	45,599	
14/3/52-17/3/52**defect**		
30/4/52-9/5/52**LC**	46,568	
30/10/53-9/11/53**LC**		
10/12/54-11/1/55**GO**	92,269	
24/8/56-14/9/56**LC**	28,941	
26/9/57-18/10/57**LI**	49,294	
11/2/59-18/2/59**LC**	78,304	
7/8/59-26/9/59**GO**	86,172	Manganese liners Spark arrester ATC New type CI (cast iron) firebars 356 copper stays renewed 16 roof stays renewed 4 holes bushed 88 lap studs fitted ½ side laps welded flanges and firehole lap 16 flanges and 20 corner rivets caulked fusible plugs 3 mud door holes welded Barrel scaled 173 new small tubes 'Tube Products' electrically welded Firehole 15 rivets caulked
28/6/60-14/7/60**NC-LC**	19,125	'Overhead live wire notices' No Boiler work
23/2/61-1/4/61**LC**		Norwood Jct
31/5/61-17/6/61**LC**	30,753	
2/1/63-9/2/63**GO**	61,942	Eastleigh Blowdown gear and silencer Briquette tube feeder 185 copper stays renewed 350 copper riveted over 134 roof stays renewed "Firehole door lap and flanges caulked" 2 fusible plugs Smokebox Tubeplate levelled "Casing covering sides levelled at fire door" Barrel scaled 173 small tubes repaired Foundation Ring 102 rivets renewed Set new large tubes

Tenders

No.3006	17/10/29
No.3100	18/2/59
No.3001	26/9/59
No.695	14/7/60
No.3032	9/2/63

Boilers

No.841 17/4/24
No.832 19/5/26
No.828 17/10/29
No.964 31/12/31
No.856 23/5/38
No.996 25/6/41
No.901 22/4/44
No.991 19/7/47
No.1062 16/6/50
No.843 11/1/55
No.1160 26/9/59
No.876 9/2/63

Allocations

25/1/25 Bricklayers Arms
22/2/36 Stewarts Lane
18/4/36 Bricklayers Arms
21/4/45 Hither Green
14/7/45 Bricklayers Arms
20/4/46 Redhill
5/10/46 Brighton
10/8/47 Redhill
4/9/48   Bricklayers Arms
8/1/49   Redhill
20/3/50 Stewarts Lane
27/7/51 Dover
30/9/55 Redhill
26/5/61 Eastleigh
22/7/63 Weymouth
22/6/64 Redhill
18/1/65 Guildford

Withdrawn 9/1/66

Left. 31816, now an Eastleigh engine, makes its presence felt at Guildford on 17 March 1963. Derek Clayton.

Below. 31816 at Fratton MPD, 31 August 1962; small first emblem, AWS, Maunsell chimney. Peter Groom.

31817

To traffic as 817 on 1/1922
Renumbered A817 no date; 1817 13/5/32; 31817 29/4/49

Works

10/6/22-12/6/22**L**	3,500	
27/3/23-24/5/23**L**	11,177	
27/2/24-21/5/24**A**	61,813	Southern Railway green livery
9/6/25-18/6/25**D**		
21/9/25-28/9/25**D**		
16/10/25-23/12/25**D**		
29/1/26-5/2/26**D**		
7/10/26-7/1/27**A**	52,864	
20/4/28-25/5/28**B**	38,714	
8/6/28-13/6/28**D**	40,502	Extension of mileage 10,000
27/4/29-15/6/29**A**	58,410	
20/12/30**C**		Brighton
6/4/32-13/5/32**A**	68,372	
6/7/33-5/9/33**B**	36,448	Extension of mileage 5,000
11/6/34-5/7/34**D**	56,484	
15/4/35-24/5/35**A**	78,930	
10/3/36-12/3/36**D**	22,174	
15/1/37-6/2/37**C**	41,093	Extension of mileage 5,000
17/2/38-26/4/38**C**	68,412	Stewarts Lane
19/10/38-25/11/38**A**	79,637	Class plate fitted
13/3/40-25/4/40**C**	35,178	Bricklayers Arms
15/3/41-11/5/41**C**		Bricklayers Arms
11/8/42-16/9/42**A**	93,535	
30/7/43-16/8/43**C**	22,751	
29/4/44-6/6/44**C**		Bricklayers Arms
1/9/44-23/9/44**C**		Bricklayers Arms
25/6/45-14/7/45**C**		Hither Green
10/7/46-30/8/46**A**	87,095	
5/11/46-6/11/46**D**	7,457	
14/5/47-13/6/47**D**	21,005	
25/3/49-29/4/49**A**	76,196	525 copper and 705 steel stays renewed 228 roof stays renewed Internal Tubeplate and smokebox Tubeplate new Barrel cleaned Set new small tubes 'Tubes Ltd' Large tubes steel with copper ends
16/12/50-24/1/51		Bricklayers Arms
27/8/51-3/8/51**LC**	70,144	101 nuts renewed 173 new small tubes 'Talbot and Stead' 21 large tubes expanded and rebeaded
18/3/52-28/3/52**LC**	84,134	21 second hand large tubes repaired steel with copper ends
10/3/53-2/4/53**HI**	106,966	50 copper stays riveted over 256 nuts renewed Internal Tubeplate 17 studs fitted in laps 173 new small tubes 'Tubes Ltd' 21 large tubes expanded and referruled Firehole 13 rivets caulked foundation ring 10 corner rivets caulked
25/1/55-17/2/55**GO**	146,561	
20/4/55-27/4/55**NC**	3,447	
9/4/56-21/4/56**LC**	30,285	
31/5/56-24/6/56**LC**	33,239	Redhill
18/6/57-6/7/57**LI-HI**	70,039	Tender no.3054 briquette container fitted
18/3/59-4/4/59**NC-LC**	124,793	
27/10/59-21/11/59**GO**	141,033	Blowdown valve gear and water treatment New type CI firebars 525 copper and 705 monel metal stays renewed 705 nuts renewed 444 roof nuts renewed 14 holes bushed New Firebox 2 fusible plugs 3 mud door holes welded Barrel scaled 173 new small tubes 'Stewart and Lloyds' electrically welded set new large tubes
1/5/62-2/6/62**LI-HI**	87,400	AWS complete Spark arrester 154 nuts renewed "door lap caulked" 2 fusible plugs 32 new small tubes 141 rebeaded 3 new large tubes 18 second hand expanded and referruled Firehole 15 rivets caulked
28/12/63		Redhill Tender change

Tenders

No.3007	25/5/28
No.3054	25/11/38
No.1963	28/12/63

Boilers		Allocations	
		25/1/25	Bricklayers Arms
		22/2/36	Stewarts Lane
		18/4/36	Bricklayers Arms
No.842	21/5/24	21/4/45	Hither Green
No.850	7/1/27	14/7/45	Bricklayers Arms
No.904	15/6/29	20/4/46	Redhill
No.975	13/5/32	28/9/46	Brighton
No.909	24/5/35	23/8/47	Redhill
No.850	25/11/38	4/9/48	Bricklayers Arms
No.895	16/9/42	8/1/49	Redhill
No.864	30/8/46	20/3/50	Stewarts Lane
No.846	29/4/49	27/7/51	Dover
No.1154	17/2/55	30/9/55	Redhill
No.1023	21/11/59		

Withdrawn 18/1/64 Cut up at Eastleigh Works w/e 8/2/64

Left. 31817 with a train between Deepdene and Dorking Town, 23 June 1962. The line throughout Reading-Redhill-Tonbridge offered an extraordinary if unsung variety of motive power in this period, with Southern classes as well as Standards and WR Manors and moguls. Derek Clayton.

Redhill's 31817 passing Canterbury West with an up working on 16 May 1959; the headcode denotes a train via the Maidstone East line to Victoria or Holborn Viaduct, possibly empty stock returning to London. Beyond the gantry to the left, on the far side of the signal box, was the one-time single road engine shed, closed some four years before and possibly still standing at the time of this photograph. The set is unique special traffic/excursion set 917, which was formed as seen during 1957-59 only and allocated to the London East Division, probably based at Blackheath sidings. The coaches are (in order) unique SECR matchboarded brake composite 6642, then Maunsell Thanet composite 5545 followed by six Maunsell unclassed open saloons (in the order given in the carriage working notices – possibly different in practice) 7980, 7979, 7976, 7974, 7966 and 7963. An SECR matchboarded brake third (now brake second) 3553 is on the rear. All coaches are to route restriction 1. The set was withdrawn in July 1959 so might even be on its last duty. D.C. Ovenden, ColourRail

31818

To traffic as 818 on 3/1922
Renumbered A818 no date; 1818 19/8/31; 31818 24/4/48

Works

28/4/22-23/5/22**L**	2,904	
26/4/23-16/5/23**L**	8,220	
23/10/23-15/12/23**L**	46,766	
30/7/24-25/10/24**A**	64,235	Southern Railway green livery
2/9/25-3/9/25**D**		
9/11/25-12/11/25**D**		
20/1/26-27/3/26**B**	34,036	
10/4/26-1/6/26**D**		
25/4/27-23/7/27**A**	60,040	
13/6/28**D**	37,135	
7/2/29-15/2/29**D**	48,101	
31/5/29-13/7/29**A**	54,047	
8/7/31-19/8/31**A**	51,756	
18/2/33-23/3/33**B**	40,502	Extension of mileage 10,000
12/12/33-16/1/34**C**		Bricklayers Arms
11/9/34-16/10/34**A**	80,009	
14/9/36-16/9/36**D**	51,618	
10/11/36-17/12/36**C**	54,870	Bricklayers Arms
3/11/37-8/12/37**A**	76,868	863 copper stays renewed and 100 copper riveted over 355 holes bushed Copper Tubeplate new Throat Plate 2 patches Firehole rivets renewed Set new small tubes 'Chesterfield Tube Co' Large tubes repaired steel with copper ends
20/2/41-26/3/41**A**	75,569	Class plate fitted
1/8/41-1/9/41**C**		Bricklayers Arms
28/4/43-25/5/43**D**	53,291	
4/4/44-6/5/44**A**	72,703	402 copper stays renewed 150 copper riveted over Copper Tubeplate 96 studs fitted Firehole rivets hammered Set new small tubes 'Howell and Co' Set new small tubes steel with copper ends
28/12/45-23/2/46**B**		Bricklayers Arms Extension of mileage 5,000 Set new small tubes Large tubes expanded and referruled
26/10/46-23/11/46**B**	62,220	Extension of mileage 10,000 6 copper stays renewed 300 riveted over Copper Tubeplate 39 studs fitted 100 caulked 20 large tubes repaired steel with copper ends
1/8/47-30/8/47**C**	82,925	200 copper stays riveted over Copper Tubeplate 1 stud fitted and 66 caulked
23/3/48-24/4/48**A**	96,888	
21/4/50-12/5/50**HI**	67,010	
20/12/51-11/1/52**HI**	107,821	
10/10/52-24/10/52**LC**	128,735	
15/12/52-1/1/53**HC**	130,595	
6/5/53-27/5/53**LC**		
11/5/54-29/5/54**GO**	161,182	270 copper and 124 steel stays renewed 124 nuts renewed 65 holes bushed Internal Tubeplate and Smokebox Tubeplate new Barrel scaled Firehole rivets repaired Foundation Ring 4 corner studs Set new small tubes 'Howell' Large tubes repaired
27/5/55-10/6/55**HC**	29,469	No Boiler work
19/8/55-8/9/55**LC**	34,130	2 copper stays renewed 200 copper riveted over 173 new small tubes 'Stewart and Lloyds' electrically welded
15/10/56-3/11/56**LI-HI**	59,447	4 copper stays renewed 295 copper riveted over 67 nuts renewed Internal Tubeplate 54 studs caulked in laps 2 fusible plugs 173 new small tubes 'Stewart and Lloyds' electrically welded Set new large tubes Foundation Ring 20 corner rivets caulked
2/12/57-13/12/57**LC**	89,518	200 copper stays riveted over Foundation Ring 15 corner rivets caulked 6 new small tubes 'Universal'
29/7/58-15/8/58**GO**	122,297	233 copper and 705 monel metal stays renewed 705 nuts renewed 28 roof nuts renewed 364 holes bushed Internal Tubeplate new 2 fusible plugs Smokebox Tubeplate levelled 2 mud door holes welded Barrel scaled 173 new small tubes 'Stewart and Lloyds' electrically welded Firehole and Foundation Ring all new rivets
19/1/60-6/2/60**LC**	31,602	135 nuts renewed Internal Tubeplate 20 corner rivets caulked 173 new small tubes 'Stewart and Lloyds' electrically welded 3 new large tubes 18 second hand expanded and referruled
16/5/61-10/6/61**LI**	52,958	95 copper stays riveted over 318 nuts renewed Internal Tubeplate 46 flange rivets and 20 Foundation rivets caulked 2 fusible plugs 173 new small tubes 'Tube Products' electrically welded 3 new large tubes 18 second hand expanded and referruled
13/6/62-23/6/62**NC-LC**	78,385	Eastleigh AWS

Tenders
No.3008 23/7/27
No.3000 23/11/46

Boilers
No.843 25/10/24
No.844 23/7/27
No.905 13/7/29
No.910 19/8/31
No.856 16/10/34
No.940 8/12/37
No.938 26/3/41
No.855 6/5/44
No.986 24/4/48
No.847 29/5/54
No.976 15/8/58

Allocations
25/1/25 Ashford
18/4/36 Bricklayers Arms
21/4/45 Hither Green
14/7/45 Bricklayers Arms
20/4/46 Redhill
20/3/50 Stewarts Lane
27/7/51 Dover
10/2/61 Tonbridge
26/5/61 Eastleigh
1/2/62 Exmouth Jct

Withdrawn 7/9/63 Cut up at Eastleigh Works w/e 28/9/63

31818 at Bournemouth Central, looking as if it's the station pilot; if so a Maunsell mogul would hardly be the most comfortable engine to have in inclement weather. That said, they seem never to have worked with tarpaulins, at least not so far as the photographic record is concerned. This is presumably during the short period when it was at Eastleigh, 1961-62. Fred Porter, transporttreasury

31819

To traffic as 819 on 27/5/22
Renumbered A819 no date; 1819 31/3/33; 31819 28/5/49

Works

6/9/23-31/10/23**L**	42,399		
3/7/24**D**			
7/10/24-23/12/24**A**	68,682	Southern Railway green livery	
21/10/25-6/11/25**D**			
16/4/26-23/4/26**D**			
27/1/27-23/4/27**A**	50,017		
30/7/28-12/9/28**B**	35,604	Extension of mileage 5,000	
8/10/28-17/11/28**C**	37,297		
3/1/30-23/2/30**A**	66,361		
17/12/30-12/2/31**C**	14,463		
27/7/32-19/9/32**C**		Bricklayers Arms Extension of mileage 10,000	
22/2/33-31/3/33**A**	68,967	93 copper and 1 monel metal stays renewed 50 copper riveted over 314 nuts renewed Firehole rivets hammered Set new small tubes 'Howell and Co' Large tubes repaired steel with copper ends	
1/6/34-26/6/34**B**	35,703	104 nuts renewed 68 new small tubes 'Mannesmann Tube Co' all other small tubes expanded and rebeaded	
4/10/35-11/11/35**A**	73,359	219 copper and 564 steel stays renewed 174 copper riveted over Copper Tubeplate 16 studs fitted Firehole 13 rivets renewed others hammered Foundation Ring 6 new rivets 173 new small tubes 'Chesterfield Tube Co' Large tubes repaired steel with copper ends	
12/8/37-2/10/37**C**	49,010	Brighton Extension of mileage 5,000 3 copper stays renewed 68 copper riveted over 79 nuts renewed Copper firehole Plate 5 studs fitted Foundation Ring corners caulked All small tubes expanded and rebeaded All large tubes expanded and referruled	
19/1/38**D**	57,259	[Rail washing app fitted]	
11/5/39-12/6/39**A**	83,367	Class plate fitted Rail washing app removed	
5/8/41-17/9/41**C**	53,393	Bricklayers Arms	
8/1/43-10/2/43**A**	86,437		
8/10/45-30/11/45**B**		Bricklayers Arms Extension of mileage 10,000	
21/1/46-15/2/46		Bricklayers Arms	
23/5/46-28/6/46**D**	69,437		
29/8/47-2/10/47**A**	98,059		
9/5/49-28/5/49**LC**	42,900		
22/11/50-22/12/50**HI**	76,848		
15/1/53-5/3/53**GO**	114,997		
12/11/54-30/11/54**HI**	40,822		
15/5/56-8/6/56**HI**	79,428		
10/4/57-18/4/57**LC**	103,251		
15/10/57-26/10/57**LC**	116,590		
4/12/58-2/1/59**GO**	146,185	New type firebars fitted	
9/11/60-7/1/61**LC**		Guildford	
19/9/61-7/10/61**LI-HI**	55,064		
5/4/62-21/4/62**NC**	68,067	AWS complete [minus batteries]	
13/8/62-3/9/62**LC**		Guildford	
31/12/63		Guildford tender change	

Tenders

No.3009	23/4/27
No.3014	31/3/33
No.3036	11/11/35
No.3037	31/12/63

Boilers

No.844	23/12/24
No.842	23/4/27
No.902	22/2/30
No.1022	31/3/33
No.989	11/11/35
No.879	12/6/39
No.889	10/2/43
No.1167	2/10/47
No.970	5/3/53
No.1061	2/1/59

Allocations

25/1/25	Dover
24/4/37	Bricklayers Arms
21/4/45	Hither Green
14/7/45	Bricklayers Arms
20/4/46	Dover
10/2/61	Redhill
6/7/61	Brighton
8/12/61	Guildford

Withdrawn 5/1/64
NB Only one Boiler Record Card covering this loco.

31819 with an up train, passing through Ashford on 13 May 1960. The first two coaches are BR 4-wheeled Ferry Vans; there were thirty of these shortened versions of the BR CCT, classed as Goods Vehicles and painted in Bauxite Brown. D.C. Ovenden, ColourRail

At Reading South, 31 May 1963. While many moguls took the 'direct route' west suddenly, en masse, on completion of the Kent Coast Scheme, for others it was an 'indirect route', as dieselisation and electrification spread, often via Redhill and Brighton. Peter Groom.

31820

To traffic as 820 on 16/8/22
Renumbered A820 no date; 1820 31/7/33; 31820 26/3/49

Works

Date	Mileage	Notes
12/9/23-20/10/23**L**	37,432	149 steel stays riveted over 149 nuts renewed
22/9/24-5/11/24**B**	65,666	
20/7/25-9/10/25**A**	83,929	Southern Railway green livery 232 copper and 94 steel stays renewed 125 copper riveted over 203 nuts renewed 20 steel stays replaced by copper Copper Tubeplate 2 studs in flanges Firehole rivets hammered Set new small tubes 'Stewart and Lloyds' Large tubes expanded and referruled
25/11/26-7/12/26**D**		
14/3/27-14/5/27**C**	36,386	Extension of mileage 10,000 Large tubes repaired "1 large tube hole bushed"
1/11/27**D**	50,455	
5/6/28-9/7/28**A**	65,400	
15/2/29-16/2/29**D**	19,573	
14/4/30-1/5/30**D**	50,122	
17/10/30-22/11/30**A**	59,792	
5/3/32-7/4/32**B**	43,264	Extension of mileage 10,000
23/6/33-31/7/33**A**	77,277	
11/12/34-5/3/35**C**	40,982	Bricklayers Arms
20/7/35-17/8/535**C**		Bricklayers Arms
11/11/36-23/12/36**A**	76,998	702 copper stays renewed and 100 copper riveted over 228 roof stays renewed 270 holes bushed Copper Tubeplate new Firehole rivets renewed Set new small tubes 'Tubes Ltd' Large tubes repaired steel with copper ends
21/1/38-26/1/38**D**	31,201	[Rail washing app fitted] 350 copper stays riveted over
7/7/38-16/8/38**C**	43,937	Class plate fitted Extension of mileage 10,000 350 copper stays riveted over
10/1/40-7/2/40**A**	78,816	Rail washing app removed
29/11/40-8/2/41**C**	23,118	Bricklayers Arms
9/5/41-29/5/41**D**	28,857	
29/10/41-24/12/41**D**	38,223	
5/3/42-16/3/42**D**	41,945	
17/9/42-28/10/42**C**		Bricklayers Arms Extension of mileage 5,000
23/3/43-16/5/43**C**		Bricklayers Arms Extension of mileage 10,000
17/9/43-27/10/43**A**	74,261	
2/6/45-21/7/45**B**		Bricklayers Arms
22/6/46-26/7/46**C**	68,157	
16/1/47-28/2/47**C**		Dover
13/9/47-22/10/47**A**	94,456	38 copper and 96 monel metal stays renewed 115 nuts renewed Copper Tubeplate "Tube Test 2093" Firehole 11 new rivets Set new small tubes 'Talbot and Stead' Large tubes repaired steel with copper ends "Test 2093" 10 large without ferrules and 11 with ferrules
25/2/49-26/3/49**LC**	34,889	
28/9/49-15/10/49**LC**	49,383	250 nuts renewed "Tubes Test 2093 closed 6/12/49" Internal Wrapping Plate "8 studs fitted in side seams" 7 small tubes repaired 166 expanded and rebeaded
26/4/50-19/5/50**HC**	62,977	No Boiler work
14/2/51-16/3/51**GO**	82,232	All roof stays and roof nuts renewed 167 holes bushed New Firebox Barrel scaled Set new small tubes 'Talbot and Stead' Set new large tubes
29/3/51-2/4/51**defect**		
18/6/51-29/6/51**LC**	5,533	No Boiler work
1/8/52-5/9/52**HC**	32,047	No Boiler work
23/7/53-29/8/53**HI**	54,473	1 copper stay renewed and 70 copper riveted over 249 nuts renewed 173 new small tubes Large tubes repaired
24/6/54-19/7/54**NC**		Ashford shed 420 steel stays riveted over 420 nuts renewed Internal Tubeplate flanges caulked 21 second hand large tubes expanded
17/6/55-9/7/55**LI-HI**	100,523	185 steel stays replaced by copper 74 steel renewed 20 holes bushed Internal Tubeplate "18 studs fitted in laps" 2 fusible plugs Foundation Ring 16 corner rivets caulked 173 new small tubes 'Stewart and Lloyds' electrically welded Set new large tubes
28/11/56-15/12/56**GO**	141,182	
25/2/58-7/3/58**LC**	35,900	
4/2/59-21/2/59**LI-HI**	60,650	New type CI (cast iron) firebars
21/5/59-1/6/59**NC**	66,420	

12/10/60-12/11/60**GO**	96,060	'Overhead live wire notices'-3 plates fitted to complete 525 copper and 705 monel metal stays renewed 705 nuts and 228 roof stays renewed 444 roof nuts renewed New Firebox 2 fusible plugs Barrel scaled Firehole new rivets 173 new small tubes 'Stewart and Lloyds' electrically welded Large tubes repaired
13/9/61-14/9/61**NC**		Bricklayers Arms
16/7/62-9/8/62**LC**		Guildford

Tenders
No.3018 9/7/28
No.3009 23/12/36

Boilers
No.845 9/10/25
No.821 9/7/28
No.857 22/11/30
No.867 31/7/33
No.876 23/12/36
No.864 7/2/40
No.863 27/10/43
No.864 7/2/40
No.863 27/10/43
No.1021 22/10/47
No.1075 16/3/51
No.1000 15/12/56
No.1012 12/11/60

Allocations
From new Redhill
25/1/25   Stewarts Lane
10/11/38   New Cross Gate
2/11/38   Bricklayers Arms
24/3/45   Hither Green
26/4/45   Bricklayers Arms
20/4/46   Dover
10/2/61   Redhill
6/7/61   Brighton
8/12/61   Guildford

Withdrawn 24/8/63 Cut up at Eastleigh Works w/e 21/12/63

Left. Taking coal at Reading South, the coal stage altogether more modest than Ashford's, below. The vast GWR signalbox has a back entrance through the Southern yard, we can observe.

Below. 31820 takes coal at Ashford, the fireman sitting down between tub loads; he's obviously up there to 'square up' after each one. There is no date but the (small) first emblem usually means it is later on in the 1950s rather than early but the moguls by the later 1950s were going four years between Generals (it was more like three in the 1930s) and after one in 1956 the next General, at which 31820 could get the second emblem, was in 1960. transporttreasury

95

31821

To traffic as 821 on 20/10/22
Renumbered A821 no date; 1821 2/8/34; 31821 8/12/48

Works

8/8/23-5/9/23**L**	22,618	
30/1/25-24/4/25**A**	56,558	Southern Railway green livery
22/7/25-28/7/25**D**		
8/1/26-3/2/26**C**	16,686	
2/5/27-10/6/27**C**	48,083	Extension of mileage 10,000
9/11/27-24/2/28**A**	58,921	
11/1/30-25/2/30**C**		Bricklayers Arms Extension of mileage 15,000
21/2/31-28/3/31**A**	77,509	
3/3/33-20/4/33**B**	50,001	Extension of mileage 5,000
29/6/34-2/8/34**A**	75,884	
24/7/35-23/8/35**C**	29,313	Extension of mileage 5,000
29/6/37-7/8/37**A**	75,039	
31/1/38-2/2/38**D**	15,091	[Rail washing app fitted]
21/9/39-19/10/39**C**		Bricklayers Arms
6/4/40-1/5/40**A**	68,633	Class plate fitted Rail washing app removed 411 copper stays renewed 250 copper riveted over Copper Tubeplate 29 studs fitted Firehole rivets hammered Set new small tubes 'Tubes Ltd' Large tubes repaired steel with copper ends
10/8/43-2/10/43**B**		Bricklayers Arms Extension of mileage 30,000 Copper stays riveted over "in fire area" Some small tubes renewed others second hand welded Large tubes expanded and rebeaded
30/4/45-2/6/45**A**	122,105	Boiler repaired at Brighton 329 copper and 619 steel stays renewed 48 copper riveted over 228 roof stays repaired 639 holes bushed Copper Tubeplate new Steel tubeplate and Barrel cleaned Firehole rivets renewed 138 new small tubes 'Talbot and Stead' 35 new 'Pieced Steel' 21 large tubes repaired steel with copper ends
31/7/47-23/8/47**C**		75 nuts renewed "Large ferrules renewed"
5/11/48-8/12/48**A**	86,420	All copper and 228 roof stays renewed New Firebox Set new small tubes 'Talbot and stead' Set new large tubes steel with copper ends
16/2/51**NC**	57,144	
4/6/51-29/6/51**GO**	64,884	125 copper and 605 monel metal stays renewed 75 copper riveted over Internal Tubeplate new Internal Wrapping Plate 2 half sides Set new small tubes 'Howells' Firehole 26 new rivets Set new large tubes
16/7/51-18/7/51**defect**		
2/10/51-11/10/51**NC**	2,431	
8/5/52-22/5/52**LC**	13,886	No Boiler work
9/9/53-30/9/53**HI**	48,413	337 nuts and 96 roof nuts renewed Internal Tubeplate 21 lap rivets and seams caulked 173 new small tubes 'Howells' Set new large tubes
10/8/55-27/8/55**GO**	88,278	
3/1/57-24/1/57**LI-HI**	41,812	
23/9/58-11/10/58**GO**	89,615	New type CI (cast iron) firebars
24/5/60-11/6/60**LC**	40,181	AWS part fitted
26/9/61-14/10/61**LI-HI**	58,531	Spark arrester
18/3/63-5/4/63**LC**	99,071	Eastleigh Blowdown gear and silencer Briquette tube feeder

Tenders
No.3011 24/2/28
No.1881 1/5/40

Boilers
No.846 24/4/25
No.843 24/2/28
No.865 28/3/31
No.904 2/8/34
No.844 7/8/37
No.987 1/5/40
No.1066 2/6/45
No.855 8/12/48
No.1021 29/6/51
No.1162 27/8/55
No.1029 11/10/58

Allocations
25/1/25 Bricklayers Arms
25/3/44 Exmouth Jct
21/4/45 Hither Green
26/4/45 Bricklayers Arms
20/4/46 Ashford
12/7/47 Dover
26/5/61 Norwood Jct
8/7/61   Brighton
8/12/61 Guildford
31/8/63 Exmouth Jct

Withdrawn 5/64

31821 with a train of strange apparitions – continental vans – at St Mary Cray Junction on 16 August 1959. Transferring west in 1961 (though it had had a year at Exmouth Junction during the War) it was one of a number repaired at Eastleigh after Ashford closed, which saw the late fitting of a briquette feeder for water treatment. RailOnline

31821 at North Camp on 26 May 1962, with ECS to Reading. RailOnline

31823

To traffic as 823 on 18/5/23
Renumbered A823 1823 31823 1/49
Some records missing

Works

Date	Mileage	Description
14/8/23-16/8/23**L**		
6/26		Southern Railway green livery
17/3/45		654 copper stays renewed and 200 copper riveted over Copper Tubeplate 83 studs fitted Steel Tubeplate 14 rivets renewed Firehole rivets hammered Set new small tubes 'Tubes Ltd' Large tubes repaired steel with copper ends
24/12/47		5 copper stays renewed 450 copper riveted over copper Tubeplate 18 studs fitted and 200 caulked 40 new small tubes 'Talbot and Stead' Large tubes expanded and referruled
15/1/49		Brighton 534 copper and 691 steel stays renewed 228 roof stays renewed 175 holes bushed New Firebox Set new small tubes 'Howell and Co' Set new large tubes steel with copper ends
4/2/50		No Boiler work
12/12/50		Set new small tubes 'Howells' 21 second hand large tubes expanded and referruled
12/6/51-13/7/51**LI**	64,945	12 steel stays and 125 nuts renewed Internal Tubeplate 75 copper studs fitted in laps 30 new small tubes 6 'Talbot and Stead' with 24 'Tubes Ltd'
2/8/52		Bricklayers Arms 173 new small tubes 'Tubes Ltd' Set new large tubes steel with copper ends
23/9/53-17/10/53**GO**	125,226	39 copper and 230 steel tubes renewed 150 copper riveted over 130 nuts renewed Internal Tubeplate 31 studs fitted in laps Barrel scaled 173 new small tubes 'Howells' Firehole 17 rivets caulked Large tubes repaired
8/7/54-10/7/54**LC**	24,685	No Boiler work
18/4/55-6/5/55**LI-HI**	44,662	110 copper stays riveted over 257 nuts renewed Internal Tubeplate 15 studs and seams caulked 2 fusible plugs 173 small tubes "repaired" Firehole 13 rivets caulked Large tubes repaired
5/10/56-20/10/56**LC**	81,522	30 copper stays and 105 nuts renewed 173 new small tubes 'Stewart and Lloyds' set new large tubes
28/1/58-22/2/58**GO**	118,069	387 copper and 705 steel stays and 705 nuts renewed 340 holes bushed Internal Tubeplate new 2 fusible plugs Smokebox Tubeplate levelled 2 mud door holes welded 173 new small tubes 'Stewart and Lloyds' electrically welded set new large tubes
23/9/58-29/9/58**NC**	21,069	Blowdown valve gear and water treatment
14/1/60-6/2/60**LI-HI**	57,710	New type CI firebars 210 nuts renewed Internal Tubeplate "tubeplate flanges and firehole laps caulked 24 flange rivets caulked" 2 fusible plugs 32 new small tubes 'Stewart and Lloyds' electrically welded 141 rebeaded 3 new large tubes 18 second hand expanded and referruled
1/8/61-2/8/61		Bricklayers Arms
6/4/62-28/4/62**LC**	113,160	AWS complete [minus batteries]

Tender
No.3029

Boilers
No.999 17/3/45
No.985 15/1/49
No.976 17/10/53
No.849 22/2/58

Allocations

25/1/25	Stewarts Lane
16/10/37	Ashford
25/3/44	Exmouth Jct
27/1/45	Bricklayers Arms
20/4/46	New Cross Gate
12/7/47	Dover
27/7/51	Bricklayers Arms
8/7/60	Stewarts Lane
22/7/63	Norwood Jct
16/9/63	Redhill

Withdrawn 21/9/63 Cut up at Eastleigh Works w/e 25/1/64

Not long out of a General at Ashford, 31823 stands in the yard at Hither Green MPD on 23 February 1958. Norman Preedy.

A dismal 31823 at Hither Green MPD in June 1960; a Bricklayers Arms engine since 1951, it was about to be transferred to Stewarts Lane. It was here, at Hither Green in this year, that electrification flashes first came to notice, wrongly ascribed at first to the presence of overhead wires in the adjacent yards; it was of course a BR edict, following fatalities in Lancashire when fire irons came into contact with the 25kV supply. Possibly because of the dirt (the tender emblem is completely obscured, and the cab number not much better) the washout plug holes on the boiler front are visible. ColourRail

31824

To traffic as 824 on 18/8/23
Renumbered A824 no date; 1824 12/9/32; 31824 9/9/49

Works

23/5/24-6/8/24**B**	23,896	
11/12/24-20/12/24**D**	35,233	
16/2/26-29/5/26**A**	66,366	Southern Railway green livery
9/11/27-6/1/28**B**	41,461	Extension of mileage 10,000
20/6/28-11/8/28**C**	51,458	
31/7/29-14/9/29**A**	77,704	
22/7/31**D**	44,964	
5/8/32-12/9/32**A**	63,768	
7/10/32-18/10/32**D**	701	
11/1/34-3/2/34**B**	32,374	Extension of mileage 5,000
18/6/35-26/7/35**A**	72,349	
16/4/37-26/8/37**C**	48,023	Bricklayers Arms
24/4/39-19/5/39**A**	80,691	Class plate fitted
1/1/42-28/1/42**C**	56,764	Extension of mileage 10,000
28/4/43-1/6/43**A**	87,267	684 copper stays renewed 75 copper riveted over "[all steel stays in half sides replaced by copper] 12 holes bushed Copper Firehole Plate new ½ sides Firehole rivets hammered Foundation Ring all rivets renewed Set new small tubes 'Howell and Co' Set new large tubes steel with copper ends
18/9/44-19/10/44**C**		Exmouth Jct 3 copper stays renewed
29/1/46-28/2/46**A**	83,728	239 copper and 653 steel stays renewed ["Test 753 steel stay nuts"] 228 roof stays renewed 464 holes bushed Copper Tubeplate new Foundation Ring all rivets renewed Set new small tubes 'Howell and Co' Set new large tubes steel with copper ends
8/3/48-10/3/48		Bricklayers Arms "Replaced stays caulked" Large tubes expanded and referruled
24/6/48-10/8/48**C**	51,692	Bricklayers Arms
25/7/49-9/9/49**A**	72,063	[Boiler repaired at Brighton] 534 copper and 697 steel stays renewed 228 roof stays and 444 roof nuts renewed 154 holes bushed Internal Tubeplate, Internal Firehole Plate and Internal Wrapping Plate all new Barrel cleaned 173 new small tubes 'Howells' 21 second hand large tubes steel with copper ends Firehole and foundation ring all rivets renewed
2/11/51-23/11/51**HI**	57,161	100 copper stays riveted over 257 nuts renewed Internal Tubeplate 100 studs fitted in lap Set new small tubes 'Talbot and Stead' Set new large tubes
22/1/53-18/2/53	89,963	Bricklayers Arms 173 new small tubes 'Stewart and Lloyds'
12/2/54-6/3/54**GO**	119,835	
31/1/56-17/2/56**HI**	54,481	
31/5/57-7/7/57**LC**	92,009	Bricklayers Arms
17/6/58-5/7/58**GO**	118,633	Blowdown valve and water treatment New type CI firebars
16/3/60-16/4/60**LI**	51,459	
4/8/61-6/8/61		Bricklayers Arms

Tenders

No.3013 14/9/29
No.3033 19/5/39

Boilers

No.847 29/5/26
No.868 14/9/29
No.938 12/9/32
No.902 26/7/35
No.820 19/5/39
No.1030 1/6/43
No.1082 28/2/46
No.847 9/9/49
No.1155 6/3/54
No.1031 5/7/58

Allocations

25/1/25	Bricklayers Arms
16/10/37	Ashford
25/3/44	Exmouth Jct
21/4/45	Stewarts Lane
20/4/46	Ashford
12/7/47	Bricklayers Arms
8/7/60	Stewarts Lane
22/7/63	Redhill

Withdrawn 26/10/63 Cut up at Eastleigh Works w/e 18/1/64

Bricklayers Arms N 31824 at Groombridge, on the Brighton line to the west of Tunbridge Wells, 16 January 1960. L. Rowe, ColourRail

31824 at the head of a line of moguls, at Three Bridges MPD on 18 March 1962; AWS fitted by now, though there is no reference to it on the Record Card. Ken Fairey, ColourRail

31825

To traffic as A825 on 3/12/23
Renumbered 1825 no date; 31825 16/3/51
ERC missing for earlier dates

Works

Date		Mileage	Notes
17/1/24**D**			
17/8/35-19/9/35**C**		59,164	
13/5/36-19/6/36**C**		73,064	
19/10/36-27/11/36**A**		80,777	
14/9/37-23/9/37**D**		22,653	
22/2/38-23/4/38**C**		33,978	Class plate fitted
3/2/40-5/3/40**A**		72,122	
1/4/40**C**		72,122	
18/7/41-22/8/41**C**			Bricklayers Arms
9/10/42-6/11/42**C**		58,458	
12/4/43-14/4/43**D**		69,233	
22/10/43-24/11/43**A**		81,346	675 copper stays renewed 96 nuts renewed [84 steel stays replaced by copper] 215 holes bushed 2 fusible plugs Firehole rivets hammered Set new small tubes 'Howell and Co' Set new llarge tubes steel with copper ends
19/12/45-24/1/46**B**		58,718	Extension of mileage 10,000
29/9/46-30/10/46**C**			New Cross Gate 8 copper stays renewed 90 nuts renewed 2 fusible plugs 173 new small tubes "Large tubes expanded and 21 new ferrules"
28/1/48-2/3/48**A**		96,774	
23/5/50-23/6/50			Stewarts Lane
14/2/51-16/3/51**GO**		68,373	All copper stays renewed 228 roof stays and 444 roof nuts renewed New Firebox Smokebox Tubeplate new Barrel scaled 173 new small tubes 'Talbot and Stead' Set new large tubes steel with copper ends
16/10/52-31/10/52**LI**			450 copper stays riveted over Internal Tubeplate laps caulked 173 new small tubes 'Tubes Ltd' 21 second hand large tubes expanded and referruled Firehole 13 rivets caulked Foundation Ring 10 corner rivets caulked "All elements removed replaced by Piece welded" second hand 21 superheater tubes
16/3/53-31/3/53		63,233	Bricklayers Arms
21/10/53-9/11/53			Bricklayers Arms "Several stays in Firebox riveted and tooled to plate" 173 new small tubes 'Howells' 21 second hand large tubes expanded
25/8/54-4/9/54**LC**		101,251	No Boiler work
14/1/55-9/2/55**GO**		110,179	222 copper stays renewed 133 steel stays replaced by copper 50 copper riveted over 156 nuts renewed Internal Tubeplate "Laps welded 41 studs fitted" 2 fusible plugs 173 new small tubes 'Howells' Firehole 13 new rivets Set new large tubes
18/10/55-9/11/55**LC**		26,115	Bricklayers Arms 173 new small tubes 'New Steel'
22/2/56-24/2/56**LC**		34,141	No Boiler work
7/11/56-24/11/56**LI-HI**		53,078	8 copper stays renewed 312 riveted over 77 nuts renewed Internal Tubeplate "7 cap studs fitted' 2 fusible plugs 173 new small tubes 'Stewart and Lloyds' electrically welded Firehole 15 rivets caulked Set new large tubes
22/4/58-10/5/58**GO**		94,789	1,102 copper stays renewed 228 roof stays and 444 roof nuts renewed 58 holes bushed New Firebox 2 fusible plugs Smokebox Tubeplate levelled 2 mud door holes welded Barrel scaled 173 new small tubes 'Stewart and Lloyds' electrically welded Set new large tubes
2/10/58-7/10/58**NC**		13,831	Water treatment fitted
29/7/60-9/9/60**LI-HI**		67,863	New type CI firebars AWS part fitted 338 copper stays riveted over 6 tubeplate stays riveted "Firehole laps and flanges caulked" 2 fusible plugs 32 new small tubes 'Stewart and Lloyds' electrically welded 141 rebeaded 3 new large tubes 18 second hand expanded and referruled Firehole 15 rivets caulked
26/10/61-29/10/61**NC**			Stewarts Lane

Tenders

No.3009	no date
No.1887	27/11/36
No.3050	4/9/54
No.3051	9/2/55

Allocations

25/1/25	Bricklayers Arms
25/3/44	Exmouth Jct
21/4/45	Stewarts Lane
20/4/46	New Cross Gate
12/7/47	Bricklayers Arms
30/6/62	Stewarts Lane
19/8/63	Redhill

Boilers

No.821	no date
No.1020	27/11/36
No.865	5/3/40
No.1028	24/11/43
No.866	2/3//48
No.888	16/3/51
No.999	9/2/55
No.937	10/5/58

Withdrawn 25/8/63 Cut up at Eastleigh Works w/e 28/12/63

31825 with a substantial train, leaving Lingfield for Oxted on 18 June 1952. Derek Clayton.

31825 in the 1950s, with small first emblem, at Bricklayers Arms, where it was allocated for the great part of its working life. Twin slidebars from new. The coaling plant was more or less unique, a long covered shed for wagons with a typical tub hoist part way along; it's not clear what the function was of the concrete blockhouse at the end, raised above the track to let the coal wagons through.

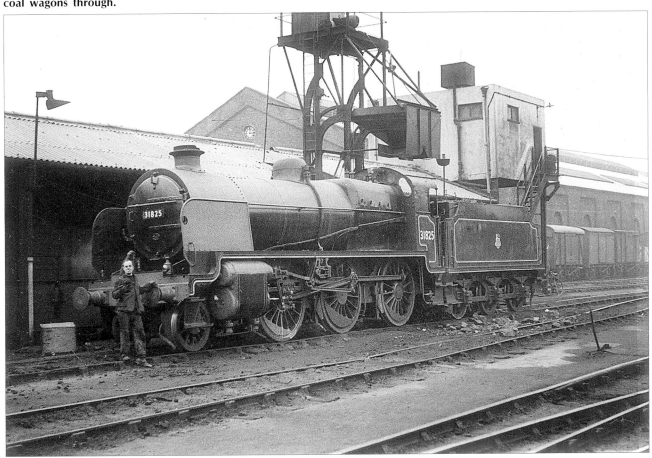

31826

To traffic as A826 3/6/24
Renumbered 1826 14/6/33; 31826 24/12/48

Works
Ex Woolwich 13/5/24

13/5/24-3/6/24**B**		
29/4/26-10/8/26**A**	46,294	
8/10/28-12/12/28**A**	65,144	31 copper and all steel stays renewed 175 copper riveted over 8 roof nuts renewed Copper Tubeplate 19 studs fitted Firehole rivets hammered Set new small tubes 'Howell and Co' Set second hand large tubes "21 large tube holes bushed"
15/10/30-15/11/30**A**	64,649	
5/5/32-13/6/32**C**	58,961	Extension of mileage 10,000
5/5/33-14/6/33**A**	90,120	
20/9/35-30/10/35**A**	77,497	
8/11/37-11/12/37**A**	79,858	
12/10/39-17/10/39**D**	59,679	
23/7/40-22/8/40**A**	81,446	Class plate fitted 300 copper and 616 monel metal stays renewed 150 copper riveted over 66 roof nuts renewed 340 holes bushed Copper Tubeplate new Firehole rivets renewed Set new small tubes 'Chesterfield Tube Co' Large tubes repaired steel with copper ends
28/10/41-25/11/41**C**	48,544	Extension of mileage 5,000
1/9/42-12/10/42**A**	77,482	
17/9/43-9/10/43**C**		Exmouth Jct
16/2/45-21/3/45**A**	98,466	
13/10/47-12/12/47	73,351	Brighton Extension of mileage 10,000
25/11/48-24/12/48**A**	95,304	
22/2/51-4/4/51**HI**	63,291	600 copper stays riveted over Internal Tubeplate 13 copper studs fitted Firehole lap welded Set new small tubes 'Tubes Ltd' Large tubes referruled Firehole 17 new rivets
30/7/51-10/8/51**LC**	71,070	Copper stays riveted over "in fire area" "Firebox laps copper welded" Casing Backplate "Fracture right side welded" firehole 17 new rivets
20/3/53-17/4/53**GO**	106,793	700 copper stays renewed 24 holes bushed Internal Tubeplate and smokebox Tubeplate new Barrel scaled 173 new small tubes 'Tubes Ltd' Set new large tubes
24/4/54-24/5/54**LC**	35,093	Bricklayers Arms 3 copper stays renewed 173 small tubes "repaired" 21 second hand large tubes expanded and referruled
31/8/54-26/9/54**LC**		Bricklayers Arms 21 large tubes repaired
13/5/55-2/6/55**LI**	62,113	16 copper stays renewed 550 copper riveted over Internal Tubeplate "14 studs fitted in laps and 84 caulked" 2 fusible plugs 173 new small tubes 'Howells' electrically welded 3 new large tubes 18 second hand expanded and referruled
28/3/56-13/4/56**HC-LC**	81,925	6 new small tubes 'Universal' 167 rebeaded 21 second hand large tubes
21/5/57-8/6/57**GO**	113,352	118 copper stays renewed 183 copper riveted over 705 nuts renewed 12 roof stays and 12 roof nuts renewed Internal Tubeplate "25 studs fitted and 2 corner rivets caulked" 2 fusible plugs 173 new small tubes 'Universal' set new large tubes Firehole 15 new rivets
12/5/58-30/5/58**LC**	24,666	173 new small tubes 'Stewart and Lloyds' electrically welded
11/5/59-30/5/59**LI-HI**	51,538	Blowdown valve gear and water treatment New type CI firebars 3 copper stays renewed 519 copper riveted over "Firehole laps caulked and 44 lap studs caulked" 2 fusible plugs 32 new small tubes 'New steel 141 rebeaded 3 large tubes repaired 18 second hand expanded and referruled Firehole 15 rivets caulked Foundation Ring 22 rivets caulked
1/7/60-30/7/60**LC**	79,159	AWS part fitted
2/9/61-4/9/61		Bricklayers Arms

Tenders
No.3015 12/12/28
No.3041 24/12/48

Boilers
No.864 10/8/26
No.845 12/12/28
No.912 15/11/30
No.853 14/6/33
No.900 30/10/35
No.893 11/12/37
No.993 22/8/40
No.958 12/10/42
No.960 21/3/45
No.853 24/12/48
No.851 17/4/53
No.988 8/6/57

Allocations
15/6/24 Exmouth Jct
21/4/45 Stewarts Lane
20/4/46 New Cross Gate
12/7/47 Bricklayers Arms
30/6/62 Stewarts Lane

Withdrawn 25/8/63 Cut up at Eastleigh Works w/e 11/1/64

31826, grimly filthy at Norwood Junction MPD on 24 April. It had been in the West for the first twenty years or so, moving to London at the end of the War where it stayed till withdrawal. Note the practice of stowing the screw coupling out of the way (actually on a hook fitted for the purpose) even before AWS appeared. Typically, that hook could appear on either side of the coupling. Barely visible on the cabside is the triangle/circle denoting briquette water treatment. ColourRail

31826, now with AWS, on an evening Reading-bound train near Farnborough, on 31 May 1963. Mainly through the closure of Tonbridge and Bricklayers Arms in June 1962 there was something of a mass transfer of moguls and BR 2-6-4Ts to Stewarts Lane. At the same time its code was altered from 73B to 75D though with events moving fast (steam barely had a year left at Stewarts Lane) no one seemed to think it worthwhile changing plates – it is unlikely that new ones were cast anyway – so 31826 still carries the defunct 73B Bricklayers Arms plate. Peter Groom.

31827

To traffic as A827 on 31/5/24
Renumbered 1827 31/10/31; 31827 16/10/48

Works
Ex Woolwich 13/5/24

Date	Mileage	Notes
13/5/24-31/5/24**B**		
5/10/24-17/10/24**D**		Eastleigh
16/3/25-25/4/25**C**		Eastleigh
24/8/25-5/9/25**D**		Eastleigh
23/8/26-10/12/26**A**	43,554	
7/2/28-18/5/28**A**	63,633	
9/12/29-25/1/30**A**	68,044	
28/9/31-31/10/31**A**	76,393	
3/2/34-10/3/34**A**	92,690	
4/2/36-18/3/36**A**	75,704	753 copper stays renewed 100 copper riveted over 24 roof nuts renewed 267 holes bushed Copper Tubeplate new Throat plate "2 patches R. and L. insides 1 patch L. outside" Firehole rivets hammered Set new small tubes 'Talbot and Stead' Large tubes repaired steel with copper ends
4/4/38-18/5/38**A**	71,739	Class plate fitted
20/2/40-21/3/40**A**	76,271	
12/9/41-14/10/41**A**	75,148	570 copper stays renewed 250 copper riveted over Copper Tubeplate 22 studs fitted Firehole 13 new rivets Foundation Ring 2 rivets renewed Small tubes expanded and rebeaded Large tube repaired steel with copper ends
10/4/42-23/5/42		Exmouth Jct "Several stays riveted over" Copper Tubeplate 27 studs renewed
29/12/42-16/1/43**C**		Exmouth Jct Extension of mileage 30,000 173 new small tubes
5/6/45-6/7/45**A**	141,742	
17/12/46-21/12/46**D**	35,790	Eastleigh
16/6/47-21/6/47**D**	45,941	Eastleigh
22/3/48-25/3/48**D**	59,247	Eastleigh
6/9/48-16/10/48**B**	66,861	
5/12/50-12/1/51**GO**	119,746	
6/3/52-9/4/52	36,051	Bricklayers Arms
19/6/53-17/7/53**HI**	69,538	
13/1/55-4/2/55**GO**	109,572	191 copper stays renewed 702 copper riveted over 708 nuts renewed 240 holes bushed Internal Tubeplate new 2 fusible plugs Barrel scaled 173 new small tubes 'Howells' Firehole and Foundation Ring all new rivets
7/3/56-21/4/56**LC**	32,077	Bricklayers Arms 173 new small tubes 'Stewart and Lloyds' electrically welded Large tubes repaired
4/4/57-27/4/57**LI-HI**	59,927	107 copper stays riveted over 114 nuts renewed 32 new small tubes 'Universal' 141 rebeaded 3 new large tubes 18 second hand expanded and referruled
18/4/58-22/5/58**LC**	27,872	Bricklayers Arms 173 small tubes repaired 3 new large tubes 18 second hand expanded and referruled
12/6/59-11/7/59**GO**	115,648	New type CI (cast iron) firebars ATC Manganese liners Blowdown valve gear and water treatment
10/7/61-11/7/61**NC**		Bricklayers Arms
13/12/61-6/1/62**LI**	61,163	

Tenders
No.3016 18/5/28
No.3051 15/6/53
No.3050 4/2/55

Boilers
No.852 10/12/26
No.830 25/1/30
No.854 31/10/31
No.866 10/3/34
No.965 18/3/36
No.897 18/5/38
No.913 21/3/40
No.965 14/10/41
No.1162 6/7/45
No.886 12/1/51
No.1014 4/2/55
No.1020 11/7/59

Allocations
18/5/24	Exmouth Jct
11/7/38	Barnstaple
18/10/38	Exmouth Jct
30/1/39	Barnstaple
12/8/39	Exmouth Jct
14/7/45	Feltham
29/12/45	Eastleigh
4/2/50	Bricklayers Arms
30/6/62	Stewarts Lane

Withdrawn 14/6/64

A version of 'sunshine' style 31827 at Eastleigh in 1948; it acquired the number on the buffer beam (see *Devil in the Detail*) and only after that, as here, did it get the proper Gill sans smokebox plate too, so for a while it carried the number twice at the front, on smokebox door and buffer beam.

31827 in the external condition customary for the period, at Norwood Junction MPD about 1962; AWS fitted. RailOnline

31828

To traffic as A828 on 2/6/24
Renumbered 1828 10/5/33; 31828 19/8/49

Works
Ex Woolwich 13/5/24

13/5/24-2/6/24**B**		
28/5/26-22/9/26**A**	36,555	
31/1/28-21/4/28**A**	63,680	
25/10/30-29/11/30**A**	62,836	
4/9/31-15/10/31**C**	33,401	Extension of mileage 10,000
9/8/32-11/10/32**C**	62,362	
31/3/33-10/5/33**A**	71,327	
23/5/35-5/7/35**A**	76,480	
26/10/37-4/12/37**A**	87,744	
16/8/38-23/8/38**D**	23.954	Class plate fitted
14/12/39-15/1/40**A**	75,177	
14/11/41-22/12/41**A**	89,221	
31/5/43-22/6/43**C**		Exmouth Jct Extension of mileage 5,000
23/5/44-24/6/44**A**	90,089	95 copper and 486 steel stays renewed 74 nuts renewed 498 holes bushed 2 fusible plugs Firehole rivets hammered set new small tubes 'Howell and Co' Large tubes repaired steel with copper ends
29/4/46-18/5/46**A**	77,765	
23/7/47-21/8/47**B**	35.532	
16/7/49-19/8/49**A**	96,437	295 copper and 587 steel stays renewed 105 copper riveted over 587 nuts renewed 72 roof nuts renewed 612 holes bushed Internal Tubeplate flanges caulked Barrel cleaned Set new small tubes 'Howell' Firehole and Foundation Ring new rivets Large tubes repaired
2/4/51-11/5/51**LC**		Brighton
10/1/52-7/3/52**HI**	67,699	50 copper stays riveted over 250 nuts renewed 132 roof stays and 132 roof nuts renewed Internal Tubeplate 20 studs fitted 173 new small tubes 'Howells' 21 second hand large tubes expanded and referruled
15/1/54-6/2/54**GO**	124,535	
20/12/55-11/1/56**LI**	57,096	
17/12/56-5/1/57**LC**	84,518	
12/9/57-5/10/57**GO**	102,095	
11/9/58-25/9/58**NC-LC**	29,528	Blowdown valve gear and water treatment
22/10/58-27/11/58**LC**		Bricklayers Arms
13/11/59-5/12/59**LI-HI**	59,556	Cast ironl firebars
9/10/61-12/10/61**LC**		Bricklayers Arms
13/2/62-10/3/62**LI**	109,635	AWS part fitted

Tenders

No.3017	21/4/28
No.3053	6/2/54

Boilers

No.897	22/9/26
No.846	29/11/30
No.887	10/5/33
No.843	5/7/35
No.913	4/12/37
No.868	15/1/40
No.913	22/12/41
No.996	24/6/44
No.850	18/5/46
No.1032	19/8/49
No.880	6/2/54
No.848	5/10/57

Allocations

15/6/24	Exmouth Jct
4/1/50	Stewarts Lane
25/3/50	Eastleigh
13/11/50	Exmouth Jct
27/6/51	Bricklayers Arms
30/6/62	Brighton
6/1/64	Redhill

Withdrawn 6/9/64

Top. 31828 at rest at St Leonards MPD, 9 August 1956; small first emblem. transporttreasury

Middle. 31828, late in the day for as N on passenger service, at London Bridge with a rush hour departure, 6 August 1962. Leslie Sandler.

Below. 31828 with some manful attempt at cleaning at least, at Brighton about 1962; the extravagant heights of the works rise up beyond. Small second emblem, AWS, later triangle on cab to denote water treatment, washout plugs on boiler top very apparent.

31829

To traffic as A829 on 15/7/24
Renumbered 1829 21/1/32; 31829 29/7/48

Works
From Woolwich 20/5/24

20/5/24-15/7/24**B**		
18/1/26-15/4/26**A**	46,074	
16/6/28-1/9/28**A**	54,038	
20/12/29-8/2/30**A**	61,368	
11/12/31-21/1/32**A**	67,695	
Stored at shed 29/1/32		
7/5/34-13/6/34**A**	83,284	
4/10/35-21/12/35**C**	47,918	
2/11/36-7/12/36**A**	78,728	
13/4/39-13/5/39**A**	83,498	Class plate fitted
20/5/41-11/6/41**A**	77,158	
3/2/43-17/3/43**A**	68,334	New right hand cylinder
7/4/43-9/4/43**D**	192	
13/4/45-14/4/45**C**		Exmouth Jct
27/4/45-18/5/45**C**		Exmouth Jct Extension of mileage 20,000
25/8/45-26/9/45**A**	95,685	
28/11/46-6/12/46**D**	29,071	Eastleigh
4/1948		Test No.1977 Water gauge protection. Fitted by Motive Power depot
21/5/48-29/7/48**B**	59,173	
9/11/48-10/11/48**D**	62,676	Eastleigh
20/3/50-21/4/50**A**	77,965	525 copper, 705 steel and 228 roof stays renewed 245 holes bushed Internal stays renewed Tubeplate new Set new small tubes 'Howells" Set new large tubes steel with copper ends
16/7/52-8/8/52**HI**	69,851	50 copper stays riveted over 185 nuts renewed 173 new small tubes 'Tubes Ltd' 21 second hand large tubes expanded and referruled Foundation Ring 6 corner rivets caulked
6/11/52-19/11/52**return**		No Boiler work
1/2/54-20/2/54**LC**	109,575	3 steel stays renewed 50 nuts renewed "16 studs fitted in Tubeplate" 173 new small tubes 'Stewart and Lloyds' Large tubes repaired
14/9/54-21/10/54**LC**	125,522	Brighton
21/2/56-10/3/56**GO**	162,409	
2/8/57-10/9/57	42,009	Bricklayers Arms
3/9/58-10/9/58**NC**	67,706	Blowdown valve gear and water treatment complete
19/2/58-8/3/58**LI**	54,306	
3/9/58-10/9/58**NC**	64,999	
7/10/59-24/10/59**LC**	94,720	New type cast iron firebars ATC
6/9/60-14/10/60**GO**	116,212	Full frame conversion New type CI firebars New type 9mm injectors both fitted lhs 759 copper stays renewed 410 copper riveted over 286 holes bushed "Tube and Back plate flanges welded" Internal Wrapping Plate 2 new half sides 2 fusible plugs Barrel scaled 173 new small tubes 'Stewart and Lloyds' electrically welded Foundation Ring new rivets
6/10/61-7/10/61**NC**		Bricklayers Arms

Tenders

No.1887	1/9/28
No.3058	7/12/36
No.3003	17/3/43
No.1882	8/8/52

Boilers

No.854	15/4/26
No.852	8/2/30
No.890	21/1/32
No.848	13/6/34
No.879	7/12/36
No.884	13/5/39
No.851	11/6/41
No.872	17/3/43
No.904	26/9/45
No.996	21/4/50
No.1072	10/3/56
No.1034	14/10/60

Allocations

13/7/24	Exmouth Jct
24/3/34	Eastleigh
15/6/35	Exmouth Jct
14/7/45	Feltham
29/12/45	Eastleigh
9/9/50	Exmouth Jct
27/6/51	Bricklayers Arms
30/6/62	Brighton

Withdrawn 5/1/64 Cut up at Eastleigh Works w/e 2/5/64

31829 at Ramsgate on 17 January 1959; the new station built by the Southern is in the background, with the contemporaneous engine shed and coaling plant to the left. ColourRail

31829 with freight passing Shalford, heading towards Guildford, date not recorded. Note the SECR signal, with Shalford Junction distant below the starter and the repeater lower down on the post. Westinghouse banner repeater for the starter going east towards Redhill. ColourRail

31830

To traffic as A830 on 30/5/24
Renumbered 1830 6/3/33; 31830 27/11/48

Works
Ex Woolwich 20/5/24

Date	Mileage	Notes
20/5/24-13/6/24**B**		"145 small tubes renewed at Feltham"
11/8/24-23/8/24**D**		Eastleigh
5/11/25-30/1/26**A**	33,937	Eastleigh
28/9/26-9/10/26		Feltham
12/7/27-7/9/27		Feltham
29/11/28-2/3/29**A**	64,977	
16/1/31-21/2/31**A**	66,570	13 steel stays renewed 350 copper riveted over 187 nuts renewed Firehole rivets hammered Set new small tubes 87 'Chesterfield Tube Co' 86 'Howell and Co' Large tubes expanded and rebeaded
1/2/33-6/3/33**A**	76,669	
9/7/35-23/8/35**A**	76,625	
9/3/36**D**		Eastleigh
18/2/37-2/4/37**A**	76,483	New left hand cylinder
5/4/38-18/4/38**C**	48,423	Exmouth Jct
27/2/39-13/4/39**A**	87,927	Class plate fitted New right hand cylinder
7/11/41-10/12/41**A**		
15/3/43-30/3/43**C**		Exmouth Jct Extension of mileage 5,000
8/1/44-2/2/44**A**	82,044	
3/10/44-11/11/44**B**	30,577	Extension of mileage 5,000
29/5/45-13/6/45**C**	50,157	
29/4/46-18/5/46**B**	78,771	Extension of mileage 5,000
31/10/46-23/11/46**A**		
3/12/46-7/12/46**D**	86,593	
11/3/48-2/4/48**C**		Stewarts Lane
19/10/48-27/11/48**C**	41,659	
1/7/49-16/7/49**NC**	55,642	
18/4/50-18/5/50**GO**	70,702	178 copper and 572 steel stays renewed 647 nuts renewed 150 holes bushed Barrel scaled Set new small tubes 'Howell and Co' Firehole 11 rivets renewed Large tubes repaired steel with copper ends
6/6/52-18/7/52**HI**	69,898	3 copper stays renewed 75 copper riveted over 121 nuts renewed "28 studs and firebox laps caulked" 32 new small tubes 'Howells' 141 rebeaded 21 second hand large tubes expanded and referruled Firehole 13 rivets caulked
3/9/53-3/10/53**GO**	109,559	525 copper stays renewed and 705 riveted over 705 nuts renewed 228 roof stays and 444 roof nuts renewed New Firebox Barrel scaled 173 new small tubes 'Tubes Ltd' Large tubes repaired
3/10/55-19/11/55**LI-GO**	65,614	New type front end 202 copper and 705 monel metal stays renewed 705 nuts renewed 256 holes bushed Internal Tubeplate new 2 fusible plugs Barrel scaled 173 new small tubes 'Stewart and Lloyds' electrically welded set new large tubes
4/1/56-19/1/56**return**	1,297	No Boiler work
7/5/58-24/5/58**LI-HI**	73,983	304 copper stays renewed 2 fusible plugs 2 corner mud holes welded 32 new small tubes 'Stewart and Lloyds' electrically welded 141 rebeaded 3 large tubes repaired 18 second hand expanded and referruled
9/12/60-21/1/61**GO**	151,489	New type cast iron firebars Water treatment AWS 1,012 copper stays renewed 228 roof stays and 444 roof nuts renewed 48 holes bushed New Firebox 2 fusible plugs Barrel scaled 173 new small tubes 'Stewart and Lloyds' electrically welded Foundation Ring rivets repaired Set new large tubes
2/2/62-24/2/62**LC-HC**	28,565	'Overhead live wire notices' Spark arrester

Tenders

No.3028	2/3/29
No.3062	13/4/39
No.3028	18/7/52
No.3027	19/11/55
No.3034	14/4/60

Boilers

No.855	13/6/24
No.887	2/3/29
No.985	21/2/31
No.914	6/3/33
No.898	23/8/35
No.874	2/4/37
No.907	13/4/39
No.1042	10/12/41
No.1072	2/2/44
No.859	23/11/46
No.1087	18/5/50
No.1044	3/10/53
No.1158	19/11/55
No.860	21/1/61

Allocations

15/6/24	Exmouth Jct
By 23/4/32	Barnstaple
24/4/43	Bricklayers Arms
29/12/45	Exmouth Jct
14/6/47	Tonbridge
31/3/48	Norwood Jct
31/7/48	Ashford
4/2/50	Faversham
9/9/50	Exmouth Jct
22/10/62	Brighton

Withdrawn 5/1/64 Cut up at Eastleigh Works w/e 11/4/64

Left. Double heading on a 'Royal' was an insurance, and probably also useful operationally out in the West, with parts of the train likely to be stabled separately and so on. Raised to dizzying heights of cleanliness, 31830 heads another N near Cowley Bridge on 8 May 1956. There were in fact four Ns involved in the 'Grove' that week, the others being 31835 and (see later) 31844. 'Grove' was the telegraphic code for HM The Queen, 'Deepdene' was the code for lesser Royals They were universal on all the BR regions and were the names of stately homes acquired (commandeered?) by the railway companies as HQs during the War. L.F. Folkard, ColourRail

Below. 31830 at its home shed, Exmouth Junction, in the 1950s; cleanliness a far cry from the Royal heights of 1956. J. Davenport, Initial Photographics.

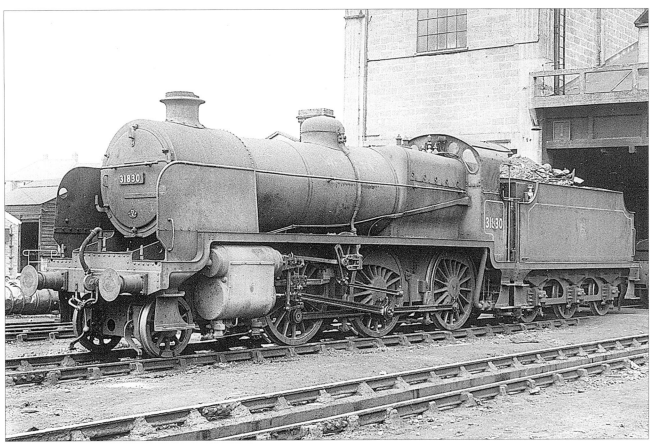

31831

To traffic as A831 on 20/6/24
Renumbered 1831 23/2/34; 31831 4/12/48

Works
Ex Woolwich 20/5/24

20/5/24-20/6/24**B**		
10/8/25-26/9/25**B**		Eastleigh
2/3/27-3/6/27**A**	78,827	
20/3/29-4/5/29**A**	59,314	17 copper stays renewed 450 copper riveted over Copper Tubeplate 12 studs fitted Firehole rivets hammered Set new small tubes 'Howell and Co'
2/6/31-7/7/31**A**	74,738	
8/10/32-21/10/32**C**		Exmouth Jct Extension of mileage 15,000
12/1/34-23/2/34**A**	111,583	40 copper and 344 steel stays renewed 75 copper riveted over 31 nuts renewed [12 steel stays replaced by copper] "8 tube holes bushed" Firehole rivets hammered Set new small tubes 'Chesterfield tube Co' Large tubes repaired steel with copper ends
28/4/34-8/6/34**C**	2,994	170 nuts renewed
15/4/35-10/5/35**D**	41,406	"2 tube holes bushed" Throat Plate R.H/ top corner welded 3 new small tubes 'Howell and Co' "170 small tubes expanded and rebeaded. All large tubes expanded and referruled"
4/6/36-22/7/36**A**	78,203	
9/3/38**D**		Eastleigh
20/12/38-27/1/39**A**	87,841	Class plate fitted
17/6/41-15/7/41**A**	87,276	
21/10/42-23/11/42		Exmouth Jct extension of mileage 10,000
27/4/44-3/6/44**A**	96,714	26 copper stays renewed 75 copper riveted over 101 nuts renewed [184 monel metal stays replaced by copper] Copper Tubeplate 53 studs fitted 2 fusible plugs Firehole rivets hammered Set new small tubes 'Howell and Co' Set new large tubes
8/1/46-13/4/46**C**		Exmouth Jct
3/6/47-18/9/47**A**	105,303	Converted to oil fuel
21/1/48-31/1/48**D**	7,798	Eastleigh Electric lighting apparatus fitted
8/11/48-4/12/48**C**	30,034	Converted to coal firing
19/12/49-19/1/50**HI**	62,580	Test No.2089 Shot blasted springs fitted 400 copper stays riveted over "in fire area" Set new small tubes Large tubes referruled
11/5/52-6/6/52**GO**	138,820	
23/3/54-12/4/54	65,257	Exmouth Jct
14/6/54-26/6/54**LI-HI**	71,419	
23/3/56-14/4/56**LI**	132,718	
31/3/58-26/4/58**GO**	197,680	
27/6/60-30/7/60**HI**	69,821	AWS fitted New type CI firebars Front end conversion Water treatment
17/5/62-18/5/62**NC**		Exmouth Jct
22/2/63-23/3/63**LI**	148,590	Eastleigh

Tenders
No.3020 3/6/27
No.1895 4/5/29
No.3004 22/7/36
No.3027 13/4/46
No.3031 18/9/47

Boilers

No.856	3/6/27
No.899	4/5/29
No.860	7/7/31
No.1035	23/2/34
No.957	22/7/36
No.960	27/1/39
No.961	15/7/41
No.1035	3/6/44
No.858	18/9/47
No.883	6/6/52
No.1032	26/4/58

Allocations

13/7/24	Exmouth Jct
28/12/47	Fratton
4/9/48	Exmouth Jct
4/2/50	Redhill
9/9/50	Exmouth Jct
22/10/62	Brighton
6/1/64	Redhill
18/1/65	Guildford

Withdrawn 25/4/65

Top. 1831 in its year as an 'oiler', September 1947-September 1948; during that time (but not immediately – from January 1948) it was fitted with electric lighting. This apparently stayed on for a while after reversion to coal burning. John Eyers, South Western Circle.

Middle. 31831 at Barnstaple Junction with an up train, as far as Exeter at least, on 17 August 1957. While many Eastern Section moguls gravitated west late in the day, others came the other way. 31831 had been one of the 'originals' at Exmouth Junction but in 1962 found itself at Brighton. Then it was the familiar sequence of short-term stays, at Redhill then Guildford. Ken Fairey, ColourRail

Below. 31831 climbing away from Dorking with a train for Guildford, 29 August 1964; new curving frames at front, BR chimney. As the photographer notes: 'working hard, with a clean exhaust and no steam leaks!' The loco was forty years old, a lot older than the photographer (then). Peter Groom.

31832

To traffic as A832 on 12/7/24
Renumbered 1832 16/12/32; 31832 9/7/49

Works
Ex Woolwich 13/6/24

Date	Mileage	Location / Notes
13/6/24-12/7/24**B**		
21/7/24-24/7/24**D**		
26/10/25-18/2/26**A**	40,625	Eastleigh
20/3/27-8/5/27		Exmouth Jct
26/1/28-5/5/28**A**	59,116	
6/8/30-19/9/30**A**	65,593	
4/11/32-16/12/32**A**	82,251	
20/12/34-5/2/35**A**	82,779	
11/2/37-24/3/37**A**	83,175	
13/7/39-17/8/39**A**	79,041	Class plate fitted 252 copper and 705 monel metal stays renewed 100 copper riveted over 92 holes bushed Copper Tubeplate new Firehole rivets renewed Set new small tubes 'Howell and Co' Large tubes repaired steel with copper ends
21/8/40-24/9/40**C**	36,938	
12/12/41-10/1/42**A**	79,825	
17/3/43-22/4/43**C**		Exmouth Jct
18/5/44-17/6/44**A**	75,563	
28/2/45-19/4/45**C**	14,574	
27/10/45-24/11/45**C**		Exmouth Jct
20/3/46-5/4/45**C**	42,146	
25/11/46-24/12/46**C**	60,529	
20/1/48-26/2/48**A**	92,975	638 copper stays renewed 275 riveted over 228 roof nuts renewed Copper Tubeplate new Copper firehole plate 115 studs fitted Steel Tubeplate "repaired and 20 studs renewed" Foundation Ring 30 rivets renewed Set new small tubes 'Talbot and Stead' Set new large tubes steel with copper ends
3/6/49-9/7/49**HI**	41,345	
30/8/50-6/10/50**HI**	77,545	Copper stays riveted over "in fire area" Internal Tubeplate "Fit 75 copper studs and caulk laps" Set new small tubes 'Talbot and Stead' 21 large tubes expanded and referruled
12/6/51-29/6/51**LC**	96,328	No Boiler work
29/1/53-20/2/53**GO**		252 copper stays renewed 275 copper riveted over Internal Firehole 4 laps caulked 173 new small tubes 'Stewart and Lloyds' Firehole 13 rivets caulked Large tubes repaired steel with copper ends
14/9/54-2/10/54**LC**	55,521	No Boiler work
11/10/55-27/10/55**HI**	89,142	294 copper stays riveted over 2 fusible plugs 32 new small tubes 141 rebeaded 3 large tubes repaired 18 second hand expanded and referruled
23/9/57-12/10/57**GO**	153,717	468 copper stays renewed 544 copper riveted over 6 roof nuts renewed "101 studs fitted and laps reinforced" 2 fusible plugs Barrel scaled 173 new small tubes 'Tube products' electrically welded Firehole 15 new rivets Set new large tubes
12/10/59-31/10/59**LI-HI**	69,307	New type CI firebars 429 copper stays riveted over "35 laps studs fitted flanges firehole lap and ½ side seams caulked 44 flange rivets caulked" 2 fusible plugs 32 new small tubes 'Tube Products' electrically welded 141 rebeaded 3 new large tubes 18 second hand expanded and referruled Firehole 15 rivets caulked also "22 corner rivets caulked"
12/8/61-15/8/61		
27/9/61-21/10/61**LI-HI**	128,641	AWS complete 'Overhead live wire notices' 263 copper stays riveted over "Tubeplate and firehole flanges caulked-93 lap rivets caulked" 2 fusible plugs 32 small tubes repaired 141 rebeaded 3 new large tubes 18 second hand expanded and referruled Firehole 15 rivets caulked

Tenders

No.3021	5/5/28
No.3000	24/3/37
No.3008	24/12/46
No.3039	1/1948*
No.3002	9/7/49
No.3005	20/2/53

*ERC shows changed at Exmouth Jct

Allocations

13/7/24	Exmouth Jct
22/10/62	Brighton

Boilers

No.857	5/5/28
No.909	19/9/30
No.863	16/12/32
No.832	5/2/35
No.939	24/3/37
No.1026	17/8/39
No.887	10/1/42
No.976	17/6/44
No.841	26/2/48
No.935	20/2/53
No.853	12/10/57

Withdrawn 5/1/64 Cut up at Eastleigh Works w/e 11/4/64

With sunshine tender lettering barely breaking through the grime, s1832 shunts wagons as part of its pick-up duty at Bere Alston in July 1948. It had the prefix from March 1948 to July 1949. J.H. Aston.

31832 at Exmouth Junction in 1949; BR numbering but tender now appears bare; a shadowy outline of SOUTHERN suggests a repaint during the period late 1948 to early 1949 when tenders and tanks were turned out blank due to a delay in the supply of transfers. 31832 was out of the ordinary, spending all but the last year or so of its working life at Exmouth Junction.

31833

To traffic as A833 on 4/7/24
Renumbered 1833 17/11/31; 31833 10/11/48

Works
Ex Woolwich 13/6/24

13/6/24-4/7/24**B**		
29/9/25-13/3/26**B**		Eastleigh
13/9/27-17/11/27**A**	81,872	
27/9/29-2/11/29**A**	58,457	
20/10/31-17/11/31**A**	79,291	
Stored from to 30/11/31-15/2/32 sent to shed [shed unrecorded]		
6/7/34-24/8/34**A**	80,839	
8/9/26-16/10/36**A**	79,615	
7/2/39-13/3/39**A**	77,829	Class plate fitted
7/8/41-3/9/41**A**	86,545	
6/2/43-16/3/43**C**		Exmouth Jct
7/7/43-7/8/43**C**		Exmouth Jct extension of mileage 20,000
26/8/44-21/10/44**A**	93,692	New cylinders
18/6/46-17/7/46**A**	62,296	
30/9/48-10/11/48**A**	80,527	
10/1/51**HI**	68,141	Works not recorded 25 copper stays riveted over 185 nuts renewed 32 new small tubes 'Tubes Ltd' 21 large tubes expanded and referruled
9/10/52-29/10/52**HI**		231 nuts renewed Internal Tubeplate 4 laps caulked 173 new small tubes 'Howells' 6 large tubes repaired 15 second hand expanded and referruled Firehole 11 rivets caulked
4/8/54-4/9/54**GO**	187,740	
12/10/56-3/11/56**LI**	70,834	
5/4/57-6/4/57**LC**	85,088	
2/4/59-6/6/59**GO**	146,874	Full frame conversion Manganese liners New type CI firebars 566 copper and 370 monel metal stays renewed 370 nuts renewed "50 lap studs fitted 15 flanges and 20 corner rivets caulked Firehole laps welded" 2 fusible plugs 2 mud door holes welded Barrel Ring scaled 173 new small tubes 'Tube products' electrically welded Firehole 15 new rivets "2 brick arch studs" Set new large tubes
19/7/61-26/8/61**LI-HI**	70,069	Spark arrester 'Overhead live wire notices' 357 copper stays riveted over "4 flanges and door laps caulked" 2 fusible plugs 35 new small tubes ;Tube products' 138 rebeaded 4 new large tubes 17 second hand expanded and referruled Firehole 15 rivets caulked

Tenders

No.3022	2/11/29
No.3056	28/2/59

Boilers

No.858	17/11/27
No.886	2/11/29
No.889	17/11/31
No.874	24/8/34
No.967	16/10/36
No.957	13/3/39
No.856	3/9/41
No.886	21/10/44
No.879	17/7/46
No.963	10/11/48
No.1020	4/9/54
No.1040	6/6/59

Allocations

13/7/24	Exmouth Jct
No date	Stewarts Lane
8/10/32	Exmouth Jct
22/10/62	Brighton

Withdrawn 23/2/64 Cut up at Eastleigh Works w/e 25/4/64

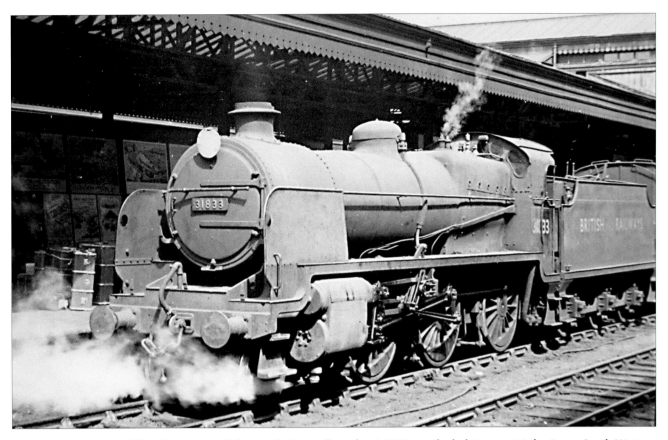

31833 at Exeter St David's with a train off the North Devon line, about 1949; no shed plate as yet. John Eyres, South Western Circle.

There were invariably Ns to be found at Barnstaple Junction; they went there from the first and revolutionised workings, with a substantial margin of power above that of the various LSW types, elderly 4-4-0s and 0-4-4Ts and even 0-4-2 tender locos. On 7 July 1959 31833 is still looking good having returned shortly before all the way from Ashford after a General there. Note twin slidebars, fitted in SR days. ColourRail

31834

To traffic as A834 on 2/7/24
Renumbered 1834 4/7/34; 31834 8/1/49

Works
From Woolwich 13/6/24

Date	Mileage	Notes
13/6/24-2/7/24**B**		
10/10/25-9/1/26**A**	44,791	Eastleigh
26/11/27-10/3/28**A**	60,470	
1/1/30-11/2/30**B**	53,768	Extension of mileage 15,000
5/12/30-17/1/31**A**	77,127	
16/2/32-19/2/32**C**	24,702	
3/5/33-15/6/33**C**	48,605	
29/5/34-4/7/34**A**	58,110	112 copper stays renewed 100 copper riveted over 62 nuts renewed [284 stays replaced by copper] Copper Tubeplate 8 studs fitted Firehole rivets hammered Set new small tubes 'Howell and co' Second hand large tubes with copper ends
19/11/35-17/1/36**C**	55,143	Extension of mileage 5,000 300 copper stays riveted over copper Tubeplate 1 stud fitted Sets of new small and large tubes
15/1/37-24/2/37**A**	88,157	
3/8/39-15/9/39**A**	79,866	Class plate fitted
17/9/40-29/1/41**A**	37,017	Eastleigh
6/10/41-29/10/41**C**		
16/1/42-24/2/42**D**		
8/10/42-16/11/42**C**	59,428	Extension of mileage 5,000
14/6/43-28/6/43**C**		Exmouth Jct Extension of mileage 10,000
20/3/45-28/4/45**A**	134,081	
5/12/45-19/12/45**C**		Exmouth Jct
4/6/46-6/7/46**C**	41,262	
21/5/47-17/6/47**C**	61,356	
20/10/47-14/11/47**B**	71,919	Extension of mileage 5,000
27/11/48-8/1/49**A**	101,663	Renumbered 31834 41 copper stays renewed [210 monel metal stays replaced by copper] 198 nuts renewed 20 roof stays renewed Copper Tubeplate 20 studs fitted Firehole rivets hammered Foundation Ring 55 rivets renewed Set new small tubes 'Talbot and Stead' Large tubes repaired steel with copper ends
21/1/50-16/2/50		Exmouth Jct
3/5/51-1/6/51**LI**	71,409	5 copper stays renewed copper riveted over "in fire area" 75 nuts renewed 115 roof stays renewed Internal Tubeplate 12 copper studs and laps caulked 4 brick arch studs fitted 32 new small tubes 141 expanded and rebeaded
5/6/51-14/6/51**return**		
1/5/53-29/5/53**GO**		13 copper and 132 steel stays renewed 75 copper riveted over 124 nuts renewed "15 studs fitted in laps Firehole laps welded" Smokebox tubeplate new Barrel scaled 173 new small tubes Large tubes repaired Firehole 15 new rivets
23/6/55-8/7/55**LI**	69,277	35 copper stays riveted over 226 nuts renewed 2 fusible plugs 32 small tubes repaired 141 rebeaded 3 large tubes repaired 18 second hand expanded and referruled Firehole 12 new rivets
21/11/56-7/12/56**LI**	112,811	138 nuts renewed Internal Tubeplate15 studs 2 fusible plugs welded 32 new small tubes 'Stewart and Lloyds' electrical welded 141 rebeaded 3 new large tubes 18 second hand
23/12/59-6/2/59**GO**	181,642	New type CI firebars Manganese steel liners
6/4/61-29/4/61**LI-HI**	67,637	AWS complete 'Overhead live wire notices'
11/5/62-14/5/62**NC**		Exmouth Jct
28/5/63-29/6/63**LI**	128,607	Eastleigh
28/8/63-14/9/63**return**	128,802	Eastleigh

Tenders

No.3023	10/3/28
No.3041	19/12/45
No.3015	8/1/49
No.3064	29/4/61

Boilers

No.859	10/3/28
No.874	17/1/31
No.999	4/7/34
No.868	24/2/37
No.842	15/9/39
No.893	28/4/45
No.1064	8/1/49
No.1040	29/5/53
No.1162	6/2/59

Allocations

13/7/24	Salisbury
6/10/34	Exmouth Jct

Withdrawn 7/9/64. Sold to Birds, Morriston 14/10/64

Top. 31834 at Exmouth Junction about 1954-55; one of the newly arrived 82000 3MT 2-6-2Ts stands beyond. This N never went east unless it were for overhaul at Ashford; it was at only two sheds, Salisbury and Exmouth Junction. John Eyres, South Western Circle.

Middle. On 29 August 1964, one week before through expresses from Waterloo to Ilfracombe ceased, 31834 (most strangely, bereft of its AWS 'protector plate') pilots the 5.57 pm Ilfracombe-Taunton train up the bank out of Ilfracombe; the little engine shed and the terminus are down there in the background and, beyond them, the sea. In charge of the six Western Region coaches is 43XX 2-6-0 7303. S.C. Nash.

Below. The Meldon Quarry ballast hoppers were unmistakable; with only a single locomotive, this is the down working – the empties returning to Meldon with extra wagons tacked on the rear – on 3 August 1955. The location is Honiton and its bank and tunnel, with the train approaching the eastern portal. transporttreasury

121

31835

To traffic as A835 on 10/7/24
Renumbered 1835 31/12/31; 31835 18/5/50

Works
Ex Woolwich 20/6/24

Date	Mileage	Notes
20/6/24-10/7/24**B**		
16/7/24-18/7/24**D**		
8/1/27-22/4/27**A**	70,515	
12/6/29-24/7/29**A**	68,033	
29/12/30-30/12/30**D**	42,454	
10/2/31-11/4/31**B**	44,528	Extension of mileage 10,000
21/11/31-31/12/31**A**	67,998	
Stored from 12/1/32-15/2/32 sent to shed		
7/6/34-20/7/34**A**	77,070	
30/7/36-11/9/36**A**	77,333	309 copper stays renewed 275 copper riveted over 4 roof nuts renewed Copper Tubeplate 104 studs fitted Firehole rivets hammered Set new small tubes 'Tubes Ltd' Large tubes repaired steel with copper ends
6/4/39-8/5/39**A**	86,987	Class plate fitted
26/5/41-18/6/41**A**	86,237	574 copper stays renewed 275 copper riveted over Copper Tubeplate 105 studs fitted Firehole 13 rivets renewed Foundation Ring 3 rivets renewed Set new small tubes 'Howell and Co' Large tubes repaired steel with copper ends
30/1/43-13/3/43**B**		Exmouth Jct Extension of mileage 15,000 Fusible plugs examined 173 new small tubes
30/5/44-8/7/44**A**	99,231	
19/4/45-2/6/45**C**		Exmouth Jct
16/3/46-6/4/46**B**	47,558	
13/10/47-12/11/47**A**	93,243	
7/10/48-16/10/48**C**	27,038	Eastleigh
14/4/50-18/5/50**A**	73,716	
13/4/51-3/5/51**HC**	30,595	
26/5/53-20/6/53**HI**		
13/5/55-3/6/55**GO**	166,592	800 copper stays renewed 385 holes bushed Internal Tubeplate new 2 fusible plugs Barrel scaled 173 new small tubes 'Howells' Set new large tubes
26/4/57-31/5/57**LI-HI**	63,392	Full frame conversion 2 new type 9mm injectors fitted to Drg.A.10317 273 copper stays riveted over "30 laps and 6 corner rivets caulked" 32 new small tubes 'Universal' 141 rebeaded 3 large tubes repaired 18 second hand expanded and referruled
22/6/59-11/7/59**HI**	133,353	New type CI firebars ATC 467 copper stays riveted over "Firehole lap and flange caulked-72 side seams caulked -114 flange rivets caulked" 2 fusible plugs 173 new small tubes 'Stewart and Lloyds' electrically welded Firehole 15 rivets caulked
8/2/60-20/2/60**LC**	147,865	
13/6/61-8/7/61**GO**	187,960	Spark arrester Water treatment 'Overhead live wire notices'
16/8/63-21/9/63**HI**	60,490	Eastleigh
23/6/64-26/6/64**NC**		Eastleigh WR loco

Tenders

No.3024	22/4/27
No.3023	20/6/53
No.3043	21/9/63

Boilers

No.860	22/4/27
No.850	24/7/29
No.858	31/12/31
No.862	20/7/34
No.831	11/9/36
No.976	8/5/39
No.962	18/6/41
No.866	8/7/44
No.898	12/11/47
No.830	18/5/50
No.855	3/6/55
No.966	8/7/61

Allocations

13/7/24	Exmouth Jct
No date	Stewarts Lane
8/10/32	Exmouth Jct

Withdrawn 7/9/64. Sold to Birds, Morriston 14/10/64

31835 awaits departure from the terminus at Ilfracombe, alongside light Pacific 34011 TAVISTOCK on 11 June 1963. This N was on the Withered Arm for practically all its working life. L. Rowe, ColourRail

Boscarne Ground Frame and exchange sidings in the winter of 1962. In the background a train for Wenford Bridge pauses on the SR up and down siding; beyond is siding No.2. The Beattie well tanks had gone by now and the train is hauled by one of the three GWR 0-6-0PT replacements acquired from Weymouth Quay in the summer of 1962. 31835 is en-route for Bodmin General with a rake of vans. It is AWS fitted; the protector plate, incidentally, was designed at Ashford Works by apprentice Raymond Sinclair Smith. RailOnline

31836

To traffic as A836 on 15/7/24
Renumbered 1836 23/1/32; 31836

Works
Ex-Woolwich 20/6/24

Date	Mileage	Notes
20/6/24-15/7/24		'Set to work'
23/7/24-25/7/24		
14/12/25-6/3/26**A**	35,794	Eastleigh
28/6/28-29/9/28**A**	59,724	
11/6/30-19/7/30**A**	61,200	
16/12/31-23/1/32**A**	64,177	
10/1/34-13/2/34**A**	76,721	
21/2/36-7/4/36**A**	73,582	
4/11/38-14/12/38**A**	89,799	Class plate fitted
28/6/40-27/7/40**C**	59,259	Extension of mileage 10,000
28/4/41-20/5/41**A**	86,873	
30/4/42-13/5/42**D**	35,776	
4/5/43-2/6/43**A**	69,999	436 copper stays renewed 300 copper riveted over Roof "cleaned" Copper Tubeplate 82 studs fitted 2 fusible plugs Firehole rivets hammered Set new small tubes 'Howell and Co' Set new large tubes steel with copper ends
22/3/45-18/4/45**C**		Exmouth Jct Extension of mileage 15,000 Copper stays riveted over "in fire area" Copper Tubeplate 50 studs fitted Casing Back Plate fracture welded 8 new small tubes
26/4/46-13/5/46**A**	119,819	
26/1/48-31/3/48		Exmouth Jct
11/11/48-11/12/48**C**	71,851	
8/2/50-10/2/50**LC**	97,792	Eastleigh
6/10/50-3/11/50**HI**	115,744	
8/1/53-20/2/53**GO**		320 copper and 705 steel stays renewed 228 roof stays and 228 roof nuts renewed 130 holes bushed Internal Tubeplate new Barrel scaled 173 new small tubes 'Tubes Ltd' Large tubes repaired
9/2/55-3/3/55**HI**	76,643	2 fusible plugs 32 new small tubes 'Howells' 141 rebeaded 3 large tubes repaired 18 second hand expanded and referruled
16/12/55-4/1/56**LC**	100,706	No Boiler work
14/3/57-30/3/57**LI**	139,676	20 copper stays riveted over 57 nuts renewed 32 new small tubes 'Universal' 3 large tubes repaired 18 second hand expanded and referruled
11/3/59-10/4/59**GO**	201,481	New type cast iron firebars Additional boiler plugs 760 copper stays renewed 252 copper riveted over 364 holes bushed Internal Tubeplate new Smokebox Tubeplate levelled 2 fusible plugs Barrel scaled Firehole new rivets 173 new small tubes 'Stewart and Lloyds' electrically welded Set new large tubes
15/3/61-7/4/61**LI-HI**	61,304	AWS 'Overhead live wire notices' 389 copper stays riveted over 2 fusible plugs 32 new small tubes 'Stewart and Lloyds' electrically welded 141 rebeaded 3 new large tubes 18 second hand expanded and referruled
4/2/62-6/2/62		Exmouth Jct

Tenders

No.1889	29/9/82
No.3100	14/12/38
No.3056	2/6/43
No.3022	10/4/59

Boilers

No.861	29/9/28
No.862	19/7/30
No.886	23/1/32
No.906	13/2/34
No.908	7/4/36
No.873	14/12/38
No.891	20/5/41
No.1034	2/6/43
No.1163	13/5/46
No.1159	20/2/53
No.889	10/4/59

Allocations

10/8/24	Exmouth Jct
14/8/36	Barnstaple
30/1/39	Exmouth Jct
8/1/49	Salisbury
13/11/50	Exmouth Jct

Withdrawn 28/12/63. Cut up at Eastleigh Works w/e 18/4/64

31836 and train near Port Isaac Road in May 1956. It had previously worked a train from Exeter to Plymouth and on the return journey had come off at Okehampton for servicing. It is now on the 1.30am ex-Waterloo to Wadebridge train but the crew have forgotten to change the headcode. The motley collection of stock includes a Maunsell Brake Composite (Diagram 2403), Bulleid Open Saloon Third (Diagram 2017), Bulleid Brake Composite (Diagram 2406), Bogie Luggage Van 'B' (Diagram 3093) with newspaper roof boards, three 'XP' rated vans and a Southern 4-wheeled passenger brake 'Van C' (BY under BR) to Diagram 3092.

31836 at home at Exmouth Junction MPD, 17 August 1957. Ken Fairey, ColourRail

31837

To traffic as A837 on 17/7/24
Renumbered 1837 13/5/32; 31837 5/11/49

Works
Ex Woolwich 20/6/24

Date	Mileage	Notes
20/6/24-17/7/24		
14/12/25-6/3/26**A**	35,396	Eastleigh
16/6/28-15/9/28**A**	56,535	
20/5/30-21/6/30**A**	64,570	
20/11/31-1/12/31**C**		Exmouth Jct Extension of mileage 15,000
12/4/32-13/5/32**A**	79,602	
20/4/34-25/5/34**A**	87,499	
6/6/35-9/8/35**C**	36,170	
14/9/36-16/9/36**D**		Eastleigh
18/12/36-27/1/37**A**	80,995	
15/4/37-20/4/37**D**	7,810	
14/6/39-10/7/39**A**	89,944	Class plate fitted
15/8/39**D**		Eastleigh
14/7/41-20/8/41**A**	86,845	
16/1/42-24/2/42**D**		
26/1/43-9/3/43**B**		Exmouth Jct Extension of mileage 20,000
5/4/44-6/5/44**A**	75,087	
9/6/45-26/6/45**C**		Exmouth Jct
13/2/47-15/3/47**A**	86,662	
1/1/48-7/2/48**C**	22,712	
6/10/49-5/11/49**A**	72,658	525 copper and 705 steel stays renewed 228 roof stays renewed 175 holes bushed Internal Tubeplate and Internal Firehole Plate new Set new small tubes 'Howells' Large tubes repaired steel with copper ends
18/12/50-19/1/51**LC**	37,300	No Boiler work
10/11/52-28/11/52**HI**	98,446	50 copper stays riveted over 126 nuts renewed 32 new small tubes 'Tubes Ltd' 141 rebeaded 6 large tubes repaired 15 second hand expanded and referruled
25/11/54-11/12/54**GO**	168,177	
12/11/56-29/11/56**LI**	66,203	
18/2/59-7/3/59**LI**	143,523	New cast iron firebars
18/1/61-17/2/61**GO**	194,030	Full frame conversion Water treatment Manganese liners AWS 'Overhead live wire notices'
27/4/62-28/4/62**NC**		Exmouth Jct
19/12/63-25/1/64**LI**	86,739	Eastleigh WR loco

Tender

No.1888	15/9/28

Boilers

No.862	15/9/28
No.892	21/6/30
No.961	13/5/32
No.844	25/5/34
No.821	27/1/37
No.1042	10/7/39
No.976	20/8/41
No.959	6/5/44
No.997	15/3/47
No.975	5/11/49
No.897	11/12/54
No.881	17/2/61

Allocations

10/8/24	Exmouth Jct
By 4/1932	Barnstaple
16/10/37	Exmouth Jct
27/2/40	Barnstaple
24/4/43	Bricklayers Arms
29/12/45	Exmouth Jct
11/12/52	Yeovil Town
3/3/53	Exmouth Jct

Withdrawn 7/9/64. Sold to Birds, Morriston, 14/10/64

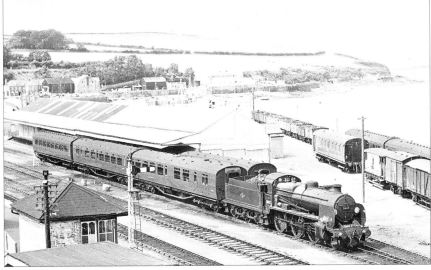

Top. Long-term resident 31837 (small first emblem) at Exmouth Junction MPD in the 1950s. John Eyers, South Western Circle.

Middle. 31837 at Padstow with a mid-day three coach train for Okehampton and ultimately, Waterloo probably in the summer of 1961 after fitting of AWS and what the Record calls 'Overhead live wire notices', during a General at Ashford.

Below. 31837 at Exmouth Junction, 4 June 1960; it would undergo frame conversion the following year. Peter Groom.

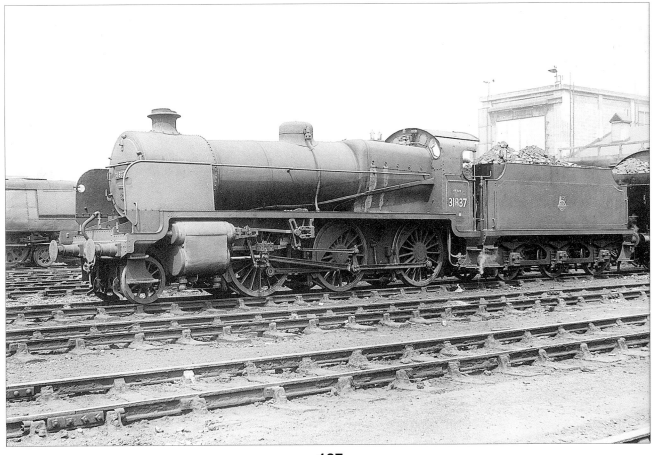

31838

To traffic as A838 on 23/7/24
Renumbered 1838 2/12/33; 31838 16/12/49

Works
Ex Woolwich 27/6/24

Date	Mileage	Notes
27/6/24-23/7/24**B**		
25/7/24-26/7/24**D**		
27/1/26-24/4/26**A**	51,933	
17/10/27-23/12/27**B**	55,958	Extension of mileage 20,000
6/11/28-2/2/29**A**	79,844	
7/3/31-23/4/31**A**	71,952	295 copper stays renewed 200 copper riveted over Firehole rivets hammered Set new small tubes 'Chesterfield Tube Co' Second hand large tubes with copper ends
30/10/33-2/12/33**A**	91,838	
24/3/34-4/5/34**C**	10,424	
2/1/36-11/2/36**A**	73,540	
20/5/38-29/6/38**A**	77,724	Class plate fitted 325 copper stays rnewed 200 copper riveted over 2 roof stays and 1 roof nut renewed Copper Tubeplate 30 studs fitted Firehole rivets hammered Set new small tubes 'Chesterfield Tube Co' Large tubes repaired steel with copper ends
1/2/39-6/2/39**D**	18,479	Eastleigh
1/8/40-12/10/40**C**	75,725	Exmouth Jct Extension of mileage 20,000 Copper stays riveted over "in fire area" [53 copper studs renewed] Copper Tubeplate seams caulked Set new small tubes Large tubes rolled and referruled
6/8/41-27/8/41**A**	107,281	
26/11/42-12/12/42**C**		Exmouth Jct Extension of mileage 5,000
29/6/43-10/7/43**C**		Exmouth Jct
22/3/44-22/4/44**A**	88,751	155 copper and 1 steel stays renewed 100 copper riveted over 180 nuts renewed [285 monel metal stays replaced by copper] Copper Tubeplate 101 studs Copper wrapping Plate "2 patches in top seam" 2 fusible plugs Firehole 13 new rivets Set new small tubes 'Howell and Co' Set new large tubes steel with copper ends
11/4/46-18/2/47**C**		Exmouth Jct Extension of mileage 5,000 63 new small tubes
2/1/48-7/2/48**A**	101,392	130 copper and 89 monel metal stays renewed 169 monel metal stays replaced by copper 237 nuts renewed 228 roof stays renewed Copper Tubeplate new Firehole 13 new rivets Set new small tubes 'Tubes Ltd' Set new large tubes
16/11/49-16/12/49**A**	59,430	3 copper stays renewed 60 copper riveted over 158 nuts renewed Internal Tubeplate flanges caulked Set new small tubes 'Howells' Firehole 15 rivets caulked Large tubes repaired
29/9/50-1/12/50**HI**	24,305	No Boiler work
29/11/51-19/1/52		Brighton
2/4/53-24/4/53**GO**		13 copper and 132 steel stays renewed 75 copper riveted over 124 nuts renewed "15 studs fitted in laps Firehole laps welded" 2 fusible plugs Barrel scaled 173 new small tubes Firehole 15 rivets caulked
30/3/55-22/4/55**HI**	68,597	
22/3/56-7/4/56**LC**	99,195	
10/5/57-28/6/57**LI-HI**	137,310	Full frame conversion 2 new 9mm injectors fitted rhs to Drg.A.10317
25/3/59-18/4/59**GO**	195,599	New type CI firebars 240 copper and 703 monel metal stays renewed 705 nuts renewed 296 holes bushed Internal Tubeplate new Smokebox Tubeplate levelled 2 fusible plugs Barrel scaled 173 new small tubes 'Stewart and Lloyds' electrically welded Set new large tubes
23/3/61-22/4/61**LI-HI**	61,522	AWS complete 68 nuts renewed "Firehole flanges and stays caulked" 2 fusible plugs 32 new small tubes 'Stewart and Lloyds' electrically welded 141 rebeaded 3 new large tubes 18 second hand expanded and referruled Firehole 15 rivets caulked
5/5/62-7/5/62**NC**		Exmouth Jct

Tenders
No.3027	2/2/29
No.3019	7/2/48
No.3046	17/8/63

Boilers
No.863	24/4/26
No.864	2/2/29
No.940	23/4/31
No.908	2/12/33
No.938	11/2/36
No.965	29/6/38
No.914	27/8/41
No.1024	22/4/44
No.1068	7/2/48
No.1040	16/12/49
No.974	24/4/53
No.847	18/4/59

Allocations
10/8/24	Exmouth Jct
2/11/38	Barnstaple
30/1/39	Exmouth Jct

Withdrawn 2/64 Cut up at Eastleigh Works w/e 21/3/64

31838 at Exmouth Junction MPD, 20 August 1953. No hint of washout plugs on boiler top. It was stationed here throughout BR days, so the missing shed plate is a mystery; it certainly carried one later. R.J. Buckley, Initial Photographics.

31839

To traffic as A839 on 29/7/24
Renumbered 1839 14/3/33; 31839 17/4/48

Works
Ex Woolwich 27/6/24

27/6/24-29/7/24**B**		
12/3/25-11/4/25**C**		Eastleigh
30/3/26-15/7/26**A**	51,485	163 copper and all steel stays renewed 175 copper riveted over 19 roof nuts renewed Copper Tubeplate "7 studs in flanges" Foundation Ring 5 rivets renewed Set new small tubes 'Howell and co' "Beaded small tubes 1½ " diameter firebox end"
25/5/27-17/6/27		Exmouth Jct
26/8/27-12/11/27**B**	34,342	Extension of mileage 10,000 6 nuts renewed
31/1/29-4/4/29**A**	72,311	374 copper stays renewed 200 copper riveted over Copper Tubeplate 14 studs fitted Firehole rivets hammered Foundation Ring 14 new rivets Set new small tubes 'Howell and Co' "Welded steel large tubes"
21/2/31-1/4/31**A**	76,873	
4/2/33-14/3/33**A**	67,512	
30/11/34-16/1/35**A**	74,603	
8/1/37-12/2/37**A**	82,478	
24/5/39-20/6/39**A**	79,529	Class plate fitted 24 copper and 24 steel stays renewed 125 copper riveted over 233 nuts renewed Copper Tubeplate 16 studs fitted Firehole 9 new rivets Set new small tubes 'Chesterfield Tube Co' Set new large tubes steel with copper ends
7/3/40-21/5/40**C**	33,185	Exmouth Jct
18/11/41-23/12/41**A**	77,613	
7/10/43-12/11/43**C**		Norwood Jct
28/6/45-27/7/45**A**	96,753	
9/3/48-17/4/48**A**	80,124	
2/7/50-1/8/50**HI**	67,966	173 new small tubes 'Talbot and Stead' 4 new large tubes 17 rebeaded
2/10/52-24/10/52**GO**	139,691	793 copper stays renewed 228 roof stays and 228 roof nuts renewed 17 holes bushed Internal Tubeplate new Barrel scaled Set new small tubes 'Howells' set new large tubes
24/8/54-9/9/54**HI**	67,297	3 copper stays renewed 350 copper riveted over 32 new small tubes 'Stewart and Lloyds' 141 rebeaded 3 new large tubes 18 second hand expanded and referruled
12/4/56-3/5/56**LI**	121,391	1 copper stays renewed 355 riveted over Internal Firehole Plate lap caulked 32 new small tubes 141 rebeaded 3 new large tubes 18 second hand expanded and referruled Firehole 15 rivets caulked
21/5/57-8/6/57**GO**	157,554	
14/7/59-8/8/59**LI**	75,732	ATC Manganese liners New type CI firebars
29/8/61-23/9/61**GO**	138,949	'Overhead live wire notices' Spark arrester Water treatment 984 copper stays renewed "52 studs fitted Firehole flanges and half side laps welded" 2 fusible plugs Barrel scaled 173 new small tubes Set new large tubes firehole 15 rivets caulked

Tenders
No.3039	4/4/29
No.3008	1/48 at Exmouth Jct

Boilers
No.841	15/7/26
No.855	4/4/29
No.900	1/4/31
No.907	14/3/33
No.958	16/1/35
No.875	12/2/37
No.1081	20/6/39
No.957	23/12/41
No.963	27/7/45
No.889	17/4/48
No.902	24/10/52
No.1167	8/6/57
No.905	23/9/61

Allocations
10/8/24	Barnstaple
15/6/35	Exmouth Jct
24/4/43	Bricklayers Arms
25/3/44	Exmouth Jct

Withdrawn 28/12/63 Cut up at Eastleigh Works w/e 18/4/64

31839 at Halwill Junction with the 12.58pm from Padstow train in June 1960; the fireman takes the opportunity to get coal forward for the run to Okehampton. The train is made up of a Bulleid corridor with two Maunsell coaches including a brake third.

Time for a brief greeting at Launceston as Ns cross on 11 June 1963; 31839 (only months away from withdrawal) with a down passenger train, its fellow with up coal empties, quite possibly from Wadebridge MPD. WR line and little engine shed in left background; the SR equivalent is out of sight behind the awning. L. Rowe, ColourRail

31840

To traffic as A840 on 6/8/24
Renumbered 1840 29/4/33; 31840 7/9/48

Works
Ex Woolwich 27/6/24

27/6/24-6/8/24**B**		
13/5/25-14/8/25**B**		Eastleigh
5/4/27-14/7/27**A**	81,442	
12/4/29-30/5/29**A**	69,953	
9/5/31-17/6/31**A**	73,438	
6/8/32-12/9/32**C**	43,801	
27/3/33-29/4/33**A**	62,311	
17/6/35-30/7/35**A**	77,290	
25/2/37-9/4/37**A**	78,794	
3/5/39-3/6/39**A**	92,796	Class plate fitted
19/10/40-11/12/40**C**		Exmouth Jct Extension of mileage 5,000
2/10/41-12/11/41**A**		528 copper stays renewed 250 copper riveted over Copper Tubeplate 38 studs fitted Firehole rivets hammered Set new small tubes 'Howell and Co' Large tubes repaired steel with copper ends
4/8/42-22/8/42**C**		Exmouth Jct 154 small tubes "[new and secondhand]"
2/6/43-3/7/43**C**	59,738	400 copper styas riveted over Copper Tubeplate 45 studs fitted
8/10/43-24/11/43**A**	65,886	
17/6/45-18/6/45**C**		Exmouth Jct
8/3/46-12/4/46**A**	86,911	
27/7/48-7/9/48**A**	74,174	1,012 [all] copper stays renewed 102 holes bushed New Firebox Steel Tubeplate new Set new small tubes 'Tubes Ltd' Set new large tubes steel with copper ends
15/9/50-12/10/50**HI**		Copper stays riveted over "in fire area" 32 new small tubes 'Talbot and Stead' 21 large tubes expanded and rebeaded
9/1/53-30/1/53**GO**		525 copper and 705 steel stays renewed 228 roof stays and 228 roof nuts renewed 214 holes bushed New Firebox Barrel scaled 173 new small tubes 'Tubes Ltd' Set new large tubes steel with copper ends
31/12/54-20/1/55**LI-HI**	68,770	90 nuts renewed 2 fusible plugs 32 new small tubes 'Howells' 141 rebeaded 3 new large tubes 18 second hand expanded and referruled
18/1/57-16/2/57**GO**		137,425 Front end conversion 9mm injectors fitted to Drg. A.10373 716 copper stays renewed 74 nuts renewed "18 lap rivets caulked" 2 fusible plugs Smokebox Tubeplate new Barrel scaled 173 new small tubes 'Stewart and Lloyds' electrically welded Foundation Ring 23 rivets caulked
15/4/59-9/5/59**LI**	72,793	New CI firebars 422 copper stays riveted over 27 nuts renewed "Firehole laps and flanges caulked 20 flange rivets and 21 corner rivets caulked 2 fusible plugs 1 mud door hole welded 32 new small tubes 'Tube Products' electrically welded 141 rebeaded 3 new large tubes 18 second hand expanded and referruled Firehole 15 rivets caulked
2/2/61-8/3/61**GO**	129,136	AWS Water treatment 'Overhead live wire notices'
17/2/62-20/2/62**NC**		Exmouth Jct
3/1/64-8/2/64**LI**	82,438	Eastleigh WR loco

Tenders

No.3029	14/7/27
No.3041	30/5/29

Boilers

No.865	14/7/27
No.888	30/5/29
No.828	17/6/31
No.903	29/4/33
No.901	30/7/35
No.958	9/4/37
No.906	3/6/39
No.845	12/11/41
No.975	24/11/43
No.906	12/4/46
No.935	7/9/48
No.1076	20/1/53
No.1075	16/2/57
No.1000	8/3/61

Allocations

10/8/24	Exmouth Jct
28/12/35	Barnstaple
14/8/36	Exmouth Jct
12/8/39	Barnstaple
24/4/43	Bricklayers Arms
25/3/44	Exmouth Jct
7/6/52	Barnstaple
7/10/52	Exmouth Jct

Withdrawn 7/9/64. Sold to Birds, Morriston 14/10/64

31840 rumbles into Okehampton with a down train past busy sidings and, beyond, the one road engine shed that every Exmouth Junction mogul made use of on a regular basis.

31840 at Boscarne Junction, Wadebrige pannier tank lurking in the background (see 31835 at the same place, earlier, for instance) in 1963; screw link hook now on other side of buffer beam... 31840 was another 'Devon' engine, and was only ever allocated to Exmouth Junction or Barnstaple Junction. transporttreasury

31841

To traffic as A841 on 8/8/24
Renumbered 1841 23/12/31; 31841 20/10/50

Works
Ex Woolwich 11/7/24

11/7/24-8/8/24**B**		
29/9/25-6/2/26**A**	42,765	Eastleigh
4/10/27-16/12/27**A**	66,902	
18/10/29-29/11/29**A**	67,310	
5/12/29-7/12/29**D**		
21/11/31-23/12/31**A**	66,285	
23/2/34-29/3/34**A**	87,464	
11/2/36-26/3/36**A**	75,372	406 copper stays renewed 200 copper riveted over Copper Tubeplate 40 studs fitted Firehole rivets "13renewed others hammered" Set new small tubes 'Howell and Co' Large tubes repaired steel with copper ends
20/1/38-7/3/38**A**	74,271	Class plate fitted 1,034 copper stays renewed 200 copper riveted over [All steel stays replaced by copper] 226 roof stays renewed 1 hole bushed Copper tubeplate new Firehole rivets renewed Set new small tubes 'Howell and Co; Set new large tubes steel with copper ends
3/1/40-30/1/40**A**	79,827	335 copper stays renewed and 500 copper riveted over Copper Tubeplate 93 studs fitted Firehole 13 new rivets Set new small tubes 'Howell and Co' Large tubes repaired steel with copper ends
16/12/41-21/1/42**A**	93,621	61 copper stays renewed 100 copper riveted over 341 nuts renewed Copper Tubeplate 4 studs fitted Firehole rivets hammered Set new small tubes 'Howell and Co' Set new large tubes steel with copper ends
2/9/43**C**		Exmouth Jct
4/11/43-22/11/43**C**		Exmouth Jct Extension of mileage 5,000 Set second hand small tubes Large tubes expanded and referruled
7/6/44-4/8/44**A**	94,979	207 copper and 22 steel stays renewed 100 copper riveted over 266 nuts renwed Copper Tubeplate 75 studs fitted Copper Wrapping Plate "2 patches top seam" Firehole 11 new rivets Set new small tubes 'Talbot and Stead' Set new large tubes steel with copper ends
5/1/46-6/2/46**C**	65,928	Extension of mileage 10,000 150 copper stays riveted over 125 nuts renewed Firehole 13 new rivets
17/7/47-23/8/47**A**	106,774	891 copper stays renewed 50 copper riveted over 72 holes bushed Copper Tubeplate new Firehole rivets renewed Set new small tubes 'Tubes Ltd' Set new large tubes steel with copper ends
19/2/50-14/3/50		Exmouth Jct
21/9/50-20/10/50**GO**	92,971	
3/3/53-20/3/53**LI**	84,138	
15/4/54-1/5/54**LC-HC**	121,472	
15/4/55-13/5/55**GO**	153,807	525 copper and 705 steel stays renewed 705 nuts renewed 228 roof stays and 444 roof nuts renewed 468 holes bushed New Firebox 2 fusible plugs Smokebox Tube new Barrel scaled 173 new small tubes 'Universal' Set new large tubes
21/8/57-24/10/57**LI**	79,981	Brighton 21/9/57 Cause of delay-Works holiday and conditions existing at Brighton 4 no.63 piston rings fitted 2 coppe stays renewed 48 riveted over 9 nuts renewed 2 fusible plugs 48 new small tubes 'Stewart and Lloyds' 125 rebeaded Set new large tubes
2/10/59-7/11/59**GO**	144,559	New type CI (cast iron) firebars ATC 323 copper stays renewed 240 copper riveted over "10 lap studs fitted flanges and seams caulked 26 flange and 20 corner rivets caulked 2 fusible plugs 3 mud door holes welded Barrel scaled 173 new small tubes 'Tube Products' electrically welded Set new large tubes
3/11/61-9/12/61**LI**	60,721	'Overhead live wire notices' Spark arrester 361 copper stays riveted over "10 studs fitted door lap 4 flanges caulked 36 flanges, 20 corner rivets caulked" 2 brick arch studs renewed 2 fusible plugs 32 new small tubes 'Tube Products' electrically welded 141 rebeaded 3 new large tubes 18 second hand expanded and referruled Firehole 15 rivets caulked

Tenders

No.3030	16/12/27
No.3043	29/3/34
No.3002	7/3/38
No.3039	14/3/50

Boilers

No.866	16/12/27
No.908	29/11/29
No.830	23/12/31
No.957	29/3/34
No.935	26/3/36
No.987	7/3/38
No.829	30/1/40
No.985	21/1/42
No.989	23/8/47
No.872	20/10/50
No.1013	13/5/55
No.862	7/11/59

Allocations

10/8/24	Barnstaple
12/8/39	Exmouth Jct
7/6/52	Barnstaple
7/10/52	Exmouth Jct

Withdrawn 3/64

Left. 31841 with a London-bound train from Padstow at Halwill Junction in 1960. The train in the background is from Bude and is being backed on for the journey up to London. Milk churns, a trolley and a general air of abandonment make it a quintessential country junction scene.

Below. 31841 at Wadebridge shed in May 1961; the coal on the left is continuously processed into the pile of clinker on the right.

31842

To traffic as A842 on 16/8/24
Renumbered 1842 1/10/31; 31842 25/1/49

Works
Ex woolwich 11/7/24

11/7/24-16/8/24**B**		
5/10/25-16/1/26**A**	41,127	Eastleigh
1/10/27-17/12/27**A**	49,609	
16/10/29-30/11/29**A**	64,538	
1/9/31-1/10/31**A**	74,776	
21/7/33-19/8/33**D**	59,265	
28/2/34-10/4/34**A**	77,612	
21/9/35**D**		Exmouth Jct 1 stay renewed
21/12/35**D**		Exmouth Jct 2 stays renewed
20/3/36-4/5/36**A**	73,756	
20/9/37-22/10/37**C**	52,047	Extension of mileage 10,000
31/12/38-3/2/39**A**	87,781	Class plate fitted
17/1/40-23/1/40**D**	30,482	
20/9/40-4/1/41**C**	47,431	Eastleigh
18/6/41-17/7/41**B**	63,714	Extension of mileage 10,000
27/11/41-26/12/41**C**	73,808	
13/10/42-16/11/42**A**	101,500	302 copper stays renewed 275 copper riveted over Copper Tubeplate 39 studs fitted Firehole rivets hammered Set new small tubes "Welded steel" Large tubes repaired steel with copper ends
11/10/43-21/10/43**C**		Exmouth Jct Copper stays riveted over "in fire area"
17/3/44-1/4/44**C**		Exmouth Jct Extension of mileage 10,000
26/7/44-9/9/44**A**	90,577	235 copper and 344 monel metal stays renewed 120 copper riveted over 74 nuts renewed 228 roof stays renewed 596 holes bushed 2 fusible plugs Barrel cleaned Firehole rivets renewed Set new small tubes 'Howell and Co' Set new large tubes steel with copper ends [Boiler repaired at Brighton]
6/6/45-8/7/45**C**		Exmouth Jct
2/4/47-2/5/47**A**	83,614	
18/5/48-29/5/48**C**	35,717	Exmouth Jct
5/1/49-25/1/49**B**	51,965	
11/5/50-9/6/50**GO**	78,226	
19/6/52-17/7/52**LC**		Brighton
14/4/53-22/5/53**HI**		Brighton
3/9/54-25/9/54**LC**	106,702	
24/10/55-11/11/55**GO**	129,945	New type 9mm injectors rhs
21/10/57-6/12/57**LI-HI**	64,394	Full frame conversion New type 9mm injectors fitted
16/12/59-16/1/60**GO**	129,304	New type CI firebars
16/2/60-1/3/60**return**	732	
28/2/62-31/3/62**LI**	67,363	AWS complete Spark arrester Water treatment 'overhead live wire notices'

Tenders

No.3031	17/12/27
No.3027	2/5/47
No.1950	11/11/55

Boilers

No.867	17/12/27
No.844	30/11/29
No.896	1/10/31
No.974	10/4/34
No.830	4/5/36
No.908	3/2/39
No.831	16/11/42
No.1021	9/9/44
No.895	2/5/47
No.1072	9/6/50
No.1017	11/11/55
No.1062	16/1/60

Allocations

7/9/24	Exmouth Jct
6/10/34	Barnstaple
15/6/35	Exmouth Jct
14/8/36	Barnstaple
12/8/39	Exmouth Jct
12/2/49	Barnstaple
27/6/51	Exmouth Jct
30/7/52	Barnstaple
11/12/52	Exmouth Jct
4/6/54	Barnstaple
11/3/55	Exmouth Jct
4/6/55	Barnstaple
17/11/56	Exmouth Jct
20/7/64	Guildford

Withdrawn 5/9/65

31842 passes Meldon Quarry with a down freight, 5 October 1962; it had got new frames and then a BR Class 4 chimney. Left to right are: Meldon Quarry signal box, defunct granite hopper, the roof of the engine shed just above the coach, platelayer hut/mess. 31842 was at either Exmouth Junction or Barnstaple Junction, moving between them at frequent intervals, until finishing up its last year at Guildford. RailOnline

31842 partly on the turntable at Barnstaple Junction, 28 September 1956. H.C. Casserley.

31843

To traffic as A843 on 23/8/24
Renumbered 1843 24/2/33; 31843 15/1/49

Works
Ex Woolwich 11/7/24

11/7/24-23/8/24**B**		
13/8/25-29/1/26**A**	35,210	Eastleigh
26/9/27-7/12/27**A**	67,017	
9/7/29-17/8/29**A**	68,603	
30/1/31-7/3/31**A**	65,153	
13/1/33-24/2/33**A**	70,788	
15/2/35-27/3/35**A**	72,168	
30/3/37-7/5/37**A**	76,114	
10/7/39-15/8/39**A**	81,255	Class plate fitted
10/5/40-23/5/40**C**	24,511	
24/1/42-25/2/42**A**	72,971	1,029 copper stays renewed 150 copper riveted over 228 roof stays renewed 344 holes bushed Copper Tubeplate new Firehole rivets renewed Set new small tubes Large tubes repaired Steel with copper ends
3/1/44-27/1/44**C**		Norwood Jct 173 new small tubes
5/10/45-3/11/45**A**	97,862	959 copper stays renewed 50 copper riveted over 228 roof stays renewed 73 holes bushed Copper Tubeplate new Firehole rivets renewed Set new small tubes 'Howell and Co' Set new large tubes steel with copper ends
25/1/47-15/2/47**C**	40,354	400 copper stays riveted over 61 roof stays renewed Copper Tubeplate 4 studs fitted Throat Plate "Fracture RH side welded" Small tubes expanded and rebeaded Large tubes expanded and referruled
17/12/48-15/1/49**A**	86,829	228 roof stays renewed New Firebox Firehole rivets renewed Set new small tubes 'Talbot and Stead' Set new large tubes steel with copper ends
21/4/50-17/5/50**LC**	39,486	No Boiler work
12/2/52-14/3/52**HI**	95,106	450 copper stays riveted over 173 new small tubes 'Howells' Large tubes repaired steel with copper ends
5/2/54-27/2/54**GO**	161,515	
9/3/54-13/3/54**defect**		
11/5/56-1/6/56**LI-HI**	50,137	
26/6/58-2/8/58**GO**	114,201	Front end conversion
2/6/60-2/7/60**LI-HI**	55,296	AWS part fitted Water treatment New type CI (cast iron) firebars 'Overhead live wire notices'
12/5/62-14/5/62**NC**		Exmouth Jct
12/11/62-15/12/62**LI**	126,920	Eastleigh

Tenders

No.3032	7/12/27
No.692	15/12/62

Boilers

			Allocations	
No.868	7/12/27			
No.865	17/8/29		7/9/24	Exmouth Jct
No.821	7/3/31		24/4/43	Bricklayers Arms
No.909	24/2/33		26/2/44	Exmouth Jct
No.905	27/3/35		8/2/46	New Cross Gate
No.857	7/5/37		20/4/46	Brighton
No.830	15/8/39		10/8/47	Redhill
No.990	25/2/42		31/7/48	Ashford
No.987	3/11/45		30/6/49	Redhill
No.936	15/1/49		11/12/52	Barnstaple
No.957	27/2/54		17/11/56	Exmouth Jct
No.913	2/8/58			

Withdrawn 7/9/64. Sold to Birds, Morriston 14/10/64

31843 with a holiday extra train in Cornwall in the 1960s, climbing away from Tresmeer and crossing the high embankment at Treneglos on the way to Otterham, Wadebridge and Padstow. The embankment was substituted for a viaduct proposed here in 1893. The first two Bulleid coaches are a 2-Set of Brake Composite 6707 and Semi-Open Brake Third 4378. The third coach is a Bulleid 'loose' Brake Composite; bringing up the rear is what looks like a Maunsell 2-Set P.

The last-but-one Saturday of through expresses from Waterloo, 29th August 1964, and the 6.50pm Ilfracombe to Taunton storms out of Slade tunnel behind 43XX 2-6-0 5336, piloted by 31843. S.C. Nash.

31844

To traffic as A844 on 5/9/24
Renumbered 1844 31/8/32; 31844 no date

Works
Ex Woolwich 25/7/24

Date	Mileage	Notes
25/7/24-5/9/24**B**		
23/6/25-5/9/25**B**		Eastleigh
1/2/27-10/5/27**A**	44,970	
22/4/29-1/6/29**A**	77,774	
4/5/31-13/6/31**A**	64,956	
21/7/32-31/8/32**A**	44,268	
3/9/34-8/10/34**A**	90,572	
17/9/36-28/10/36**A**	84,970	Set new small tubes Set new large tubes steel with copper ends
27/4/39-31/5/39**A**	84,943	Class plate fitted 246 copper and 801 monel metal stays renewed 175 copper riveted over 225 roof stays renewed 391 holes bushed Copper Tubeplate new Firehole rivets renewed Set new small tubes 'Howell and Co' Large tubes repaired steel with copper ends [5 roller expanders]
18/5/40-5/6/40**C**		Exmouth Jct
1/11/41-3/12/41**A**	71,319	
22/6/43-16/7/43**C**	43,186	Extension of mileage 15,000
21/3/44-31/3/44**C**		Exmouth Jct
12/4/45-15/5/45**A**	89,223	
24/10/46-20/11/46**B**		New Cross Gate
5/11/47-17/12/47**C**		New Cross Gate
1/2/49-21/2/49**HI**	76,474	50 copper stays riveted over 125 nuts renewed 12 new small tubes 161 expanded and rebeaded
6/5/50-3/3/50**A**	80,236	124 copper and 121 steel stays renewed 441 nuts renewed Internal Tubeplate "56 rivets replaced by studs" Set new small tubes 'Talbot and Stead' Firehole 13 new rivets Large tubes repaired steel with copper ends
25/11/52-12/12/52**HI**	87,907	1 copper stay renewed 43 steel stays replaced by copper 241 nuts renewed Internal Tubeplate laps welded and 6 studs fitted 173 new small tubes 'Tubes Ltd' 3 new large tubes 18 second hand expanded and referruled Firehole 15 new rivets
12/5/53-10/6/53**return**	94,716	24 roof stays renewed 2 fusible plugs
5/5/55-21/5/55**GO**	157,291	687 copper stays renewed 16 roof stays renewed 325 holes bushed Internal Tubeplate new 2 fusible plugs Barrel pitting welded scaled 173 new small tubes 'Universal' Set new large tubes new steel [welded]
2/1/57-19/1/57**LI**	56,121	349 copper stays riveted over 2 fusible plugs 32 new small tubes 'Stewart and Lloyds' electrically welded 141 rebeaded 3 new large tubes 18 second hand expanded and referruled
9/2/59-13/3/59**LI**	123,682	New CI (cast iron) firebox 316 copper stays riveted over "Flanges and firehole laps caulked 22 flange rivets caulked" 2 fusible plugs 32 new small tubes 'Stewart and Lloyds' electrically welded 141 rebeaded Set new large tubes Firehole 15 rivets caulked
26/10/60-18/11/60**LC-HC**	172,284	'Overhead live wire notices'
5/5/61-3/6/61**GO**	189,205	Water treatment 240 copper stays renewed 766 copper riveted over "52 lap studs fitted 2 brick arch studs renewed tubeplate and firehole plate flanges and firehole laps welded" 2 fusible plugs 2 mud door holes welded Barrel scaled Firehole 15 new rivets Foundation Ring 90 new rivets Large tubes repaired
22/5/62-1/6/62**NC-LC**	26,692	Eastleigh AWS

Tenders

No.3033	10/5/27
No.3013	31/5/39

Boilers

No.869	10/5/27
No.856	1/6/29
No.863	13/6/31
No.911	31/8/32
No.884	8/10/34
No.1081	28/10/36
No.985	31/5/39
No.963	3/12/41
No.1160	15/5/45
No.1158	3/3/50
No.905	21/5/55
No.891	3/6/61

Allocations

7/9/24	Exmouth Jct
1/12/34	Nine Elms
15/6/35	Barnstaple
12/8/39	Exmouth Jct
24/4/43	Bricklayers Arms
25/3/44	Exmouth Jct
21/4/45	Norwood Jct
31/7/48	Ashford
30/6/49	Redhill
5/2/51	Exmouth Jct
30/7/52	Fratton
20/7/53	Barnstaple
1/10/53	Exmouth Jct

Withdrawn 28/12/63 Cut up at Eastleigh Works w/e 18/4/64

With its fine BR lined black looking good enough for Pacific company, 31844 stands outside its home shed Exmouth Junction early in the 1950s; small first emblem. It looks to have better coal even than the accompanying Bulleids.

31844 with a down train for the Plymouth line at Exeter St David's, 21 May 1956, with small first emblem. It had been one of the four Ns used on the Royal train a few weeks before and the evidence is still there, in the burnishing of the buffers. RailOnline

31845

To traffic as A845 on 16/9/24
Renumbered 1845 29/6/32; 31845 2/6/49

Works
Ex Woolwich 25/7/24

Date	Mileage	Notes
25/7/24-16/9/24**B**		
8/1/26-8/4/26**A**	32,868	
11/7/29-28/8/29**A**	71,405	
25/5/32-29/6/32**A**	73,025	
13/6/33-21/6/33**C**		Exmouth Jct
10/1/34-10/2/34**A**	75,963	867 copper stays renewed 125 copper riveted over 228 roof stays renewed 171 holes bushed Copper Tubeplate new Casing Back Plate "4 angle patches 2 inside 2 outside" firehole rivets renewed Set new small tubes 'Chesterfield Tube co' Large tubes repaired new steel with copper ends
22/5/36-16/7/36**A**	79,651	
12/1/39-17/2/39**A**	80,809	Class plate fitted
1/4/41-29/4/41**A**	80,220	
28/2/42-21/3/42**C**		Exmouth Jct
11/3/43-5/4/43**C**		Exmouth Jct Extension of mileage 10,000
21/11/43-22/12/43**A**	87,777	23 copper and 126 monel metal stays renewed 100 copper riveted over 186 nuts renewed Copper Tubeplate 51 studs fitted 2 fusible plugs Firehole rivets hammered Set new small tubes 'Howell and Co' Large tubes repaired steel with copper ends
27/5/45-4/6/45**C**		Exmouth Jct
21/10/45-30/11/45**C**		Exmouth Jct 24 copper and 44 steel stays renewed set new small tubes Large tubes expanded and referruled
8/5/46-31/5/46**A**	87,673	
5/6/48-2/7/48**B**		Exmouth Jct
10/5/49-2/6/49**HI**	89,938	
31/5/50-22/6/50		Exmouth Jct
27/8/51-28/9/51**GO**	155,486	
13/10/53-5/11/53**HI**		
24/11/55-16/12/55**GO**	141,947	
21/3/58-12/4/58**LI**	76,417	
10/2/60-5/3/60**GO**	136,126	New type CI (cast iron) firebars Full frame conversion Water treatment Manganese liners
4/4/62-19/5/62**LI**	61,743	AWS complete Spark arrester

Tenders

No.3034	28/8/29
No.1914	29/6/32
No.3042	17/2/39

Boilers

No.870	8/4/26
No.911	28/8/29
No.829	10/2/34
No.828	16/7/36
No.886	17/2/39
No.849	29/4/41
No.1025	22/12/43
No.821	31/5/46
No.894	28/9/51
No.1039	16/12/55
No.1017	19/5/62

Allocations

7/9/24	Salisbury
12/8/39	Exmouth Jct
20/7/53	Barnstaple
1/10/53	Exmouth Jct

Withdrawn 7/9/64. Sold to Birds, Morriston 14/10/64

31845 arrives at Ashwater with the up afternoon goods from Wadebridge; the period is the early 1960s, after the loco got new frames in 1960. The pretty signal box on the down platform is worth a mention – it was in the fully glazed style adopted by the LSWR in the 1880s. R.K. Blencowe.

If ever an N was required to feature in a Southern holiday poster – this would be it! Scouts in unfeasibly large berets, seemingly made for boys ten years older, wait to leave Ilfracombe about 1959, before 31845 received new frames, doubtless after a week camping in the area.

31846

To traffic as A846 on 27/1/25
Renumbered 1846 25/11/31; 31846 8/5/48

Works
Ex Woolwich 2/1/25

2/1/25-27/1/25**B**		
6/8/25-8/8/25**D**		
16/4/26-21/4/26**C**		Feltham Extension of mileage 5,000
14/7/27-6/10/27**A**	57,078	
25/5/29-6/7/29**A**	60,217	
23/10/31-21/11/31**A**	75,031	
4/4/34-17/5/34**A**	90,130	
28/2/36-16/4/36**A**	65,331	
9/11/38-14/12/38**A**	87,950	
7/2/39-13/2/39**D**	2,502	
6/1/40-20/2/40**D**	32,936	
14/3/41-11/4/41**A**	73,351	
12/12/41-23/12/41**D**	21,846	Eastleigh
10/8/42-17/10/42**C**	48,571	Eastleigh Test 2269 Extension of mileage 5,000
13/3/43-27/3/43**C**		Exmouth Jct Extension of mileage 5,000
6/10/43-11/10/43**C**		Exmouth Jct
19/4/44-26/5/44**A**	110,539	New LH cylinder 736 copper stays renewed 50 copper riveted over 232 holes bushed Copper Tubeplate new 2 fusible plugs Firehole rivets renewed Set new small tubes 'Howell and Co' Set new large tubes steel with copper ends
8/9/44-19/10/44**D**	8,937	
26/3/47-24/4/47**C**	65,559	Extension of mileage 20,000
10/3/48-8/5/48**C**	86,120	3 copper stays renewed 225 roof stays renewed Set new small tubes 'Howell and Co' Large tubes repaired steel with copper ends
6/6/50-7/7/50**GO**	134,492	49 copper stays renewed "15 on tubeplate" 336 nuts renewed 116 holes bushed Internal Tubeplate new Internal Firehole Plate "Replace rivets with 36 studs" Barrel scaled Set new small tubes 'Tubes Ltd' Set new large tubes steel with copper ends
27/10/52-14/11/52**HI**	76,969	29 steel stays renewed 25 copper riveted over 241 nuts renewed Internal Tubeplate "9 studs fitted and 20 caulked in laps" 32 new small tubes 'Tubes Ltd' 141 rebeaded 21 second hand large tubes expanded and referruled Firehole 7 new rivets
1/12/54-24/12/54**GO**	144,723	
11/12/56-4/1/57**LI-HI**	67,412	
13/3/59-22/5/59**GO**	138,867	Full frame conversion Manganese liners New type CI (cast iron) firebars
13/9/60-7/10/60**LI-HI**	38,364	AWS Water treatment
21/2/62-23/2/62**NC**		Exmouth Jct
18/9/63-26/10/63**LI**	128,710	Eastleigh

Tenders

No.3035	6/10/27
No.3007	14/12/38

Boilers

No.885	6/10/27
No.891	6/7/29
No.913	21/11/31
No.851	17/5/34
No.914	14/12/38
No.860	11/4/41
No.876	26/5/44
No.1018	7/7/50
No.971	24/12/54
No.894	22/5/59

Allocations

22/2/25	Exmouth Jct
24/4/43	Bricklayers Arms
21/4/45	Salisbury
13/11/50	Exmouth Jct

31846 at home, at Exmouth Junction MPD, in 1956. RailOnline

Withdrawn 7/9/64. Sold to G. Cohen, Morriston, 14/10/64

In the last summer of steam, on the morning of Saturday 22 August 1964, the 8.30am Atlantic Coast Express from Padstow arrives behind 31846. Waterloo, or Okehampton passengers, had not been required to change at Halwill for the most part, and holiday trains or locals would consist of North Cornwall and Bude portions divided or combined here. A portion from Bude waits in fact to be attached by a 2-6-4T, 80039. Both trains are Bulleid 3-set Ls; set 781 (4323, 5762, 4324) from Bude comprises the earlier (1947) coaches while set 838 (3987, 5856, 3988) from Padstow is of the later (1950) series. P.W. Gray.

31846 at Exeter Central about to head west on what is probably the 5.58pm to Okehampton, on 26 August 1959. A Z 0-8-0T and M7 0-4-4T 30044 have been attached for the descent to St David's to perform banking duties. It was common practice to attach returning bankers to down trains at Central as this saved a path. The tender is full of rubbish masquerading as coal. A carriage and wagon examiner relaxes against the frame provided for corridor ends, for attachment to coaches as required. Ken Fairey, ColourRail

31847

To traffic as A847 on 4/2/25
Renumbered 1847 7/8/31; 31847 10/7/48

Works
Ex Woolwich 2/1/25

2/1/25-4/2/25**B**		
22/5/26-30/6/26		Feltham Extension of mileage 10,000
18/3/27-22/6/27**A**	52,293	
20/7/29-29/8/29**A**	74,670	
27/6/31-7/8/31**A**	74,074	343 copper stays renewed 175 copper riveted over Firehole rivets hammered Foundation Ring 11 new rivets Set new small tubes 'Howell and Co' Large tubes repaired steel with copper ends "Plugs 12 threads"
20/9/33-19/10/33**A**	85,020	
25/10/35-10/12/35**A**	75,376	267 copper and 699 steel stays renewed 100 copper riveted over 228 roof stays renewed 253 holes bushed Copper Tubeplate new Throat Plate two patches Firehole rivets renewed Set new small tubes 'Tubes Ltd' Large tubes repaired steel with copper ends
2/3/38-20/4/38**A**	75,550	Class plate fitted
6/2/40-6/3/40**A**	80,253	
25/3/41-3/5/41**D**	39,561	
4/3/43-27/4/43**A**	101,155	
17/11/44-13/12/44**C**		Exmouth Jct Extension of mileage 5,000
22/5/45-30/5/45**C**		Exmouth Jct
19/2/46-20/3/46**A**	86,034	
14/6/48-10/7/48**C**	75,531	Extension of mileage 10,000
12/7/48-30/7/48	75,607	Nine Elms
26/5/49-9/7/49**A**	103,945	
17/10/51-9/11/51**LI**	66,986	
2/1/53-23/1/53**HI**	102,514	
15/9/54-2/10/54**GO**	160,913	
5/8/55-16/8/55**LC**	24,371	
16/10/56-7/11/56**LI**	61,312	
9/1/59-7/2/59**LI-HI**	139,568	New type CI (cast iron) firebars Manganese steel liners
1/11/60-10/12/60**GO**	188,023	AWS 'Overhead live wire notices'-4 new plates fitted to complete set Water treatment 399 copper and 617 steel stays renewed 220 copper riveted over 617 nuts renewed 193 roof stays and 48 roof nuts renewed 515 holes bushed Internal Tubeplate new 2 fusible plugs Smokebox Tubeplate levelled Barrel scaled 173 new small tubes 'Stewart and Lloyds' electrically welded Set new large tubes
13/4/62-15/4/62**NC**		Exmouth Jct

Tenders

No.3036	29/8/29
No.3014	10/12/35
No.3061	9/7/49

Boilers

No.886	22/6/27
No.885	29/8/29
No.935	7/8/31
No.864	19/10/33
No.841	10/12/35
No.883	20/4/38
No.867	6/3/40
No.908	27/4/43
No.820	20/3/46
No.1073	9/7/49
No.1071	2/10/54
No.968	10/12/60

Allocations

22/2/25	Exmouth Jct
3/11/34	Barnstaple
15/6/35	Exmouth Jct
21/4/45	Salisbury
29/12/45	Exmouth Jct

Withdrawn 5/10/63 Cut up at Eastleigh Works w/e 16/11/63

31847 setting stock back in the sidings at Ilfracombe terminus, to be drawn out later as an up service (perhaps Monday morning) or perhaps bringing it out prior to shunting into the platform, just out of sight to the right, in July 1957. The stock is a Bulleid 5-set (two brake thirds, two corridor thirds and a corridor composite: seconds after June 1956). These 5-sets were regulars on the SW section but some were reduced to just three coaches during the winter period. The extent of the sidings indicate the importance of holiday services to this elegant resort. The station, as is clear, was perched on high ground above the town; down below was the very Atlantic Coast served by portions of the famous train. Frank Hornby, ColourRail

31847 with the 12.58pm Padstow-Waterloo train at Wadebridge on 27 May 1961. Replacing the obsolescent 0-4-2 'Jubilees', the Ns proved ideal for the lines west of Okehampton and dominated services, from heavy goods to the lengthy holiday trains, for twenty years. Even after light Pacifics became available in numbers, they were vital to the operation of the Withered Arm for the best part of another twenty years.

31848

To traffic as A848 on 11/2/25
Renumbered 1848 4/7/33; 31848 28/8/48

Works
Ex Woolwich 2/1/25

2/1/25-11/2/25**B**		
30/8/26-9/12/26**A**	55,648	
6/11/28-9/2/29**A**	63,377	
9/5/30-13/6/30**B**	57,625	Extension of mileage 15,000
2/4/31-9/5/31**A**	85,836	
1/6/33-4/7/33**A**	74,921	
26/3/35-2/5/35**C**	59,373	Extension of mileage 10,000
31/5/35-19/6/35**C**	59,990	
16/9/35**D**		Eastleigh
16/4/36-4/6/36**A**	88,186	
26/11/36-23/12/36**C**	16,430	New left hand cylinder
22/3/39-25/4/39**A**	88,608	New right hand cylinder
16/1/41-21/2/41**A**	77,959	829 copper stays renewed 100 copper riveted over 192 roof stays renewed 61 holes bushed Copper Tubeplate new Firehole rivets renewed Set new small tubes 'Tubes Ltd' Set new large tubes steel with copper ends
16/6/41-2/8/41**C**		Exmouth Jct "Stays in firebox renewed"
30/3/42-16/5/42**C**		Exmouth Jct
28/8/42-11/9/42**C**		Exmouth Jct 140 second hand tubes welded
6/11/42-24/11/42**C**	57,040	
30/9/43-9/10/43**C**		Exmouth Jct Extension of mileage 10,000 "7 bottom rows of small tubes renewed"
18/12/43-13/2/44**C**		Exmouth Jct 84 small tubes renewed
11/9/44-14/10/44**A**	110,743	1,012 [all] copper stays renewed 228 roof stays renewed New Firebox Firehole rivets renewed Set new small tubes 'Howell and Co' Large tubes repaired with copper ends
1/11/46-2/1/47**C**		Salisbury
12/7/48-28/8/48**A**	82,593	
20/12/50-19/1/51**LI**	62,915	
1/3/51-29/3/51**HI**	13,945	
19/5/52-4/7/52**LC**		Brighton
11/6/53-31/7/53**GO**		Brighton 702 copper stays renewed 191 copper riveted over 2 fusible plugs 173 new small tubes 'Howells' 21 second hand large tubes Firehole 15 new rivets
15/9/53-3/10/53**LC**		Brighton
26/8/54-11/9/54**HC**	32,671	No Boiler work
9/9/55-13/10/55**LI-GO**	62,692	Front end conversion 450 copper and 453 monel metal stays renewed 23 holes bushed Internal Tubeplate new 2 fusible plugs Barrel scaled 32 new small tubes 'Stewart and Lloyds'
31/1/58-21/2/58**LI**	63,830	212 copper stays riveted over 45 nuts renewed 2 fusible plugs 32 new small tubes 'Stewart and Lloyds' electrically welded 141 rebeaded 3 new large tubes 18 second hand expanded and referruled
15/6/60-16/7/60**GO**	132,266	New type CI (cast iron) fire bars AWS fitted "Overhead live wire notices' 1,012 [all] copper stays renewed 228 roof renewed 444 roof nuts renewed 42 holes bushed New Firebox 2 fusible plugs Barrel scaled 173 new small tubes 'Tube Products' electrically welded Set new large tubes
10/7/61-11/7/61**NC**	26,009	Spark arrester
26/9/61-14/10/61**LC**	29,887	
6/2/64**LI**		Eastleigh (presumably not carried out – engine withdrawn two weeks later!)

Tenders

No.3050	9/2/29
No.1887	11/9/54
No.3016	13/10/55

Boilers

No.887	9/12/26
No.851	9/2/29
No.864	9/5/31
No.912	4/7/33
No.906	4/6/36
No.892	25/4/39
No.999	21/2/41
No.937	14/10/44
No.865	28/8/48
No.969	31/7/53
No.1034	13/10/55
No.854	16/7/60

Allocations

22/2/25	Exmouth Jct
12/8/39	Barnstaple
24/4/43	Bricklayers Arms
21/4/45	Salisbury
18/1/49	Three Bridges
3/5/49	Redhill
11/4/51	Exmouth Jct
1/11/55	Ashford
9/11/61	Exmouth Jct

Withdrawn 15/2/64 Cut up at Eastleigh Works w/e 15/2/64

31848 at Ashford MPD on 19 May 1957. The Ns operated at both extremities of the Southern, from Kent to Cornwall and were not much to be found 'in the middle', the old Brighton lines having presumably enough of its own home-grown K moguls. 31848 was one N which ranged across the system, starting at Exmouth Junction and ending up there, by way of Bricklayers Arms, Redhill, Ashford and others. transporttreasury

31848 was the first of the Ns and the third Maunsell mogul to get new frames (full or part) and was turned out without smoke deflectors in October 1955. This took the 'look' of the engines back the 1920s and must have startled a few lineside observers. The difference was the presence of external steampipes; the idea was to see if smoke deflectors were still necessary. Presumably they were, for deflectors returned in February 1957. The new frames (or frame sections) were some five inches longer. This placed the buffer beam and footstep that much further forward which resulted in more of the pony truck wheel being exposed to view.

31849

To traffic as A849 on 28/2/25
Renumbered 1849 7/1/32; 31849 20/7/50

Works
Ex Woolwich 19/1/25

Date	Mileage	Notes
19/1/25-28/2/25**B**		
29/4/26-8/9/26**A**	18,826	
12/3/29-27/4/29**A**	13,429	833 steel stays in fire area renewed Set new small tubes 'Howell and Co'
2/1/31-31/1/31**A**	65,309	405 copper stays renewed 275 riveted over 5 roof nuts renewed Copper Tubeplate 23 studs fitted Firehole 14 new rivets Foundation Ring 3 new rivets 173 new small tubes 87 'Chesterfield Tube Co' 86 'Howell and Co' Large tubes expanded and referruled "Plugs 12 threads"
23/11/32-7/1/33**A**	78,220	
16/1/35-18/2/35**A**	75,600	
23/3/37-3/5/37**A**	80,740	
13/9/38-29/9/38**D**	46,331	Class plate fitted
27/2/39-8/3/39**D**	60,377	
16/6/39**D**		Eastleigh
29/6/39-26/7/39**A**	68,153	
3/10/41-5/11/41**A**		
27/2/42-16/3/42**D**	6,468	
27/4/43-1/6/43**C**		Exmouth Jct
23/11/43-1/12/43**C**		Exmouth Jct
16/2/44-11/3/44**C**	63,135	Extension of mileage 10,000
29/11/44-15/1/45**A**	87,832	102 copper stays renewed 25 riveted over 223 nuts renewed [148 monel metal stays replaced by copper] Copper Tubeplate 80 studs 2 fusible plugs Firehole 13 new rivets Set new small tubes 'Talbot and Stead'
6/6/45-15/6/45**D**	10,478	200 copper stays riveted over 24 steel stays caulked Firehole 17 new rivets "2 large ferrules renewed"
30/11/45-24/1/46**D**	25,305	200 copper stays riveted over 150 nuts renewed Copper Tubeplate studs and seams caulked
28/9/46-15/10/46		New Cross Gate
7/3/47-12/4/47**B**	49,169	
12/7/48-11/8/48**C**	80,016	Redhill
10/6/49-13/8/49**A**	99,668	164 copper and 664 steel stays renewed 114 holes bushed Copper Tubeplate new Set new small tubes 'Howell and Co' Set new large tubes steel with copper ends
28/6/50-20/7/50**HC**	31,968	No Boiler work
14/9/51-20/12/51**HI**		Brighton 9 copper and 12 steel stays renewed 12 nuts renewed 2 fusible plugs 139 new small tubes 'Howells' 34 expanded and rebeaded 21 new large tubes
6/11/53-3/12/53**GO**	138,535	525 copper and 705 steel stays renewed 705 nuts renewed 444 holes bushed New Firebox Smokebox Tubeplate new Barrel scaled Set new small tubes 'Howells' Large tubes repaired
18/11/55-2/12/55**LI-HI**	61,742	78 nuts renewed 2 fusible plugs 32 new small tubes 141 rebeaded 3 new large tubes 18 second hand expanded and referruled
5/10/57-24/10/57**LI-HI**	127,984	71 nuts renewed 2 fusible plugs 32 new small tubes 'Universal' 141 rebeaded 3 new large tubes 18 second hand expanded and referruled firehole 13 rivets caulked
4/10/59-7/11/59**GO**	189,719	New type CI (cast iron) firebars
24/8/61-28/8/61		Exmouth Jct
8/1/62-3/2/62**LI**	62,788	AWS part fitted 'Overhead live wire notices'

Tenders
No.3040 27/4/29
No.3060 13/8/49
No.3012 7/11/59

Allocations
22/3/25 Barnstaple
12/8/39 Exmouth Jct
24/4/42 Bricklayers Arms
21/4/45 Redhill
11/4/51 Exmouth Jct

Withdrawn 8/8/64. Sold to Birds, Morriston 4/9/64

Boilers
No.888 8/9/26
No.985 27/4/29
No.876 31/1/31
No.849 7/1/33
No.891 18/2/35
No.848 3/5/37
No.958 26/7/39
No.960 5/11/41
No.988 15/1/45
No.900 12/4/47
No.1012 13/8/49
No.994 3/12/53
No.844 7/11/59

31849 stands at Wadebridge shed on 15 September 1960. The introduction of light Pacifics after the War was made possible by the enlargement of turntables at Padstow and Okehampton but the working of the line remained very much dependent on the moguls, in a complex and clever pattern of diagrams and crew changing. Like many Ns 31849 moved from the West only to bolster war traffic, returning 'home' in 1951.

A work-stained 31849 on loaded clay wagons from Boscarne Junction to Bodmin General, where they were to be handed over to WR locos for onward transit to Fowey and Lostwithiel. The date is 5 May 1964 and the mogul bears the WR 83D code of Exmouth Junction – how it must have irked the Fitters at 'The Junction' to bolt on the badge of their rivals. It is a heavy load and the gradients severe, so another N, 31840, is on the rear. Both were withdrawn in September 1964 with the Western Region's 'wholesale dieselisation' (as it was described) of its LSW lines and the closure of Barnstaple Junction MPD. S.C. Nash.

31850

To traffic as A850 on 14/2/25
Renumbered 1850 25/7/31; 31850 4/12/48

Works
Ex Woolwich 19/1/25

19/1/25-14/2/25**B**		
2/9/26-22/12/26**A**	57,480	
5/8/27-14/9/27**B**		Extension of mileage 5,000
25/2/29-25/4/29**A**	64,559	13 copper and 8 steel stays renewed 250 copper riveted over 133 nuts renewed 24 roof nuts renewed Firehole 13 new rivets Set new small tubes 'Howell and Co' Large tubes expanded and rebeaded
2/8/29-19/10/29**C**	9,737	3 copper stays renewed Casing Back Plate patch L H corner
26/6/31-25/7/31**A**	68,789	309 copper stays renewed 700 copper riveted over Copper tubeplate 28 studs fitted
29/3/32-29/4/32**C**		Stewarts Lane 71 second hand small tubes
15/8/32-20/8/32		Exmouth Jct
16/10/33-3/2/34**A**	91,692	Eastleigh Marshall valve gear fitted 500 copper stays riveted over Copper Tubeplate flanges welded All small tubes repaired and replaced "All large taken out and replaced"
24/3/34-11/4/34**D**		Brighton Marshall valve gear removed
5/2/35-6/2/35**D**		Brighton
10/5/35-13/6/35**B**	6,079	Eastleigh
23/11/37-7/12/37**D**	38,119	3 copper stays renewed 450 copper riveted over Copper Tubeplate 11 studs fitted
9/3/38**D**		Eastleigh
9/6/38-17/6/38**D**	47,776	Class plate fitted Casing Back Plate crack welded
14/12/38-11/1/39**D**	58,076	4 copper stays renewed 250 copper riveted over Copper Tubeplate 10 studs fitted
4/10/39-1/11/39**A**	75,570	858 copper stays renewed and 150 copper riveted over 12 roof stays renewed 406 holes bushed Copper Tubeplate new Firehole rivets hammered Set new small tubes 'Howell and Co' Large tubes repaired steel with copper ends
16/1/42-17/2/42**A**	69,514	42 copper stays renewed 200 copper riveted over 264 nuts renewed Copper Tubeplate 49 studs fitted Set new small tubes 'Howell and Co' Large tubes repaired steel with copper ends
25/10/43-11/11/43**C**		Exmouth Jct "12 small tubes withdrawn and renewed for inspection."
20/3/44-1/5/44**C**		Exmouth Jct Extension of mileage 10,000 173 new small tubes
11/9/45-13/10/45**A**	113,415	259 copper and 705 steel stays renewed 50 copper riveted over Copper Tubeplate new Set new small tubes 'Howell and Co' Set new large tubes steel with copper ends
4/11/48-4/12/48**A**	75,051	
10/2/49-12/2/49**NC**	3,155	Internal Tubeplate flanges caulked Casing Back Plate R H side fracture welded
28/10/49-11/11/49**HC**	18,080	
11/3/50-14/3/50		Stewarts Lane
10/7/51-27/7/51**HI**	52,445	1 copper stay renewed 500 copper stays riveted over Internal Tubeplate 55 copper studs renewed 38 rivets caulked 173 new small tubes 'Talbot and Stead' 3 new large tubes
18/12/52-9/1/53**GO**	84,806	
4/12/53-6/1/54**LC**	22,318	Bricklayers Arms
5/10/54-6/11/54		Stewarts Lane
20/3/55-18/4/55**HI**	48,427	
3/5/56-11/5/56**HC**	73,886	791 copper stays renewed 392 holes bushed Internal Tubeplate new 2 fusible plugs Barrel scaled 173 new small tubes 'Stewart and Lloyds' electrically welded
14/5/57-1/6/57**LI**	98,825	411 copper stays riveted over Internal Tubeplate 35 lap rivets caulked 2 fusible plugs 173 new small tubes 'Tube Products' electrically welded 3 new large tubes 18 expanded and referruled
16/7/59-8/8/59**LI**	160,160	ATC New type CI firebars 381 copper stays riveted over Internal Tubeplate flanges and 26 rivets caulked 2 fusible plugs 54 new small tubes 'Tube Products' electrically welded 119 rebeaded
6/9/61-7/9/61**NC**		Bricklayers Arms
30/10/61-2/12/61**GO**	224,388	Water treatment

Tenders

No.3039	14/9/27
No.3020	25/4/29
No.1963	20/7/63 at Redhill
No.3054	28/12/62 at Redhill

		Boilers	
		No.889	22/12/26
		No.841	25/4/29
Allocations		No.899	25/7/31
22/2/25	Exmouth Jct	No.831	11/1/39
6/10/34	Brighton	No.1026	17/2/42
23/2/25	Eastleigh	No.1076	13/10/45
20/6/36	Salisbury	No.906	4/12/48
8/2/46	Reading	No.1084	9/1/53
31/3/48	Faversham	No.940	11/5/56
14/6/59	Exmouth Jct	No.1167	2/12/61
26/11/59	Redhill		

Withdrawn 5/1/64 "To be scrapped at Redhill HO 10/271/NO Our Ref.M634/2 2/3/64"
Cut up at Redhill shed on 26/12/64

Left. Redhill's 31850 works a freight up from Dover, with some Foreign wagons in the train, through Shorncliffe Camp, near Folkestone, on 7 August 1956. transporttreasury

Below. AWS-fitted Maunsell moguls at Reading South for the Redhill line; Redhill's N 31850 left, Guildford's U 31633 to the right, in July 1963. Note contrast between Maunsell chimney (31850) and BR chimney (31633). ColourRail

31851

To traffic as A851 on 20/2/25
Renumbered 1851 2/6/33; 31851 26/8/48

Works
Ex Woolwich 19/1/25

19/1/25-20/2/25**B**		
10/9/26-23/12/26**A**	55,209	
25/3/29-7/5/29**A**	75,664	
28/10/30-25/11/30**C**		Salisbury Extension of mileage 10,000
13/5/32-23/6/32**C**	59,970	
5/8/32-31/8/32**C**	60,888	
4/5/33-2/6/33**A**	73,091	
6/6/35-23/7/35**A**	62.911	
5/11/35**D**		Eastleigh
7/7/36-1/8/36**C**	38,866	Eastleigh
22/4/37-15/6/37**B**	57,276	Extension of mileage 15,000
28/3/39-2/5/39**A**	95,994	Class plate fitted
11/6/41-9/7/41**C**		Guildford Extension of mileage 5,000
13/8/42-16/9/42**A**	88,117	
12/3/43-9/4/43**D**	19,472	
2/12/43-1/1/44**C**	37,935	
26/2/45-3/3/45**C**		Exmouth Jct
14/8/45-18/9/45**C**	93,342	Exmouth Jct
14/11/45-18/12/45**A**	99,873	510 copper stays renewed 200 copper riveted over Copper tubeplate 98 studs fitted Firehole 15 new rivets Set new small tubes 'Talbot and Stead' Set new large tubes steel with copper ends
28/6/47-21/8/47**C**		Bricklayers Arms
13/8/48-26/8/48**C**	68,659	7 copper stays renewed Copper stays riveted over "in fire area" Copper Wrapping Plate 40 studs fitted 31 new small tubes 'Talbot and Stead' "All others expanded and rebeaded" Large tubes referruled
24/6/49-28/7/49**A**	89,665	419 copper stays renewed 200 riveted over 24 roof stays renewed Internal Tubeplate 118 rivets replaced by studs Smokebox Tubeplate bottom flange repaired Barrel cleaned Firehole 26 rivets hammered Set new large tubes steel with copper ends
15/2/51-20/4/51**GO**		Brighton 254 holes bushed New Firebox Barrel scaled set new tubes 'Talbot and Stead' Large tubes repaired steel with copper ends
24/9/51-10/10/51**LC**		Brighton
10/6/53-27/6/53**HI**		Smokebox Tubeplate "Fractures R and L welded" 173 new small tubes 3 new large tubes 18 expanded and referruled
29/4/55-20/5/55**LI-HI**	109,011	88 steel stays renewed 50 copper riveted over 88 nuts renewed 2 fusible plugs 32 small tubes "repaired" 141 rebeaded 3 new large tubes 18 expanded and referruled
7/5/57-25/5/57**GO**	157,613	10 copper stays renewed 293 nuts renewed 2 fusible plugs Barrel scaled 173 new small tubes 'Stewart and Lloyds' electrically welded Firehole 15 new rivets Set new large tubes
26/2/59-20/3/59**LI-HI**	48,280	New type firebox Blowdown valve gear and water treatment 1 copper stay renewed 90 copper riveted over "Firehole laps and flanges caulked 31 flange and 24 copper rivets caulked 2 fusible plugs 173 new small tubes 'Tube Products' electrically welded firehole 15 rivets caulked
1/4/60-30/4/60**LC**	77,465	
7/7/60-15/7/60**return**	82,853	
6/6/61-6/7/61**GO**	117,700	245 copper and 667 monel metal stays renewed 200 copper riveted over 24 roof nuts renewed 494 holes bushed Internal Tubeplate and Snokebox Tubeplate new 2 fusible plugs Barrel scaled 173 new small tubes Set new large tubes
21/9/61-22/9/61**NC**		Bricklayers Arms
13/2/62-28/2/62**NC**	20,280	AWS part fitted

Tenders

No.3060	7/5/29
No.3040	28/7/49

Boilers		Allocations	
No.890	23/12/26	22/2/25	Salisbury
No.986	7/5/29	29/12/45	Exmouth Jct
No.898	2/6/33	15/6/46	Brighton
No.975	23/7/35	10/8/47	Redhill
No.882	2/5/39	11/4/51	Exmouth Jct
No.830	16/9/42	8/10/51	Fratton
No.990	18/12/45	20/7/53	Exmouth Jct
No.891	28/7/49	8/2/55	Bricklayers Arms
No.1027	20/4/51	14/6/59	Exmouth Jct
No.973	25/5/57	26/11/59	Redhill
No.1067	6/7/61		

Withdrawn 25/8/63 Sold 7/3/64

Left. Redhill's 31851 calls at Eridge on the LBSC south of Groombridge on 9 September 1961. ColourRail

Below. 31851 takes nine coaches through Dartford Junction (Sidcup and Crayford to the left, Slade Green to the right) on 18 May 1959. L.Rowe, ColourRail

31852

To traffic as A852 on 9/3/25
Renumbered 1852 2/9/33; 31852 17/11/50

Works
Ex Woolwich 12/2/5

Date	Mileage	Notes
12/2/25-9/3/25**B**		
12/7/26-5/11/26**A**	32,758	
23/4/29-8/6/29**A**	74,177	
1/4/31-9/5/31**A**	63,298	326 copper stays renewed 200 copper riveted over Copper Tubeplate 33 studs fitted Foundation Ring 36 new rivets Set new small tubes 'Howell and Co' Set second hand large tubes with copper ends "Plugs 12 threads"
21/7/33-2/9/33**A**	77,240	
15/3/35-18/4/35**C**	54,664	Extension of mileage 10,000
9/4/36-27/5/36**A**	87,324	
27/10/38-5/12/38**A**	81,095	Class plate fitted
3/4/40-12/4/40**C**	51,241	
5/4/41-2/5/41**A**	87,786	21 copper stays renewed 100 copper riveted over 267 nuts renewed Copper Tubeplate 57 studs fitted
18/8/42-19/9/42**C**	60,583	Extension of mileage 5,000
15/1/43-27/2/43**C**		Exmouth Jct Extension of mileage 15,000 40 nuts renewed
2/2/44-9/3/44**C**		Exmouth Jct Extension of mileage 25,000 3 steel stays renewed Copper Tubeplate 36 studs fitted
11/11/44-22/12/44**A**	122,235	
23/5/46-6/7/46**C**		Norwood Jct
24/10/47-2/12/47**A**	70,623	525 copper and 705 steel stays renewed 228 roof stays renewed 310 holes bushed New Firebox Set new small tubes 'Tubes Ltd' Set new large tubes steel with copper ends
2/11/49-3/1/50		Hither Green 30 nuts renewed Set new small tubes
23/2/50-3/4/50		Redhill Set new large tubes steel with copper ends
24/10/50-17/11/50**LI**	73,751	75 copper stays riveted over 154 nuts renewed Internal Tubeplate renewed 32 new small tubes 'Talbot and Stead'
25/6/52-18/7/52**GO**	126,849	
22/10/52-5/11/52**Return**		
17/3/54-5/4/54**GO**	41,268	
22/9/55-19/10/55**HI**	34,995	
14/6/56-23/6/56**HI**	38,868	
2/10/56-18/10/56**LC**	54,095	
20/6/57-2/7/57**LC**	69,503	
28/2/58-22/3/58**GO**	83,024	Tender no.3035 Blowdown valve gear and water treatment 232 copper and 627 steel stays renewed 627 nuts renewed 386 holes bushed Internal Tubeplate new 2 fusible plugs smokebox Tubeplate levelled 2 mud hole doors welded Barrel scaled 173 new small tubes 'Stewart and Lloyds ' electrically welded
30/8/60-23/9/60**LI**	70,637	AWS part fitted New type CI firebars 'Overhead live wire notices' 11 copper stays renewed 164 nuts renewed Internal Tubeplate "Wrapper levelled where stays repaired" 2 fusible plugs 32 new small tubes 'Stewart and Lloyds' electrically welded 141 rebeaded 3 new large tubes 18 expanded and referruled
31/8/61-1/9/61**NC**	2,272	Bricklayers Arms
1/10/62-27/10/62**LI**	137,425	Eastleigh Blowdown gear and silencer Briquette tube feeder 52 copper and 295 monel metal stays riveted over 295 nuts renewed "Firehole strip patch fitted" 2 fusible plugs 173 new small tubes 'Stewart and Lloyds' 3 new large tubes Foundation Ring 32 rivets recaulked

Tenders

No.3100	8/6/29
No.3035	5/12/38
No.684	23/9/60

31852 out on the road with an evening Guildford-bound train near Farnborough, 31 May 1963. Peter Groom.

Boilers			Allocations	
No.891	5/11/26		23/2/25	Exmouth Jct
No.998	8/6/29		24/4/43	Bricklayers Arms
No.855	9/5/31		21/4/45	Norwood Jct
No.828	2/9/33		25/1/47	Redhill
No.886	27/5/36		11/4/51	Exmouth Jct
No.851	5/12/38		8/10/51	Fratton
No.988	2/5/41		3/3/53	Feltham
No.878	22/12/44		26/5/53	Ashford
No.988	2/12/47		20/7/53	Faversham
No.878	18/7/52		14/6/59	Exmouth Jct
No.1031	15/4/54		26/11/59	Redhill
No.1035	22/3/58			

Withdrawn 21/9/63 Cut up at Eastleigh Works w/e 14/12/63

Left. 31852 at Ashford station on 30 June 1960. It would soon go into Ashford works for a Light Intermediate which included fitting AWS and attaching the 'overhead live wire notices'. There is the faintest outline of the (small) second emblem on the tender. D.C. Ovenden, ColourRail

Below. 31852 at Redhill MPD, 22 April 1963; this was one of the engines to acquire a mechanical lubricator, prominent above the cylinder. It had to be re-sited when deflectors were added. It was originally further forward. Mysterious ARFA marked on smokebox door, washout plug on boiler top visible and leaking, strange 'bubble' feature on firebox shoulder... Peter Groom.

31853

To traffic as A853 on 9/4/25
Renumbered 1853 19/11/31; 31853 19/3/49

Works

Date	Mileage	Notes
Ex Woolwich 12/2/25		
12/2/25-9/4/25**B**		
19/4/26-19/8/26**A**	39,598	
10/2/28-27/4/28**A**	60,673	
17/1/30-1/3/30**A**	61,746	
21/10/31-19/11/31**A**	72,042	
Stored from 1/12/31-5/12/31		
1/2/34-9/3/34**A**	88,126	
18/4/35-6/6/535**C**	45,257	
22/5/36-9/7/36**A**	79,209	
20/1/39-24/2/39**A**	87,213	Class plate fitted
25/6/41-25/7/41**A**	87,529	
12/1/43-29/1/43**C**		Exmouth Jct Extension of mileage 5,000
18/10/43-17/11/43**A**	85,195	
28/8/44-16/9/44**C**		Exmouth Jct Tender only
9/3/45-27/3/45**C**		Exmouth Jct
3/1/46-24/2/46**C**		Exmouth Jct
13/6/46-11/7/46**A**	76,526	
8/11/47-12/12/47**C**		Exmouth Jct
11/2/49-19/3/49**A**	70,950	
8/12/50-18/1/51**HI**	48,355	
2/10/51-6/11/51**LC**		
12/3/52-18/2/52	74,000	Bricklayers Arms
19/12/52-21/1/53**HI**	92,743	
26/6/53-19/7/53**NC**		Bricklayers Arms
3/2/55-1/3/55**GO**	153,783	705 copper stays renewed 398 holes bushed Internal Tubeplate new 2 fusible plugs Barrel scaled 173 new small tubes 'Howells' Set new large tubes
12/7/56-12/8/56**LC**	40,322	Bricklayers Arms Set new small tubes 'New Steel' Set new large tubes
16/4/57-10/5/57**LI**	58,620	1 copper stays renewed 496 copper riveted over Internal Tubeplate 80 lap and 13 corner rivets caulked 2 fusible plugs 36 new small tubes 'Universal' 137 rebeaded 3 new large tubes 18 expanded and referulled Firehole 15 rivets caulked
20/5/58-5/6/58**LC**	90,784	20 copper stays riveted over Internal Tubeplate 30 rivets chipped and caulked 1 mud hole door welded 173 new small tubes 'Stewart and Lloyds' electrically welded set new large tubes
19/3/59-8/4/59**LC**	116,521	
8/6/60-23/7/60**GO**	146,223	New CI firebars Water treatment AWS fitted New type 9mm injectors Front end conversion 525 copper and 705 monel metal stays renewed 705 nuts renewed 228 roof stays and 444 roof nuts renewed 12 holes bushed New Firebox 2 fusible plugs Barrel scaled 173 new small tubes 'Tube Products' electrically welded Set new large tubes
19/4/62-21/4/62**NC**		Exmouth Jct
26/3/63-27/4/63**LI-HI**	75,849	Eastleigh WR loco 30 copper and 238 monel metal stays riveted over 238 nuts renewed Internal Tubeplate seams and studs repaired 2 fusible plugs 173 new small tubes 'Stewart and Lloyds' 3 new large tubes Foundation Ring 28 rivets repaired

Tenders

No.3042	27/4/28
No.3025	24/2/39

Boilers

No.892	19/8/26
No.858	1/3/30
No.884	19/11/31
No.852	9/3/34
No.842	9/7/36
No.914	24/2/39
No.901	25/7/41
No.971	17/11/43
No.939	11/7/46
No.1019	19/3/49
No.896	1/3/55
No.1063	23/7/60

Allocations

19/4/25	Exmouth Jct
5/10/35	Barnstaple
12/8/39	Exmouth Jct
8/10/51	Bricklayers Arms
14/6/59	Exmouth Jct

Withdrawn 7/9/64. Sold to Birds, Morriston 14/10/64

31853 under repair at Wadebridge, 15 March 1950; noteworthy for an early version of the new cabside lettering; early lined black applications had the lining spaced out which allowed a Gill sans number in 10in size. The tender was bare, though the cast BR smokebox plate had been fitted. A.E. West, courtesy Mike King.

31853 coming into Exeter St David's with an up ballast which includes one of the Meldon bogie hoppers, 4 September 1963. It had undergone frame alterations in 1960, getting a BR Class 4 chimney in the process. Apparently at that time – about 1960 – the supply of such chimneys from Crewe dried up due to the casting pattern wearing out, resulting in fourteen getting Maunsell chimneys instead (see page 18).

31854

To traffic as A854 on 3/1925
Renumbered 1854 no date; 31854 20/5/48
Early Engine Record Card missing

Works

5/2/41-14/5/41**C**	25,671	Eastleigh	
4/3/48-20/5/48**C**	67,566		
23/8/48-11/9/48**D**	72,333		
19/10/49-24/11/49**A**	90,788	195 copper and 664 steel stays renewed 34 nuts renewed Internal Tubeplate new Smokebox Tubeplate levelled Set new small tubes 'Tubes Ltd'	
18/7/50-9/8/50**LC**	12,751	3 copper stays renewed	
21/11/51-14/12/51**HI**	39,360	1 copper stay renewed 50 copper stays riveted over 183 nuts renewed "Firebox laps caulked" 173 new small tubes 'Tubes Ltd' 3 new large tubes 18 expanded and referulled	
16/8/52-20/9/52**NC**		Faversham	
6/10/53-31/10/53**GO**	76,098		
20/11/54-23/12/54**LC**		Redhill	
12/9/55-30/9/55**LI**	46,429		
18/6/56-17/7/56**LC**	67,052	Brighton	
29/7/57-31/8/57**GO**	97,062	Full frame conversion 2 new type 9mm injectors fitted rhs 1,012 copper stays renewed 228 roof stays and 444 roof nuts renewed New Firebox 2 fusible plugs Smokebox Tubeplate levelled Barrel scaled 173 new small tubes 'Tube Products' electrically welded Set new large tubes	
4/9/59-26/9/59**LI-HI**	63,151	New type CI firebars ATC 391 copper stays riveted over "Firebox lap caulked" 2 fusible plugs 32 new small tubes 'Stewart and Lloyds' electrically welded 141 rebeaded 3 new large tubes 18 expanded and referulled Firehole 15 rivets caulked	
7/7/61-8/7/61**NC**	114,495	Spark arrester	
2/1/62-27/1/62**LI**	126,331	313 copper stays riveted over "Tubeplate flanges caulked" 2 fusible plugs 32 new small tubes 'Tube Products' electrically welded 141 rebeaded 3 new large tubes 18 expanded and referulled	

Tenders

No.3043	no date
No.3030	no date
No.3016	31/10/53
No.1887	30/9/55

Boilers

No.844	no date
No.995	24/11/49
No.1042	31/10/53
No.863	31/8/57

Allocations

22/3/25	Exmouth Jct
15/6/35	Barnstaple
12/8/39	Exmouth Jct
15/6/46	Brighton
10/8/47	Redhill
28/12/47	Reading
31/3/48	Faversham
31/10/54	Hither Green
19/7/57	Ashford
26/5/61	Stewarts lane
31/8/63	Exmouth Jct

Withdrawn 15/6/64. Sold to G. Cohen, Morriston 18/8/64

31854, an engine amongst the earliest to undergo frame renewal, at Fratton in 1961. Based in the West until 1946, it returned briefly to Exmouth Junction before being withdrawn. Fratton had a peculiarly lingering end; deemed 'officially closed' it was nothing of the sort, it merely functioned at a much reduced level of activity. It is not hard to see how the view came about, for frequently it presented a more or less deserted appearance though, to be fair, this could be said of a number of steam sheds in the 1960s. ColourRail

31854 leaving St Leonards West Marina for Warrior Square and Hastings on 26 July 1958. The leading brake is of LMS origin while most of the rest are BR Mk1 vehicles – this would be an inter-Regional train, or the empty stock for it. A remarkable view really, showing how the entire St Leonards MPD and the station fitted into so discreet a slice of land under the former cliff line. This physical attribute allowed the water tanks to be placed up on the cliffside to gain the best head of water. RailOnline

31855

To traffic as A855 on 21/3/25
Renumbered 1855 7/11/31; 31855 12/3/49

Works

Ex Woolwich 19/2/25		
19/2/25-21/3/25**B**		
8/10/26-5/2/27**A**	42,627	
12/6/29-23/7/29**A**	73,854	All steel stays renewed 100 copper riveted over Firehole rivets hammered Set new small tubes 'Howell and Co' Large tubes expanded and rebeaded
6/10/31-7/11/31**A**	76,791	
Stored from 19/11/31-5/12/311		
28/12/33-27/1/34**A**	79,599	
24/4/36-29/5/36**A**	76,611	
2/12/38-18/1/39**A**	86,346	Class plate fitted
14/10/40-30/12/40**B**	66,227	Exmouth Jct Extension of mileage 20,000
23/9/41-22/10/41**A**	94,355	
21/4/43-24/5/43**C**	40,980	
24/3/44-22/4/44**A**	71,705	23 copper sand 101 monel metal stays renewed 150 copper riveted over 331 nuts renewed Copper Tubeplate 60 studs fitted 2 fusible plugs Firehole 10 new rivets Set new small tubes 'Howell and Co' Large tubes repaired steel with copper ends
3/1/46-22/3/46**C**		Exmouth Jct
18/5/46-12/6/46**A**	83,679	
3/2/49-12/3/49**A**	84,510	385 copper stays renewed 350 copper riveted over 228 roof stays renewed Internal Tubeplate 128 studs fitted Smokebox Tubeplate levelled Barrel cleaned Set new small tubes 'Talbot and Stead' Set new large tubes steel with copper ends
22/4/49**defect**		"74 steel replaced by copper on Tubeplate and 6 steel taken out for examination and 9 replaced steel on Tubeplate" [Reported on BRC but not on ERC]
7/3/50-17/3/50**LC**	28,279	No Boiler work
27/2/51-24/3/51**LI**	60,381	Eastleigh 430 copper stays riveted over "Firebox rivets and studs caulked" 2 fusible plugs 30 small tubes repaired 21 large tubes rebeaded and refurreled
25/3/52-16/4/52**LC**		No Boiler work
29/7/52-14/8/52		Bricklayers Arms 4 copper stays renewed Copper stays riveted over "in fire area" "Tubeplate seams and studs caulked" 173 new small tubes 'New Steel' 21 large tubes expanded and refurreled
3/11/52-14/11/52**LC**	103,903	No Boiler work
23/10/53-21/11/53**GO**	131,755	
27/12/54-26/1/55		Hither Green
22/11/55-10/12/55**GO**	63,420	New type front end 22 copper stays renewed 100 copper riveted over 156 steel stays replaced by copper 214 nuts renewed 2 fusible plugs Barrel scaled 173 new small tubes 'Stewart and Lloyds' electrically welded Set new large tubes
31/1/57-2/3/57**LI-HI**	36,121	2 copper stays renewed 231 copper riveted over 86 nuts renewed 2 fusible plugs Foundation Ring 20 corner rivets caulked 173 new small tubes 'Stewart and Lloyds' electrically welded Firehole 15 rivets caulked
2/1/59-31/1/59**LI-HI**	89,175	New CI (cast iron) firebars 162 copper stays renewed 245 copper riveted over 2 roof nuts renewed "Patch fitted top half of firehole" 58 lap studs fitted flanges caulked 43 flange and 20 corner rivets caulked 2 fusible plugs 173 new small tubes 'Stewart and Lloyds' electrically welded 3 new large tubes 18 expanded and refurreled Firehole 15 new rivets
16/6/59-4/7/59**LC**	97,927	15 new large tubes 6 expanded and refurreled
30/6/60-28/7/60**GO**	117,874	AWS part fitted 'Overhead live wire notices' 275 and 498 monel metal stays renewed 134 copper riveted over 498 nuts renewed 320 holes bushed 2 fusible plugs Smokebox Tubeplate levelled Barrel scaled 173 new small tubes 'Stewart and Lloyds' electrically welded Set new large tubes
9/2/62-12/2/62**NC**		Exmouth Jct
26/8/63-28/9/63**LI-HI**	91,087	Eastleigh Blowdown gear and silencer Briquette tube feeder 229 copper and 310 monel metal stays riveted over 310 nuts renewed Internal Tubeplate studs and seams recaulked strip patch fitted 2 fusible plugs Foundation Ring 28 rivets repaired 173 new small tubes 'Tube Products' 21 large tubes refurreled

Tenders

No.3044	5/2/27
No.3046	2/3/57
No.3019	17/8/63

Boilers

No.894	5/2/27
No.962	23/7/29
No.959	7/11/31
No.877	27/1/34
No.860	29/5/36
No.895	18/1/39
No.1017	22/10/41
No.995	22/4/44
No.975	12/6/46
No.1081	12/3/49
No.850	21/11/53
No.968	10/12/55
No.1030	28/7/60

Allocations

22/3/25	Exmouth Jct
24/4/43	Reading
29/12/45	Exmouth Jct
8/10/51	Bricklayers Arms
22/6/54	Hither Green
10/2/61	Exmouth Jct

Withdrawn 7/9/64. Sold to Birds, Morriston

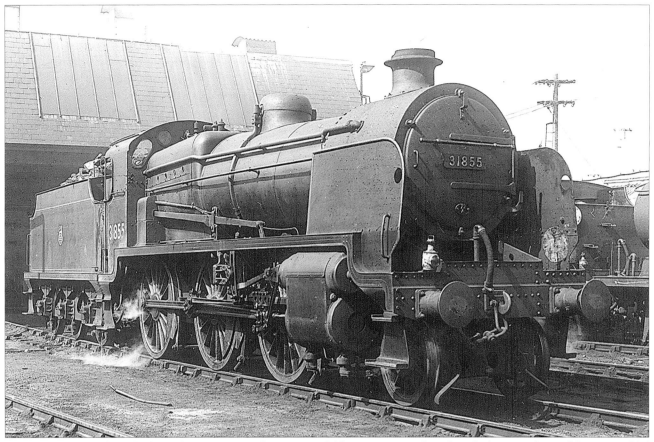

31855 at Three Bridges shed, 8 July 1952. It was by now a Bricklayers Arms engine, though the 72A plate soldiers on. Initial Photographics.

31855 with the 1pm Padstow train at Egloskerry on 11 July 1964. The train is made up of a Southern 4 wheel luggage van (PMV), a BR Mk1 bogie van (GUV) and a 2-Set of Bulleid brake composite and semi open brake third from former BRCW 3-set 4282. R. A. Lumber.

31856

To traffic as A856 on 26/3/25
Renumbered 1856 15/8/31; 31856 15/6/49

Works
Ex Woolwich 19/2/25

Date	Mileage	Notes
19/2/25-26/3/25**B**		
26/10/26-18/2/27**A**	43,822	
4/3/27-11/3/27**D**		
4/9/29-19/10/29**A**	75,580	
1/7/31-15/8/31**A**	76,161	
25/10/32-4/11/32**C**		Exmouth Jct
29/6/33-22/8/33**B**	56,270	
26/8/33-1/9/33**C**	56,270	Extension of mileage 5,000
20/7/34-30/8/34**A**	89,212	
8/3/35-3/4/35**C**	19,983	
27/11/35-7/1/36**C**	40,650	Extension of mileage 5,000
17/3/36-21/4/36**C**	46,154	
16/4/37-4/6/37**A**	80,042	
13/11/39-6/12/39**A**	87,684	Class plate fitted
16/9/41-21/10/41**A**	71,235	
25/10/43-24/11/43**A**	71,835	
2/12/45-8/1/46**C**		Exmouth Jct
21/8/46-21/9/46**A**	90,240	
29/9/48-5/11/48**C**	74,734	Exmouth Jct
10/5/49-15/6/49**A**	79,679	
19/10/50-10/11/50**HC**	39,007	
29/1/52-28/3/52**LC**	75,219	
14/5/53-5/6/53**HI**	107,846	
27/10/54-13/11/54**GO**	142,491	
18/10/55-3/11/55**LC**	26,040	
2/2/56-1/3/56**LC**	32,872	Hither Green
3/4/57-2/5/57**LI-HI**	66,012	
30/4/58-10/5/58**LC**	95,207	
8/9/58-17/9/58**LC**	103,213	
16/1/59-21/2/59**LI-HI**	112,416	New type CI firebars Manganese steel liners
16/6/60-7/7/60**LC**	145,278	AWS fitted
5/9/60-10/9/60**HC**	146,743	New type CI firebars 217 copper and 514 monel metal stays renewed 60 copper riveted over 514 nuts renewed 137 holes bushed Copper Tubeplate and Back Plate flanges welded 20 corner rivets caulked 2 fusible plugs Smokebox Tubeplate levelled Barrel scaled Set new small tubes 'Howells' 6 new large tubes welded 15 repaired
17/8/61-21/8/61		Exmouth Jct
10/1/62-10/2/62**LI-HI**	180,499	Water treatment 121 copper stays riveted over 129 nuts renewed "Tubeplate flanges and Firehole laps caulked" 2 fusible plugs 173 new small tubes 3 new large tubes 18 expanded and referruled Firehole 15 rivets caulked

Tenders

No.3045	18/2/27
No.3023	8/1/46
No.3024	5/6/53
No.3048	10/9/60

Boilers

No.895	18/2/27
No.847	19/10/29
No.856	15/8/31
No.858	20/8/34
No.867	4/6/37
No.821	6/12/39
No.884	21/10/41
No.859	24/11/43
No.891	21/9/46
No.912	15/6/49
No.881	13/11/54
No.1077	10/9/60

Allocations

19/4/25	Exmouth Jct
17/7/37	Barnstaple
16/10/37	Exmouth Jct
24/4/43	Reading
29/1/44	Exmouth Jct
8/10/51	Hither Green
3/3/53	Guildford
26/5/53	Redhill
20/7/53	Hither Green
10/2/61	Exmouth Jct

Withdrawn 8/8/64. Sold to Birds, Morriston 4/9/64

Time for a sit down for the crew at Padstow before working back up country with 31856 about 1962. 31856 had returned to Exmouth Junction a year or so before, having left there during the War; it had been made redundant by dieselisation at Hither Green. RailOnline

31856 with a down train at Exeter Central (a local with Plymouth headcode – possibly the 5.50pm to Okehampton) probably in late 1962. The train is a Maunsell '2P' set, one of those numbered between 22 and 30 or between 168 and 200, used mostly on west of England local services after 1948. The sets were made up of a Maunsell brake third and brake composite; in this instance 1935 flush-sided vehicles. The banker is a W 2-6-4T, several of which had arrived from September 1962 to replace the ailing Z 0-8-0Ts. RailOnline

31857

To traffic as A857 on 2/4/25
Renumbered 1857 9/6/33; 31857 30/7/48

Works
Ex Woolwich 19/2/25

19/2/25-2/4/25**B**		
14/3/37-10/6/27**A**	61,301	
2/1/29-15/3/29**A**	63,877	
29/11/30-10/1/31**A**	69,592	
4/5/33-9/6/33**A**	94,319	
13/6/35-19/7/35**A**	77,641	25 copper and 651 steel stays renewed 200 copper riveted over [150 steel stays replaced by copper] Copper Tubeplate 6 studs fitted Firehole rivets hammered 173 new small tubes 'Tubes Ltd' Large tubes repaired steel with copper ends
5/7/37-18/8/37**A**	77,434	
2/7/40-3/9/40**B**	77,810	Exmouth Jct Extension of mileage 30,000
14/5/41-10/6/41**A**	105,899	Class plate fitted
1/4/42-15/4/42**C**	34,450	
4/11/42-9/12/42**C**	51,032	
30/12/42-26/1/44**A**	78,769	
30/3/44-22/4/44**D**	3,680	
10/5/46-7/6/46**B**	46,640	
16/8/46-30/8/46**D**	47,780	
25/6/48-30/7/48**A**	94,279	
25/2/49-26/3/49**LC**		
26/7/49-27/8/49**NC**	25,800	
18/4/51-11/5/51**HI**	66,279	100 copper stays riveted over 247 nuts renewed Internal Tubeplate 49 copper studs fitted laps copper welded 173 new small tubes 'Howells' 3 large tubes repaired steel with copper ends18 large tubes expanded and referruled
3/10/51-24/10/51**NC**	77,256	No Boiler work
10/11/51-1/12/51	78,226	Hither Green 8 copper stays renewed 173 new small tubes 'Howells' 12 new large tubes 9 expanded and referruled
4/11/52-28/11/52**GO**	105,168	525 copper and 705 steel stays renewed 705 nuts renewed 228 roof stays renewed New Firebox Smokebox Tubeplate new Barrel scaled 173 new small tubes 'Tubes Ltd' Set new large tubes
7/11/53-24/11/53		Hither Green 173 new small tubes 21 large tubes expanded and referruled
16/12/54-13/1/55**LI-HI**	65,289	34 steel stays renewed 117 copper riveted over 150 nuts renewed 173 new small tubes 'Howells' Firehole 11 rivets caulked
29/3/56-20/4/56**LC**		Hither Green 173 new small tubes 'Stewart and Lloyds' electrically welded Set new large tubes
2/8/56-22/8/56**GO**	109,494	274 copper and 610 monel metal stays renewed 610 nuts renewed 376 holes bushed Internal Tubeplate new 2 fusible plugs Barrel scaled 173 new small tubes 'Stewart and Lloyds' electrically welded Set new large tubes
22/5/58-14/6/58**LI-HI**	57,856	94 copper stays riveted over 308 nuts renewed "Flange and firehole lap caulked 44 flanges and 20 corner rivets caulked" 2 fusible plugs 173 new small tubes 'Stewart and Lloyds' electrically welded Firehole 15 rivets caulked set new large tubes
25/7/60-16/9/60**GO**	115,057	'Overhead live wire notices' New type CI firebars AWS part fitted 467 copper and 615 monel metal stays renewed 162 copper riveted over 615 nuts renewed 514 holes bushed Internal Tubeplate new Smokebox Tubeplate levelled 2 fusible plugs 173 new small tubes Set new large tubes
11/7/61-14/7/61**NC**		Exmouth Jct

Tenders

No.3046	10/6/27
No.3049	15/3/29

Boilers

No.896	10/6/27
No.900	15/3/29
No.897	10/1/31
No.976	9/6/33
No.990	19/7/35
No.901	18/8/37
No.886	10/6/41
No.849	26/1/44
No.873	30/7/48
No.1074	28/11/52
No.1161	25/8/56
No.963	16/9/60

Allocations

19/4/25	Barnstaple
18/10/38	Exmouth Jct
24/4/43	Reading
20/3/50	Redhill
22/7/51	Hither Green
17/1/61	Feltham
10/2/61	Exmouth Jct
22/10/62	Guildford

Withdrawn 5/1/64 Cut up at Eastleigh Works w/e 22/2/64

The revolutionary worth of the Ns in the West is demonstrated in this picture; a big wholly modern locomotive untroubled by its three aging and lightweight coaches. The contrast is striking. Shrugging off the three ancient rattling ex-LSW non-corridors, new 1857 crosses the River Taw viaduct at Barnstaple about 1925.

31857 at Hither Green MPD, its home throughout the 1950s, on 2 November 1957; it was another of the Ns to be equipped with a mechanical lubricator. Peter Groom.

31858

To traffic as A858 on 1/5/25
Renumbered 1858 4/5/33; 31858 23/6/50

Works

Ex Woolwich 13/3/25		
13/3/25-1/5/25**B**		
23/4/26-28/7/26**A**	35,874	
16/10/28-19/1/29**A**	72,838	
23/10/30-28/11/30**A**	62,988	
30/3/33-4/5/33**A**	81,760	
15/2/35-28/3/35**A**	71,475	
20/5/37-2/7/37**A**	78,845	
26/4/40-26/5/40**A**	76,549	Class plate fitted 728 copper stays renewed 212 copper riveted over 228 roof stays renewed 344 holes bushed Copper Tubeplate new Firehole rivets renewed Set new small tubes 'Chesterfield Tube Co.' Large tubes repaired steel with copper ends
1/11/41-25/11/41**C**	60,712	Exmouth Jct Extension of mileage 10,000
27/2/42-13/4/42**D**	65,103	"Right corner of Foundation bar caulked"
24/7/42-24/9/42**C**		Exmouth Jct Extension of mileage 30,000 166 second hand small tubes
24/2/44-25/3/44**A**	105,970	
4/2/46-5/3/46**B**	49,671	Extension of mileage 5,000
28/6/47-21/8/47		Bricklayers Arms Extension of mileage 5,000
19/1/48-26/2/48**A**	93,553	
30/5/50-23/6/50**HI**	59,979	
27/6/51-20/7/51**HI**	94,690	
31/7/51-8/8/51**LC**	94,696	
29/12/52-30/1/53**GO**		525 copper and 705 steel stays renewed 228 roof stays and 228 roof nuts renewed 183 holes bushed New Firebox Smokebox Tubeplate "Bottom section of flange renewed" Barrel scaled 173 new small tubes 'Tubes Ltd' Set new large tubes
16/9/53-25/9/53**LC**	18,908	No Boiler work
12/2/54-6/3/54**LC**	30,807	Hither Green
24/3/55-14/4/55**LI-HI**	63,474	100 copper stays riveted over 214 nuts renewed 2 fusible plugs 173 new small tubes 'Universal' Firehole 15 rivets caulked Set new large tubes
23/8/56-23/9/56**LC**	100,681	Hither Green 2 fusible plugs 173 new small tubes 'Stewart and Lloyds' electrically welded
2/7/57-10/8/57**GO**	122,688	
27/8/57-28/8/57**return**	122,739	
27/4/59-16/5/59**LI-HI**	51,198	
9/6/61-24/6/61**GO**	98,819	Manganese liners AWS part fitted Water treatment Full frame conversion 'Overhead live wire notices' 400 copper and 615 steel stays renewed 216 copper riveted over 50 holes bushed Internal Tubeplate new 2 fusible plugs Smokebox Tubeplate levelled 3 mud door holes welded 173 new small tubes Set new large tubes
2/4/62-3/4/62**NC**		Stewarts Lane

Tenders

No.3019	19/1/29
No.3004	26/2/48
No.3015	24/6/61

Boilers

No.851	28/7/26
No.874	19/1/29
No.842	28/11/30
No.902	4/5/33
No.849	28/3/35
No.832	2/7/37
No.855	26/5/40
No.1042	25/3/44
No.970	26/2/48
No.1079	30/1/53
No.1163	10/8/57
No.996	24/6/61

Allocations

17/5/25	Exmouth Jct
24/4/43	Bricklayers Arms
22/5/43	Reading
21/4/45	Bricklayers Arms
20/4/46	Brighton
10/8/47	Redhill
27/7/51	Hither Green
22/10/59	Guildford

Withdrawn 26/12/65

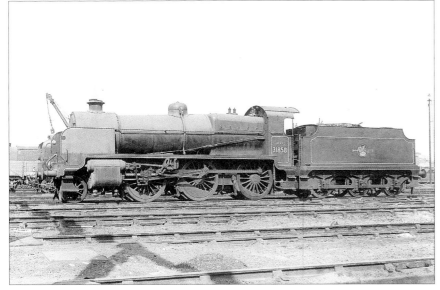

Top. 1858, as yet with no BR smokebox plate, leaving Reigate in June 1948. Derek Clayton.

Middle. 31858 at Nine Elms MPD, 31 May 1960. It was yet another Exmouth Junction wartime 'evacuee' though it was never to return. Peter Groom.

Below. 31858 at Norwood Junction MPD in 1963; behind it is an unrebuilt light Pacific, unlikely company at this particular shed. The AWS 'bash plate' is doing its job, for the screw coupling is not hooked up out of the way, as stipulated. 31858 underwent frame improvements in 1961, hence the curving shape at the front and the snifting valve on the valence. RailOnline

31859

To traffic as A859 on 24/4/25
Renumbered 1859 19/9/31; 31859
Engine Record Card missing

Works

Ex Woolwich 13/3/25		
13/3/25-24/4/25**B**		
5/8/27-30/11/27**A**	66,661	
8/10/29-16/11/29**A**	67,233	
25/8/31-19/9/31**A**	74,038	
6/2/33-25/2/33**C**	50,478	
3/5/33-19/5/33**C**	51,536	
24/3/34-28/4/34**A**	79,096	
7/9/34-10/10/34**D**	11,065	
23/1/36-11/3/36**C**	57,117	Extension of mileage 5,000
26/10/36-2/12/36A	76,520	
15/3/39-19/4/39**A**	76,718	Class plate fitted 877 copper stays renewed 350 copper riveted over 327 holes bushed Copper Tubeplate new Set new small tubes 'Howell and Co' Set new large tubes steel with copper ends
24/4/40-15/5/40**C**	43,031	Extension of mileage 10,000
25/8/41-17/9/41**A**	94,760	
20/6/42-15/7/42**C**	24,221	
17/6/44		443 copper and 74 nickel plated stays renewed 250 copper riveted over Copper Tubeplate 20 studs fitted 2 fusible plugs firehole rivets hammered set new small tubes 'Howell and Co' Set new large tubes steel with copper ends
28/12/46		Set new small tubes 'Tubes Ltd' Large tubes expanded and referruled
21/1/53-6/2/53**HI**		
21/2/55-15/3/55**HI**	93,501	
20/6/56-7/7/56**GO**	131,018	525 copper and 705 monel metal stays renewed 228 roof stays and 444 roof nuts renewed 518 holes bushed New Firebox 2 fusible plugs Barrel scaled 173 new small tubes 'Stewart and Lloyds' electrically welded Set new large tubes
4/11/57-26/11/57**LC**		Hither Green 2 fusible plugs 173 new small tubes 'New steel'
12/2/58-12/3/58**LC**		Hither Green 18 new large tubes
5/1/59-24/1/59**LI-HI**	70,507	New type CI (cast iron) firebars 73 copper stays riveted over 155 nuts renewed "18 lap studs fitted flanges and 20 corner rivets caulked" 2 fusible plugs 173 new small tubes 'Stewart and Lloyds' electrically welded 3 new large tubes 18 expanded and referruled
28/3/60-23/4/60**LI**	101,057	AWS part fitted 100 copper stays riveted over 335 nuts renewed "15 lap studs fitted flanges and firehole lap caulked 20 corner and 18 flange rivets caulked" 2 fusible plugs 173 new small tubes 'Stewart and Lloyds' electrically welded 3 new large tubes 18 expanded and referruled Firehole 15 rivets caulked
22/1/62-24/2/62**LC-HC**	135,033	173 new small tubes 'Tube products' electrically welded Firehole 15 rivets caulked Foundation Ring 20 corner rivets caulked
12/3/63-20/4/63**LI**	163,465	Eastleigh Blowdown gear and silencer Briquette tube feeder 364 copper and 62 monel metal stays riveted over 62 nuts renewed Internal Tubeplate seams and rivets caulked 2 fusible plugs 173 new small tubes 21 new large tubes

Tenders

No.3048	30/11/27
No.3024	no date

Boilers

No.898	30/11/27
No.870	16/11/29
No.847	19/9/31
No.896	28/4/34
No.884	2/12/36
No.845	19/4/39
No.847	17/9/41
No.1040	17/6/44
No.1068	7/7/56
No.1070	24/2/62

Allocations

17/5/25	Exmouth Jct
5/10/35	Barnstaple
12/8/39	Exmouth Jct
24/4/43	Bricklayers Arms
22/5/43	Reading
21/4/45	Bricklayers Arms
20/4/46	Exmouth Jct
14/6/47	Tonbridge
31/3/48	Redhill
25/3/50	Stewarts Lane
18/12/50	Dover
27/7/51	Hither Green
26/5/61	Norwood Jct
6/7/61	Brighton
8/12/61	Guildford
31/8/63	Exmouth Jct

Withdrawn 7/9/64. Sold to Birds, Morriston 14/10/64

An N that had worked from one extremity of the Southern to the other, and most places in between; 31859 is in natural mogul habitat at Trewanion, summit of the North Cornwall 860 feet above sea-level, with barely a tree in the landscape. The train is the 1.00pm Padstow-Okehampton, up over from Camelford and coasting into Otterham on a hot August afternoon in the early 1960s. The train comprises Southern 4 wheel luggage van (PMV), BR Mk1 bogie van with the national newspapers (now returning to Clapham Junction), Bulleid open saloon third and a Bulleid 'loose' brake composite. P.W. Gray.

31860

To traffic as A860 on 18/4/25
Renumbered 1860 25/7/31; 31860 11/5/50

Works

Ex Woolwich 13/3/25		
13/3/25-18/4/25**B**		
17/8/27-4/11/27**A**	61,538	393 copper stays renewed and 400 riveted over Firehole rivets hammered Set new small tubes 'Howell and Co' Large tubes expanded and referruled
14/2/29-6/4/29**A**	52,056	
6/3/30-31/3/30**C**	28,405	Extension of mileage 10,000
19/6/31-25/7/31**A**	72,238	
15/6/32-30/7/32		Exmouth Jct
31/10/32-18/11/32**C**	52,489	
19/10/33-18/11/33**A**	85,799	329 copper stays renewed 200 copper riveted over Copper Tubeplate 20 studs fitted Firehole rivets hammered Foundation Ring 2 rivets renewed Set new small tubes Large tubes repaired steel with copper ends
13/12/35-31/1/36**A**	74,829	
18/8/37-17/9/37**C**	57,607	Extension of mileage 10,000
17/2/39-29/3/39**A**	100,144	Class plate fitted
4/2/41-8/3/41**A**	72,107	
21/10/42-3/11/42**C**		Exmouth Jct
8/4/43-24/5/43**A**	75,706	877 copper stays renewed 100 copper riveted over [all steel stays replaced by copper] 52 holes bushed 2 fusible plugs 21 large tubes repaired steel with copper ends Small tubes expanded and rebeaded
10/5/44-10/6/44**C**	30,434	
14/12/44-21/2/45**C**		Nine Elms 2 copper stays renewed copper stays riveted over "in fire area" 2 fusible plugs 173 new small tubes 14 large tubes referruled
14/5/45-1/6/45**C**	48,510	
14/1/46-2/2/46**B**	60,928	Extension of mileage 5,000
7/11/47-12/12/47A	103,388	
3/2/49-5/2/49		Guildford
6/4/50-11/5/50**A**	70,772	404 copper stays renewed 200 copper riveted over "14 firebox lap rivets replace studs" Smokebox Tubeplate new Barrel scaled Set new small tubes 'Talbot and Stead' Set new large tubes steel with copper ends
7/11/50-28/11/50**LC**	14,293	No Boiler work
19/10/51-9/11/51**LI**	40,612	Copper stays riveted over "in fire area" 173 new small tubes 21 large tubes expanded and referruled
3/12/52-31/12/52**HI**	70,808	485 copper stays riveted over Internal Tubeplate 35 studs fitted and caulked 173 new small tubes 'Stewart and Lloyds' 21 large tubes expanded and referruled
14/1/54-2/2/54**LC**	102,088	Bricklayers Arms "Stays in firebox:re-rivet and tool" 21 new large tubes
9/3/55-31/3/55**GO**	135,401	
7/7/56-26/7/56**LC**	37,685	Bricklayers Arms
2/4/57-27/4/57**LI**	59,307	
9/4/58-27/4/58**LC**	28,340	Hither Green
5/3/59-21/3/59**GO**	116,782	New type CI firebars 275 copper and 541 monel metal stays renewed 125 copper riveted over 541 nuts renewed 323 holes bushed 2 fusible plugs Smokebox Tubeplate levelled Barrel scaled 173 new small tubes 'Tube products' electrically welded
1/9/60-30/9/60**LI-HI**	40,130	AWS Water treatment 'Overhead live wire notices' 116 copper stays riveted over 2 fusible plugs 32 new small tubes 'Stewart and Lloyds' electrically welded 141 rebeaded 3 new large tubes 18 expanded and referruled
29/7/61-1/8/61**NC**		Exmouth Jct

Tenders

No.3049	4/11/27
No.3038	6/4/29

Boilers

No.899	4/11/27
No.896	6/4/29
No.888	25/7/31
No.935	18/11/33
N0.882	31/1/36
No.860	29/3/39
No.863	8/3/41
No.841	24/5/43
No.875	11/5/50
No.844	31/3/55
No.1026	21/3/59

Allocations

17/5/25	Exmouth Jct
24/4/43	Reading
25/3/50	Stewarts Lane
17/6/50	Ashford
5/2/51	Redhill
27/7/51	Hither Green
14/6/59	Exmouth Jct

Withdrawn 2/11/63 Cut up at Eastleigh Works w/e 18/1/64

The most cursory comparison will confirm the welcome the new moguls had in the West. The Adams Jubilee 0-4-2 looks positively ancient and certainly puny against the shiny new 1860 on 21 July 1925 at Barnstaple Junction shed. The new locos had taken over the summer timetable only the week before; from thereon the main passenger trains ran Exeter-Ilfracombe rather than Exeter-Torrington (see *The North Devon Line*, Nicholas and Reeve, Irwell Press, 2010). The miracle is that the old Jubilee survived until 1938, indeed some were still at work in 1948! It is sobering to reflect that the Ns in turn were similarly eclipsed twenty years later when the West Country Pacifics arrived. The new engines dwarfed the N in 1945 and outclassed it. By the time Exmouth Junction had a large quota on its books the light Pacifics (apart from summer peaks) had a near monopoly of passenger trains at Ilfracombe where existed the only turntable at the time on the Southern west of Exeter that could turn them.

31860, heading for Ilfracombe, holds up the holidaymakers at Braunton about 1962. ColourRail

31861

To traffic as A861 on 23/6/25
Renumbered 1861 no date; 31861 15/7/48

Works

Ex Woolwich 7/4/25

7/4/25-23/6/25**B**		
11/6/26-16/10/26**A**	30,593	
24/3/28**D**	43,582	
29/11/28-16/2/29**A**	61,089	
2/4/31-9/5/31**A**	60,588	
28/9/32-2/12/32**C**	36,200	
31/7/33-31/8/33**C**	51,096	Extension of mileage 10,000
11/12/34-18/1/35**A**	82,472	
10/7/35-15/8/35**C**	10,828	
28/2/36-7/4/36**C**	22,385	Extension of mileage 5,000
21/8/36-27/8/36**D**	31,033	
5/7/37-28/8/37**C**	47,916	Brighton
8/4/38-13/4/38**C**	60,235	Class plate fitted
24/1/39-1/3/39**A**	75,545	
19/6/41-16/7/41**C**		Bricklayers Arms
28/10/41-26/11/41**D**	61,994	
31/12/42-27/1/43**A**	88,309	
13/6/44-1/7/44**C**	42,931	
19/2/45-16/4/45**B**		Nine Elms
24/5/46-21/6/46**A**	84,424	261 copper and 723 nickel plated stays renewed 228 roof stays renewed 383 holes bushed Set new small tubes 'Talbot and Stead' set new large tubes steel with copper ends
16/4/48-28/4/48	55,420	Guildford 1 copper stay renewed Small and large tubes expanded and referruled
15/6/48-15/7/48**C**	59,236	
13/3/50-6/4/50**A**	107,923	16 copper stays renewed 50 copper riveted over 366 nuts renewed 228 nickel plated roof stays renewed All roof nuts renewed 173 new small tubes 'Tubes Ltd' Firehole 26 rivets caulked
8/8/51-7/9/51**LC**		No Boiler work
20/6/52-10/7/52**HI**	49,040	1 copper stay renewed 50 copper stays riveted over 193 monel metal nuts renewed Internal Tubeplate "20 studs fitted and laps caulked" 173 new small tubes 'Tubes Ltd' 21 large tubes expanded and referruled
2/10/52-17/10/52**LC**	61,327	No Boiler work
2/3/53-13/3/53**LC**	71,033	
25/8/54-11/9/54**GO**	112,133	
14/11/55-8/12/55**LC**	36,813	
4/6/56-21/6/56**LC**	50,595	Hither Green
18/2/57-8/3/57**LI**	71,384	
26/3/58-19/4/58**GO**	102,515	816 copper stays renewed 573 holes bushed Internal Tubeplate new 2 fusible plugs Smokebox Tubeplate levelled Barrel scaled 173 new small tubes 'Stewart and Lloyds' electrically welded Set new large tubes
26/4/60-28/5/60**LI-HI**	54,415	AWS part fitted New type CI firebars 40 copper stays renewed 475 copper riveted over "Flanges caulked 61 flange rivets and 20 corner rivets caulked" 2 fusible plugs 173 new small tubes 'Howells' Firehole 15 rivets caulked Set new large tubes
7/11/60-18/11/60**LC-NC**	63,734	6 copper stays renewed
22/8/61-16/9/61**LC-HC**	84,171	Spark arrester 199 copper stays renewed 257 copper riveted over "Tubeplate flanges and rivets caulked" 173 new small tubes 'Tube products' electrically welded Set new large tubes

Tenders

No.3046	16/2/29
No.3044	8/3/57

Boilers

No.900	16/10/26
No.863	16/2/29
No.843	9/5/31
No.970	18/1/35
No.888	1/3/39
No.997	27/1/43
No.1018	21/6/46
No.1014	6/4/50
No.986	11/9/54
No.960	19/4/58

Allocations

12/7/25	Redhill
6/10/34	Bricklayers Arms
15/6/35	Ashford
25/1/36	Norwood Jct
22/2/36	Hither Green
21/3/36	Stewarts Lane
13/6/36	Bricklayers Arms
24/4/43	Reading
25/3/50	Stewarts Lane
17/6/50	Ashford
5/2/51	Redhill
27/7/51	Hither Green
14/6/59	Redhill

Withdrawn 11/5/63 Cut up at Eastleigh Works w/e 29/6/63

31861 with a down train, a local stopper probably – headcode is for a train to Folkestone and Dover – at Ashford on 11 October 1958. The stock is BR Mk1 set 527 in 'crimson and cream' new in 1955, coaches brake thirds S34645/46 with composite S15569 in the centre. The set moved to the SW division from June 1960. Three SR utility vans and two BR cattle wagons bring up the rear. D.C. Ovenden, ColourRail

31861 at Hither Green, its home from 1951 to 1959, on 2 November 1957. Peter Groom.

31862

To traffic as A862 on 26/5/25
Renumbered 1862 16/2/33; 31862 23/4/48

Works

Ex Woolwich 7/4/25		
7/4/25-26/5/25**B**		
16/6/26		Exmouth Jct Extension of mileage 10,000
17/5/27-22/8/27**A**	53,044	
28/6/28	29,066	
19/1/29-31/1/29		Stewarts Lane
14/12/29-25/1/30**A**	58,757	
30/6/30-5/7/30		New Cross Gate
28/8/30-30/8/30**D**	11,806	
29/1/32-7/4/32**B**	46,361	
13/1/33-16/2/33**A**	63,009	329 copper stays renewed 250 riveted over Copper tubeplate 49 studs fitted Firehole rivets hammered Set new small tubes 'Chesterfield Tube Co' Large tubes expanded and referruled
6/9/34-19/10/34**C**	39,660	Bricklayers Arms Copper stays riveted over "in fire area" Copper Tubeplate "seams and studs caulked" Small tubes expanded and rebeaded large tubes expanded and referruled
6/1/35-19/2/35**C**		Bricklayers Arms 2 copper stays renewed 21 new large tubes steel with copper ends
8/7/36-21/8/36**A** Firehole	76,298	368 copper stays renewed 250 copper riveted over Copper Tubeplate 76 studs fitted rivets hammered Foundation ring 8 rivets renewed Set new small tubes 'Tubes Ltd' Large tubes repaired steel with copper ends
9/5/38-22/6/38**C**	51,082	Bricklayers Arms 1 copper stay renewed
20/4/39-24/5/39**D**	68,832	Brighton
15/8/39-12/9/39**A**	70,729	Class plate fitted
17/11/41-31/12/41**C**	56,226	
9/5/42-17/6/42**C**		Bricklayers Arms extension of mileage 5,000
23/4/43-26/5/43**A**	84,476	
5/5/44-10/6/44**C**	26,051	
31/10/44-25/11/44**B**	35,081	
1/3/45-14/3/45**C**	39,206	
12/5/45-19/5/45**D**	43,042	
27/11/46-21/12/46**A**	76,910	
6/8/47-11/9/47**B**		Bricklayers Arms
12/3/48-23/4/48**D**	25,513	
22/12/49-13/2/50		Bricklayers Arms 173 new small tubes Large tubes expanded and referruled
8/6/50-30/6/50**LC**	72,117	
19/3/51-18/4/51**GO**	97,009	
8/8/52-12/9/52**HI**	45,444	
23/5/53-25/6/53**LC**		Redhill
15/6/54-2/7/54**GO**	103,950	
8/9/55-27/9/55**LC**	44,492	
14/11/56-1/12/56**LI-HI**	81,868	
8/8/57-24/8/57**LC-HC**	106,010	Briquette container fitted
9/5/58-31/5/58**GO**	128,879	Blowdown valve and water treatment 150 copper and 576 monel metal stays renewed 170 copper riveted over 576 nuts renewed 38 roof nuts renewed 2 fusible plugs Smokebox Tubeplate new Barrel scaled 173 new small tubes 'Stewart and Lloyds' electrically welded Firehole 15 rivets caulked Set new large tubes
17/2/60-30/4/60**LI-HI**	64,202	AWS part fitted Front end conversion New type 9mm injectors New type CI firebars 4 copper stays riveted over 235 nuts renewed "40 lap studs fitted flanges and firehole lap caulked 12 flange rivets caulked 2 fusible plugs 32 new small tubes 141 rebeaded 3 new large tubes 18 expanded and referruled Firehole 15 rivets caulked
4/4/61-29/4/61**LC-HC**	99,330	
11/12/61-16/12/61**LC**	120,038	
20/2/62-10/3/62**NC-LC**	121,058	Spark arrester
26/4/63-25/5/63**LI**	164,490	Eastleigh 118 copper and 297 monel metal stays riveted over 2 fusible plugs 36 new small tubes 'Tube products' 32 rebeaded Foundation Ring 28 rivets repaired

Tenders

No.3051	22/8/27
No.3016	15/6/53
No.3030	3/7/54
No.1962	25/5/63
No.3098	17/4/65

Boilers		Allocations	
		14/6/25	Stewarts Lane
No.901	22/8/27	12/8/39	Bricklayers Arms
No.898	25/1/30	20/4/46	Exmouth Jct
No.876	16/2/33	14/6/47	Ashford
No.829	21/8/36	12/7/47	Tonbridge
No.875	12/9/39	31/3/48	Redhill
No.852	26/5/43	27/7/51	Hither Green
No.905	21/12/46	3/3/53	Guildford
No.897	18/4/51	26/5/53	Redhill
No.1029	3/7/54	8/1/65	Guildford
No.1083	31/5/58		

Withdrawn 11/4/65

Left. An N on the move. Not much detail to be gleaned at this distance but it's hard to resist this study of 31862, spied from above the tunnel mouth at Guildford in July 1962. Derek Clayton.

Below. 31862 at Redhill MPD; date not certain but the interest lies in the late appearance of 4,000 gallon tender no.1962 attached in May 1963 in place of the almost universal straight-sided 3,500 gallon type. This broadside reveals (almost) the view of the pony truck wheel that the longer replacement front end frame provides. For comparison see page 137. Collection Richard Vitler.

31863

To traffic as A863 on 16/5/25
Renumbered 1863 22/4/33; 31863 20/5/48

Works

Ex Woolwich 7/4/25		
7/4/25-16/5/25**B**		
30/3/27-22/7/27**A**	52,604	
2/9/27-15/9/27**D**	479	
12/1/28-3/2/28**C**	14,933	
4/10/29-13/11/29**A**	51,498	
24/9/31-7/11/31**B**		Brighton Extension of mileage 15,000
16/2/32-3/3/32**C**		Stewarts Lane
29/4/32-13/5/32**D**	52,711	
20/3/33-22/4/33**A**	74,069	57 copper stays renewed 50 copper riveted over 337 nuts renewed [Test 1403 169 Hadfields heat resisting steel nuts fitted on LH side] Set new small tubes 'Howell and Co' Large tubes expanded and referruled
8/10/34-7/12/34**C**	46,725	Brighton Extension of mileage 5,000 65 copper stays riveted over 373 nuts renewed
17/12/35-29/1/36**A**	76,868	
8/4/38-17/5/38**B**	54,222	Class plate fitted. Extension of mileage 10,000
19/10/38-31/10/38**D**	66,492	
8/9/39-3/10/39**A**	79,696	
17/8/42-23/9/42**A**	76,250	
25/1/44-25/2/44**C**		Bricklayers Arms
15/1/46-14/2/46**A**	83,555	
4/6/47-13/7/47**C**		Bricklayers Arms
1/4/48-20/5/48**B**	57,836	
6/11/48-20/1/49		Norwood Jct
12/12/49-13/1/50**A**	90,977	
8/11/51-14/12/51**LI**	59,105	
3/6/52-20/6/52**LC**	72,779	
10/9/53-3/10/53**HI**	106,991	
26/2/54-13/3/54**LC**	119,809	
26/10/54-6/11/54**NC-LC**	142,558	
23/5/55-17/6/55**GO**	158,249	
28/4/56-21/5/56**LC**	31,727	Redhill
17/5/57-8/6/57**LI-HI**	66,922	Tender no.3047 fitted for briquette carrier
10/2/59-28/2/59**LI**	119,000	New type CI firebars Blowdown valve only
23/1/61-25/2/61**GO**	188,061	AWS 'Overhead live wire notices' 833 copper stays renewed 179 copper riveted over 8 roof nuts renewed Internal Tubeplate new 2 fusible plugs Smokebox tubeplate "levelled bottom flange repaired" Barrel scaled and pitting welded 173 new small tubes 'Tube Products' electrically welded Set new large tubes
11/4/61-22/4/61**NC-LC**	188,126	
13/10/61-14/10/61**NC**		

Tenders

No.3052	22/7/27
No.3057	13/11/29
No.3047	13/3/54

Boilers

No.902	22/7/27
No.895	13/11/29
No.1013	22/4/33
No.864	29/1/36
No.967	3/10/38
No.821	23/9/42
No.830	14/2/46
No.1041	13/1/50
No.886	17/6/55
No.877	25/2/61

Allocations

17/5/25	Stewarts Lane
15/6/35	Hither Green
25/1/36	Norwood Jct
12/9/36	Bricklayers Arms
25/3/44	Redhill
3/3/53	Feltham
26/5/53	Ashford
20/7/53	Redhill

Withdrawn 7/7/63 Cut up at Eastleigh Works w/e 7/3/64

31863, an N for once that was never based in the West, at Guildford on the 12.26pm from Redhill, a Sunday working on 26 July 1959. No latter day modifications as yet.

31863 at Groombridge with mysteriously white-painted lamp irons, 18 September 1961.

31864

To traffic as A864 on 6/1925
Renumbered 1864 and 31864 dates unknown
ERCs not available

Works

27/6/33		34 copper and 1 monel metal stays renewed 75 copper riveted over 156 nuts renewed [Test 1403] "167 heat resisting steel firebox stay nuts fitted right hand side" Firehole rivets hammered Set new small tubes 'British Mannesmann Tube co' Large tubes repaired steel with copper ends
8/12/34		Bricklayers Arms "All small tubes expanded and rebeaded"
8/12/43		556 copper stays renewed 125 copper riveted over 228 roof stays renewed Copper Tubeplate 24 studs fitted Firehole rivets hammered set new small tubes 'Howell and Co' Large tubes repaired steel with copper ends
2/5/45		1 copper stay renewed 300 copper stays riveted over 1 hole bushed Copper Tubeplate 24 stays fitted flanges caulked Set new small tubes 'Tubes Ltd'
19/10/45		300 copper stays riveted over Copper Tubeplate seams and studs caulked Foundation Ring corner rivets caulked
4/2/50		365 copper stays renewed 375 riveted over 24 roof nuts renewed Internal Tubeplate 75 studs fitted 12 caulked Barrel scaled Set new small tubes 'Tubes Ltd' set new large tubes steel with copper ends
14/6/51		350 copper stays riveted over Internal Tubeplate 35 copper studs fitted and 66 caulked Set new small tubes 'Howells' 18 second hand large tubes rebeaded and referruled 3 repaired
15/4/52		53 copper stays renewed 350 copper riveted over 12 roof nuts renewed Internal Tubeplate 12 studs renewed and 50 caulked 6 new small tubes 'Tubes Ltd' 167 rebeaded 21 second hand large tubes expanded and referruled Firehole 15 rivets caulked
22/10/52-7/11/52**GO**		65 copper stays renewed 281 nuts renewed "45 firebox lap rivets caulked" 173 new small tubes 'Stewart and Lloyds' Foundation Ring corner rivets caulked
21/1/54-12/2/54**HI**	42,613	69 steel stays renewed 227 nuts renewed Internal Tubeplate 104 studs fitted in laps 173 new small tubes 'Stewart and Lloyds' 3 new large tubes 18 second hand expanded and referruled Firehole 15 rivets caulked
28/10/54-11/11/54**LC**	73,153	No Boiler work
1/9/55-28/9/55**HI**	97,450	16 copper stays renewed 134 steel stays replaced by copper 150 copper stays riveted over 245 nuts renewed Internal Tubeplate 63 studs fitted in laps, laps welded Foundation Ring 10 corner rivets caulked 173 small tubes "Repaired"
26/2/57-16/3/57**GO**	144,777	317 copper and 615 steel stays renewed 212 holes bushed Internal Tubeplate new barrel scaled 173 new small tubes 'Stewart and Lloyds' electrically welded
7/5/58-20/6/58**LC**		Redhill 173 new small tubes 'New Steel' Large tubes repaired
9/12/58-15/1/59**HI**	56,349	Full frame conversion Manganese steel liners New type 9mm injectors New type CI firebars Blowdown valve gear and water treatment complete 42 copper stays riveted over 132 nuts renewed Internal Tubeplate flanges and 2 corner rivets caulked 2 fusible plugs 32 new small tubes 'Stewart and Lloyds' electrically welded 141 rebeaded 3 new large tubes 18 second hand expanded and referruled Firehole 15 rivets caulked
15/10/59-31/10/59**NC**	87,298	ATC
8/3/60-2/4/60**GO**	92,439	New type CI firebars
6/2/61-24/2/61**LC**	29,913	'Overhead live wire notices'

Tender

No.1897	no date

Boilers

No.1012	27/6/33
No.989	8/12/43
No.875	out 3/1/50
No.910	4/2/50
No.1037	7/11/52
No.1030	16/3/57

Allocations

14/6/25	Redhill
15/6/35	Hither Green
22/2/36	Stewarts Lane
20/6/36	Hither Green
12/9/36	Bricklayers Arms
25/3/44	Redhill
3/3/53	Feltham
26/5/53	Redhill

Withdrawn 1/64

31864 at Reading South shed on 27 May 1950 with large first emblem; the eagle-eyed will spot that the cab lining, for once, scrupulously follows the outline of the cab rather than disappearing into the running plate.

31864 now with small second emblem and conventional cab lining, at Norwood Junction in the 1960s; tender full of the despised 'ovoids'. This was another N not to venture West, though it did spend a couple of months at the Western Section's Feltham MPD in 1953. Front end replacement dates from January 1959. ColourRail

31865

To traffic as A865 on 16/6/25
Renumbered 1865 13/10/31; 31865 30/10/48

Works
Ex Woolwich 21/4/25

Date	Mileage	Notes
21/4/25-16/6/25**B**		
30/12/26-22/4/27**A**	52,138	
2/4/29-11/5/29**A**	63,205	
21/10/30**D**		Brighton
9/9/31-13/10/31**A**	57,266	52 copper and 705 steel stays renewed 450 copper riveted over 6 roof nuts renewed "20 steel stays replaced by copper stays" Copper Tubeplate 15 studs fitted Firehole rivets hammered Set new small tubes 'Howell and Co' "Cut back large with copper ends Plugs 12 threads"
23/6/33-28/7/33**B**	41,753	Extension of mileage 10,000 1 copper stay renewed 68 nuts renewed
23/8/33-29/8/33**C**	42,114	
18/10/33-9/11/33**D**	45,440	138 nuts renewed 14 large tubes expanded and ferrules renewed
7/12/33-26/1/34**D**	46,742	20 copper stays riveted over [174 steel stays replaced by copper]
24/3/34-25/5/34**C**		Bricklayers Arms 90 new small tubes
22/12/34-16/1/35	65,905	Bricklayers Arms 8 copper stays renewed Copper stays riveted over "in fire area" 5 nuts renewed 84 new small tubes above 7th row renewed All expanded and beaded Large tubes expanded and referruled
23/5/35-9/7/35**A**	74,562	
6/5/36-11/6/36**D**	24,095	
23/8/37-21/10/37**B**	53,205	Extension of mileage 5,000
25/10/38-30/11/38**A**	82,483	Class plate fitted
13/2/40-12/3/40**B**	36,493	Extension of mileage 15,000
8/1/42-10/2/42**A**	83,335	
22/5/44-21/6/44**C**	60,659	Extension of mileage 5,000
22/3/45-6/4/45**C**		Eastleigh
29/3/46-4/5/46**A**	104,703	
14/4/47-19/4/47**C**	27,262	
17/8/48-30/10/48**B**	48,641	
4/5/49-2/6/49**LC**	58,174	Bricklayers Arms
25/10/50-17/11/50**GO**	99,369	
25/8/51-25/10/51**HI**	31,279	Redhill
8/1/53-6/2/53**HI**	77,851	
2/3/53-31/3/53	79,672	Redhill
27/1/54-13/2/54**HC**	111,528	
29/6/54-17/7/54**GO**	125,985	
18/7/55-26/8/55	39,677	Redhill
10/1/56-27/1/56**LI**	55,669	
5/3/56-12/3/56**NC**	58,115	
24/8/56-7/9/56**NC-LC**	75,646	
23/10/56-24/10/56**NC**	78,316	
21/1/57-26/1/57**LC**	85,895	
27/2/57-9/3/57**LC**	87,458	
18/11/57-7/12/57**GO**	110,504	Blowdown valve gear and briquette container fitted 20 copper and 580 monel metal stays renewed 705 nuts renewed 2 fusible plugs Smokebox tubeplate renewed 173 new small tubes 'Universal'
2/6/59-13/6/59**LC**	53,524	6 new small tubes 'Stewart and Lloyds' electrically welded 167 rebeaded 3 new large tubes 18 expanded and referruled
9/11/60-3/12/60**LI-HI**	101,505	New type CI firebars AWS part fitted 'Overhead live wire notices' 2 copper stays renewed 209 copper riveted over 201 nuts renewed "21 lap studs fitted flanges firehole lap ½ side seams and 75 flange rivets caulked" 2 fusible plugs 32 new small tubes 'Tube Products' 141 rebeaded 3 new large tubes 18 expanded and referruled Firehole 15 rivets caulked
20/2/61-6/3/61**LC**	109,164	
16/11/61-21/11/61**NC**		Bricklayers Arms
5/3/63-15/3/63**NC**		Bricklayers Arms

Tenders

No.3054	22/4/27
No.1889	30/11/38
No.3035	3/12/60

Boilers

No.904	22/4/27
No.889	11/5/29
No.841	13/10/31
No.960	9/7/35
No.889	30/11/38
No.868	10/2/42
No.908	4/5/46
No.971	17/11/50
No.878	20/8/55
No.1079	7/12/57

Allocations

12/7/25	Bricklayers Arms
14/8/36	Hither Green
12/8/39	Dover
1/7/40	Folkestone
25/3/44	Eastleigh
14/6/47	Hither Green
12/7/47	Bricklayers Arms
4/2/50	Redhill

Withdrawn 25/8/63 Cut up at Eastleigh Works w/e 21/3/64

Left. Early lettering on 31865 at Ashford shed on 29 June 1950; snifting valves still in place. Norman Preedy.

Below. An N in the landscape; 31865 with a Birkenhead-Hastings train near Patcham tunnel, Brighton, on 5 September 1959. B. Wadey, transporttreasury

31866

To traffic as A866 on 28/11/25
Renumbered 1866 3/10/31; 31866 29/1/49

Works

From Woolwich 21/4/25
'Sent to Wembley Exhibition on 22/5/25'

Date	Mileage	Notes
14/11/25-28/11/25**B**		
23/11/26-10/3/27**A**	24,623	
26/4/29-8/6/29**A**	60,711	
4/3/31**D**	48,164	
7/9/31-3/10/31**A**	59,198	
3/1/33-2/2/33**C**	32,727	Extension of mileage 5,000
26/1/34-17/3/34**C**		Brighton Extension of mileage 5,000
12/4/34-26/4/34**D**	51,006	
9/11/34-15/12/34**A**	66,786	18 copper and 328 steel stays renewed 50 copper riveted over 14 nuts renewed [12 steel stays in back corners replaced by copper] Set new small tubes 'Howell and Co' Large tubes repaired steel with copper ends
2/6/36-7/7/36**C**	37,687	Dover "Retubed"
10/11/36-16/12/36**C**	47,735	Extension of mileage 10,000
21/4/38-1/6/38**A**	83,545	Class plate fitted
28/8/39-19/9/39**C**	36,731	Extension of mileage 5,000
8/3/41-2/4/41**A**	75,293	
12/12/41-6/1/42**C**		Bricklayers Arms
14/3/42-21/3/42**D**	18,769	
13/7/42-29/8/42**C**	25,899	
10/8/43-31/8/43**D**	50,928	
20/5/44-21/6/44**C**	64,159	Extension of mileage 5,000
1/1/45-2/6/45**A**	77,593	Brighton
8/7/47-6/8/47**C**	54,688	
10/9/47-17/9/47**D**	54,668	Eastleigh
16/12/48-29/1/49**A**	80,598	30 copper stays renewed and 30 copper riveted over 210 nuts renewed Set new small tubes Set new large tubes steel with copper ends
17/11/50-21/12/50**LI**	47,398	2 copper stays renewed 138 nuts renewed Internal Tubeplate 24 copper studs caulked 2 fusible plugs Set new small tubes 'Tubes Ltd' Foundation Ring corner rivets caulked
1/11/51-23/11/51**HC**	79,504	106 steel stays replaced by copper 130 nuts renewed Smokebox Tubeplate fracture welded
10/10/52-31/10/52**GO**		All copper stays and all roof nuts renewed 202 holes bushed Internal Tubeplate and Smokebox Tubeplate new Barrel cleaned 173 new small tubes 'Tubes Ltd' 21 new large tubes Firehole and Foundation Ring all rivets renewed
16/11/53-5/12/53**LC**		Redhill 173 new small tubes 'Howells'
15/7/54-31/7/54**LI**	58,522	350 copper stays riveted over 32 new small tubes 'Howells' 141 rebeaded 21 new large tubes
15/4/55-13/5/55**LC**		Redhill 2 fusible plugs 173 small tubes repaired
8/11/55-23/11/55**LC**	98,663	No Boiler work
5/6/56-22/6/56**GO**	115,577	1,012 copper stays renewed 228 nickel plated roof stays renewed 444 roof nuts renewed New Firebox 2 fusible plugs Barrel scaled 173 new small tubes 'Stewart and Lloyds' electrically welded Set new large tubes
13/5/57-18/5/57**LC**	32,068	
14/11/57-13/12/57**LC**	46,177	Redhill 173 new small tubes 'New steel'
22/12/58-17/1/59**HI**	77,156	New type CI firebars Blowdown valve gear and water treatment complete 470 copper stays riveted over "Flanges and firehole laps caulked 18 lap studs fitted" 2 fusible plugs 32 new small tubes 'Tube Products' electrically welded 141 rebeaded 3 new large tubes 18 expanded and referruled
1/7/59-8/7/59**LC**	95,654	
27/1/61-3/3/61**GO**	140,283	AWS part fitted 'Overhead live wire notices' 230 copper and 657 monel metal stays renewed 290 copper riveted over 657 nuts renewed 288 holes bushed Internal Tubeplate new 2 fusible plugs Smokebox tubeplate levelled Barrel scaled 173 new small tubes 'Stewart and Lloyds' electrical welded Set new large tubes
13/10/61-18/10/61**LC**	17,465	
8/1/62-9/1/62**NC**		Bricklayers Arms
26/2/62-17/2/62**LC**	34,809	
30/8/62-31/8/62**LC**	49,921	Eastleigh
12/6/63-3/8/63**LI**	75,581	Eastleigh 34 copper and 247 monel metal stays riveted over 247 nuts renewed 2 fusible plugs Foundation Ring 28 rivets repaired 34 new small tubes 'Tube Products' 3 new large tubes
6/2/64-15/2/64**LC**	83,257	Eastleigh
6/4/65-13/4/65**LC**		Eastleigh

Tenders

No.3055	10/3/27
No.3047	3/10/31
No.3057	31/7/54

Boilers

No.905	10/3/27
No.890	8/6/29
No.905	3/10/31
No.1018	15/12/34
No.1017	1/6/38
No.892	2/4/41
No.1019	2/6/45
No.1076	29/1/49
No.895	31/10/52
No.891	22/6/56
No.1066	3/3/61

Allocations

29/11/25	Stewarts Lane
6/10/34	Ashford
3/11/34	Bricklayers Arms
23/2/35	Dover
1/7/40	Folkestone
25/3/44	Eastleigh
13/11/50	Exmouth Jct
11/4/51	Redhill
18/1/65	Guildford

Withdrawn 9/1/66

Left. 31866 at Crowhurst Junction on the SECR main line, going over the LBSC about 1962. We are looking north and the N is heading towards Redhill from Tonbridge, crossing the Oxted to East Grinstead line. Crowhurst North box is in the distance with the spur going off right to join the SER line to the right. RailOnline

Below. 31866 undergoing attention at Ashford works, in less than salubrious surroundings, 18 March 1962; this was during the final throes of locomotive work at Ashford, closure coming a few months later. As A866, the loco (who'd have guessed, looking at it now!) had been exhibited at the 1925 Wembley British Empire Exhibition, in a special finish. Ken Fairey, ColourRail

31867

To traffic as A867 on 26/6/25
Renumbered 1867 10/3/33; 31867 24/12/48

Works

Ex Woolwich 12/5/25

Date	Mileage	Notes
12/5/25-26/6/25		
15/2/27-26/5/27**A**	52,906	
12/4/29-27/4/29**C**	50,691	Extension of mileage 5,000
15/7/29-22/8/29**C**		Stewarts Lane Extension of mileage 10,000
9/12/29-9/1/30		Stewarts Lane
28/6/30-1/8/30**A**	68,520	
3/2/33-10/3/33**A**	59,852	
22/6/34-26/7/34**C**	27,760	Extension of mileage 5,000
2/12/35-23/12/35**C**		Dover
31/12/36-10/2/37**A**	80,568	
11/4/38-30/4/38**C**	34,273	Dover
1/6/39-30/6/39**B**	65,716	Class plate fitted Extension of mileage 15,000
4/4/40-1/5/40**A**	86,021	
17/4/41-24/5/41**C**	31,519	
29/10/41-18/11/41**D**		
12/5/43-15/6/43**A**	64,614	
23/1/46-15/2/46**C**	65,633	Extension of mileage 10,000
5/4/46-17/6/46**C**		Eastleigh
13/12/46-11/1/47**B**	68,580	
2/12/47-6/12/47**D**	83,911	Eastleigh
22/11/48-24/12/48**A**	106,826	
2/8/49-12/8/49**LC**	11,439	Eastleigh
11/5/51-8/6/51**HI**	61,940	
1/9/52-19/9/52**HI**	106,839	
12/1/54-4/2/54**GO**	156,301	
22/2/55-12/3/55**HI-LI**	43,832	
21/3/56-24/4/56	76,246	Redhill
17/4/57-10/5/57**GO**	110,088	275 copper stays renewed 172 nuts renewed 2 fusible plugs Smokebox Tubeplate levelled Barrel scaled 173 new small tubes 'Universal' Set new large tubes Firehole 15 new rivets
30/1/58-22/2/58**LC**	25,530	Redhill 2 fusible plugs 173 new small tubes 'New Steel'
19/3/58-12/4/58**LC**	25,721	
14/7/58-25/7/58**LC**	31,603	Redhill 15 new large tubes
13/2/59-6/3/59**LC**	50,178	6 new small tubes 'Stewart and Lloyds' electrically welded
17/11/60-17/12/60**LI**	107,325	'Overhead live wire notices' AWS part fitted New type CI (cast iron) firebars Water treatment 14 copper stays renewed 285 copper riveted over 92 nuts renewed "5 lap studs fitted Flanges and firehole lap caulked 22 flanges and 20 corner rivets caulked 2 fusible plugs 32 new small tubes 'Tube products' electrically welded 141 rebeaded 3 new large tubes 18 expanded and referulled
22/8/61-9/9/61**LC**	129,952	Spark arrester

Tenders

No.3056	26/5/27
No.3100	15/6/43
No.3006	6/3/59
No.1889	17/12/60
No.3068	22/6/63

Boilers

No.906	26/5/27
No.853	1/8/30
No.894	10/3/33
No.846	10/2/37
No.883	1/5/40
No.967	15/6/43
No.1020	24/12/48
No.848	12/3/55
No.1082	10/5/57

Allocations

12/7/25	Stewarts Lane
6/10/34	Dover
1/7/40	Ashford
26/2/44	Exmouth Jct
4/11/44	Guildford
21/4/45	Eastleigh
13/11/50	Exmouth Jct
11/4/51	Redhill

Withdrawn 7/7/63 Cut up at Eastleigh Works w/e 22/2/64

31867 on a London-Reading train near Coulsdon North in August 1951; most likely the train is the 5.25pm London Bridge to Reading and Tonbridge which divided at Redhill with each part going off separately. Derek Clayton.

31867 at Eastleigh; with no lettering or emblem on the tender the period is presumably about 1949. Note drain from ejector pipe and eccentric arrangement of oil delivery pipes. This was later corrected. John Eyers, South Western Circle.

31868

To traffic as A868 on 3/7/25
Renumbered 1868 7/10/33; 31868 27/11/48

Works

Ex Woolwich 12/5/25		
12/5/25-3/7/25**B**		
18/5/27-20/8/27**A**	65,673	
10/10/29-20/11/29**A**	56,262	300 copper stays renewed 275 riveted over Copper Tubeplate new Copper firehole Plate 41 studs fitted Firehole rivets hammered Set new small tubes 'Howell and Co' Set new large tubes with copper ends Plugs 12 thread
15/7/30-24/7/30**D**	12,382	350 copper stays riveted over Copper Tubeplate seams caulked
23/1/31-25/2/31**C**	19,939	Extension of mileage 7,000 300 copper stays riveted over
27/2/32-9/4/32**C**	42,771	Copper stays riveted over in "bottom rows" Small tubes expanded and rebeaded
28/7/32-1/9/32**C**		Stewarts Lane 120 new small tubes
10/11/32-20/12/32**B**	54,543	Extension of mileage 5,000 10 copper stays renewed 500 copper riveted over Copper Tubeplate 21 studs fitted 26 new small tubes 'Howell and Co'
1/9/33-7/10/33**A**	73,583	
12/6/34-26/6/34**D**	15,849	
19/7/35-23/9/35**C**	47,550	New Cross Gate
3/11/36-14/12/36**A**	72,331	846 copper stays renewed 100 copper riveted over 322 holes bushed Copper Tubeplate new Set new small tubes 'Tubes Ltd' Large tubes repaired steel with copper ends
30/12/36**D**	361	
2/12/38-10/1/39**B**	52,940	Class plate fitted Extension of mileage 10,000
8/9/39-3/10/39**C**	67,808	400 copper stays riveted over
27/2/40-21/3/40**C**	73,493	4 copper stays renewed 400 copper riveted over Set new small tubes 'Howell and Co'
28/11/40-23/12/40**A**	86,294	
22/4/43-14/7/43**C**		Bricklayers Arms Extension of mileage 10,000
13/3/44-20/3/44**C**		Exmouth Jct
30/1/45-7/3/45**A**	95,512	742 copper and 55 steel stays renewed 50 copper riveted over 144 holes bushed Copper Firehole new Set new small tubes 'Talbot and Stead' Set new large tubes steel with copper ends
30/11/46-18/1/47**C**	47,373	
10/4/47-23/4/47**C**		Guildford Set new small tubes 'New Steel' Large tubes re-rolled and referruled
13/12/47-10/2/48		Guildford
27/10/48-27/11/48**A**	79,470	All [1,012] copper stays renewed New Firebox set new small tubes 'Tubes Ltd' Large tubes repaired steel with copper ends
26/4/50-28/4/50		Stewarts Lane
23/1/52-8/2/52**GO**	79,442	
15/7/53-7/8/53**HI**	51,478	
21/10/53-4/11/53**NC**		
4/8/54-1/10/54**LC**	82,199	Brighton
31/5/55-9/7/55**LC**	105,076	Brighton Leading crankpin modified to Drg.A.13093
19/9/55-7/10/55**GO**	111,014	525 copper and 705 monel metal stays renewed 705 nuts renewed 228 nickel plated roof stays renewed 444 roof nuts renewed New Firebox 2 fusible plugs Barrel scaled 173 new small tubes 'Howells'
23/11/56-8/12/56**LC**		34,879 No Boiler work
8/5/57-6/7/57**LI**	48,764	Brighton w/e 12/6/57 waiting for boiler, waiting for tubes Piston rings fitted for L63 R61 84 copper stays riveted over 812 nuts renewed 2 fusible plugs 173 new small tubes 'Stewart and Lloyds' 3 second hand large tubes welded ends
1/8/58-23/8/58**LI-HI**	82,813	New type CI (cast iron) firebars Tender no.3018 Blowdown valve gear and briquette container 85 copper stays riveted over 275 nuts renewed "Flanges and firehole laps caulked 20 lap studs fitted 20 corner rivets caulked" 2 fusible plugs Barrel scaled 173 new small tubes 'Tube products' electrically welded Firehole 15 rivets caulked
15/1/59-24/1/59**LC**	95,074	
8/10/59-31/10/59**LC**	120,240	
6/10/60-23/12/60**GO**	158,634	AWS part fitted Front end conversion New type CI firebars 321 copper and 615 monel metal stays renewed 289 copper riveted over 615 nuts renewed 42 roof nuts renewed 314 holes bushed Internal Tubeplate new 2 fusible plugs Smokebox Tubeplate levelled Barrel front plate scaled 173 new small tubes 'Tube products' electrically welded Set new large tubes
30/3/62-2/4/62**NC**		Bricklayers Arms

Tenders	
No.3057	20/8/27
No.3058	20/11/29
No.3018	14/12/36

Boilers	
No.907	3/7/25
No.829	20/11/29
No.846	7/10/33
No.937	14/12/36
No.832	23/12/40
No.1081	7/3/45
No.831	27/11/48
No.966	8/2/52
No.1085	7/10/55
No.1161	23/12/60

Allocations

12/7/25	Stewarts Lane
24/3/34	Eastleigh on loan
15/6/35	New Cross Gate
5/10/35	Bricklayers Arms
20/6/36	Dover
13/3/37	Bricklayers Arms
12/8/39	Dover
1/7/40	Bricklayers Arms
26/2/44	Exmouth Jct
4/11/44	Guildford
14/6/47	Hither Green
12/7/47	Bricklayers Arms
28/12/47	Reading
25/3/50	Faversham
11/4/51	Redhill

Withdrawn 5/1/64

Left. 31868, a Redhill engine since 1951, at Farnborough North with one of the Reading locals it must have worked thousands of times. John Eyers, South Western Circle.

Below. 31868 leaving Eridge with a train for Lewes and Brighton on 6 May 1961. D.C. Ovenden, ColourRail

31869

To traffic as A869
Renumbered 1869 5/1/33; 31869 6/5/48

Works

Ex Woolwich 12/5/25

Date	Mileage	Notes
12/5/25-11/7/25**B**		
8/3/26-21/4/26**C**		Exmouth Jct Extension of mileage 10,000
26/5/27-27/8/27**A**	56,883	
4/3/29-12/4/29		Stewarts Lane
30/9/29-8/11/29**A**	54,074	
3/2/32-20/4/32**C**	57,051	
24/11/32-5/1/33**A**	71,827	274 copper stays renewed and 225 riveted over Firehole rivets hammered Foundation Ring 17 rivets renewed Set new small tubes 'Howell and Co' Second hand large tubes with copper ends
23/11/34-1/1/35**C**	53,080	Extension of mileage 10,000 6 copper stays renewed 350 copper riveted over 61 new small tubes 'Howell and Co' All other small tubes expanded and rebeaded
13/9/35-23/10/35**A**	69,246	67 copper and 693 steel stays renewed 150 copper riveted over Copper Tubeplate new Firehole rivets hammered Foundation Ring 2 new rivets 173 new small tubes 'Howell and Co' 21 new large tubes steel with copper ends
7/5/36-29/5/36**C**	16,075	
26/8/37**D**		Bricklayers Arms [12 copper stays replaced steel]
26/11/37-14/1/38**C**	51,413	3 copper stays renewed 72 nuts renewed copper wrapping plate 3 stay holes bushed all small tubes expanded and rebeaded
19/2/38-20/4/38**A**	53,174	Class plate fitted
24/4/41-14/5/41**A**	64,218	38 copper and 125 steel stays renewed 278 nuts renewed Copper tubeplate 37 studs fitted Firehole rivets hammered Set new small tubes 'Chesterfield Tube Co' Set new large tubes steel with copper ends "[Tubes rolled with 5 roller expander]"
30/10/43-4/12/43**C**		Norwood Jct
5/10/44-18/11/44**A**	82,755	417 copper stays renewed 150 copper riveted over 216 roof stays renewed Copper Tubeplate 23 studs fitted 2 fusible plugs Firehole rivets hammered Set new small tubes 'Tubes Ltd' Set new large tubes steel with copper ends
14/2/46-9/3/46**C**	41,928	
6/2/47-5/3/47**B**	67,830	Extension of mileage 5,000 Set new small tubes 'Howell and Co' Large tubes expanded and referruled
25/3/48-6/5/48**A**	100,788	31 copper stays renewed 50 copper riveted over 248 nuts renewed Copper Tubeplate 16 studs fitted Set new small tubes 'Howell and Co' Set new large tubes steel with copper ends
31/7/50-8/9/50**HI**	63,634	150 copper stays and 99 nuts renewed 173 new small tubes 'Talbot and Stead' 21 large tubes rebeaded and referruled
27/8/51-7/9/51**LC**		No Boiler work
5/10/51-2/11/51**NC**	93,967	
17/4/52-2/5/52**HC**	107,619	6 new small tubes 'Tubes Ltd'
24/7/52-8/8/52**HC**	117,827	416 copper stays renewed 136 copper riveted over Internal Tubeplate laps welded and 34 rivets renewed Set new small tubes 'Howells' Firehole 15 rivets renewed Set new large tubes
26/8/53-19/9/53**LI**	152,192	450 copper stays riveted over Internal Tubeplate 16 studs fitted and 24 caulked in laps 173 new small tubes 3 new large tubes 18 expanded and referruled
5/8/54-13/9/54**LC**		Redhill
21/6/55-8/7/55**GO**	211,308	
14/5/56-25/5/56**LC**	29,193	
19/9/56-23/10/56	38,513	
1/1/58-15/2/58**HI**	73,570	Full frame conversion Tender no.3052 Briquette container Blowdown valve gear
6/3/58-12/3/58**return**	74,432	
24/2/60-19/3/60**GO**	143,278	New type CI firebars AWS 239 copper and 657 steel stays renewed 290 copper riveted over 705 nuts renewed 421 holes bushed Internal Tubeplate new 2 fusible plugs 173 new small tubes Set new large tubes
22/11/61-29/11/61**LI**	63,312	Spark arrester 236 nuts renewed "Tubeplate flanges and 57 rivets caulked Firehole Plate and door lap and flange sides seams caulked" 2 fusible plugs 32 new small tubes 141 rebeaded 3 new large tubes 18 expanded and referruled

Tenders

No.3058	27/8/27
No.3052	8/11/29

Boilers

No.908	11/7/25
No.894	8/11/29
No.965	5/1/33
No.1032	23/10/35
No.961	20/4/38
No.998	14/5/41
No.831	18/11/44
No.1016	6/5/48
No.858	8/8/52
No.872	8/7/55
No.1069	19/3/60

Allocations

9/8/25	Stewarts Lane
12/8/39	New Cross Gate
25/3/44	Exmouth Jct
11/4/51	Redhill
6/1/64	Guildford

Withdrawn 2/8/64

Left. 31869 running into Guildford station off the Reading line on 6 August 1960, coming south with the main line to Woking just behind the train, New Guildford line coming in at extreme right, line to Ash and Reading in from left; thence on to Redhill. Stock is a Maunsell restriction 1 4-set, much used on these services right up to January 1965 as several of the duties took the stock over the restricted width tunnels either side of Tunbridge Wells Central which meant that they had to be retained in direct contravention to the accountant's '30-year rule'. RailOnline

Below. At the Guildford coal stage in 1964, after its late transfer to the MPD here – hence the absent shed plate. A. Scarsbrook, Initial Photographics.

31870

To traffic as A870 on 28/7/25
Renumbered 1870 18/2/33; 31870 17/3/50

Works

Ex Woolwich 12/6/25

12/6/25-28/7/25**B**		
18/9/26-19/1/27**A**	41,544	
4/7/28-3/8/28**B**	40,330	Extension of mileage 10,000
7/8/29-4/9/29**C**	66,739	Extension of mileage 5,000
12/3/30-12/4/30**A**	79,658	
18/2/32-20/4/32**B**	44,387	
16/9/32-23/9/32**D**		Brighton
23/12/32-18/2/33**A**	55,097	
18/7/34-3/9/34**B**	39,532	Extension of mileage 10,000
15/3/35-12/4/35**D**	55,386	
5/11/35-30/11/35**C**	68,320	
4/9/36-16/10/36**A**	80,456	
20/3/39-18/4/39**B**	62,273	Class plate fitted Extension of mileage 20,000
18/6/40-29/7/40**A**	89,402	
27/2/42-4/4/42**C**		Guildford
15/1/43-3/2/43**B**	61,182	Extension of mileage 15,000
9/12/43-26/1/44**C**	80,681	Extension of mileage 15,000
24/5/45-23/6/45**A**	112,419	
29/8/47-29/9/47**C**	54,653	
12/11/47-4/1/48**C**		Eastleigh shed
19/5/48-22/5/48**D**	63,426	Eastleigh
3/8/48-7/8/48**D**	65,863	Eastleigh
21/2/50-17/3/50**A**	109,469	187 copper stays renewed 300 copper riveted over Smokebox tubeplate levelled Barrel scaled Set new small tubes Set large tubes with copper ends
29/7/52-29/8/52**HI**	108,949	Copper stays riveted over "in fire area" 14 roof nuts renewed Internal Tubeplate 119 studs fitted in laps 173 new small tubes 'Tubes Ltd' 21 large tubes expanded and referruled
26/5/54-17/6/54**GO**	163,267	405 copper and 525 steel stays renewed 525 nuts renewed 64 roof nuts renewed 23 holes bushed Internal Tubeplate and Smokebox Tubeplate new 173 new small tubes 'Howells' Foundation Ring 48 new rivets
7/9/55-23/9/55**LI-HI**	37,849	260 copper stays riveted over 6 nuts renewed Internal Tubeplate 4 laps and 46 studs caulked 173 new small tubes 'Stewart and Lloyds' electrically welded Set new large tubes Foundation Ring 26 rivets caulked
28/8/57-14/9/57**GO**	90,278	661 copper stays renewed 569 nuts renewed 44 holes bushed Internal Tubeplate new 2 fusible plugs Smokebox Tubeplate levelled 173 new small tubes 'Tube Products' electrically welded Set new large tubes
25/5/59-26/6/59**LC**		Bricklayers Arms 173 new small tubes 'New steel
19/11/59-19/12/59**LI-GO**	66,291	New type CI (cast iron) firebars 234 copper and 705 monel metal stays renewed 80 copper riveted over 705 nuts renewed 546 holes bushed Internal Tubeplate new 2 fusible plugs Smokebox tubeplate levelled Barrel scaled 173 new small tubes 'Stewart and Lloyds' electrically welded Set new large tubes
6/1/60-28/1/60**return**	66,291	
27/9/60-14/10/60**NC-LC**	21,334	
7/1/62-8/1/62**NC**		Bricklayers Arms 32 repaired small tubes 141 rebeaded 3 new large tubes 18 expanded and referruled Firehole 15 rivets caulked
30/4/62-26/5/62**LI**	79,062	AWS complete Water treatment 160 nuts renewed "Tubeplate firehole plate and doors lapped " 2 fusible plugs

Tenders

No.3059	19/1/27
No.3072	13/7/63

Boilers

No.909	19/1/27
No.907	12/4/30
No.868	18/2/33
No.877	16/10/36
No.991	29/7/40
No.890	23/6/45
No.877	17/3/50
No.1028	17/6/54
No.1037	14/9/57
No.1043	19/12/59

Allocations

9/8/25	Stewarts Lane
3/11/34	Dover
23/2/35	Hither Green
2/11/35	Bricklayers Arms
12/8/39	New Cross Gate
25/3/44	Exmouth Jct
21/4/45	Eastleigh
4/9/48	Fratton
12/11/50	Plymouth Friary
5/2/51	Fratton
8/10/51	Bricklayers Arms
14/6/59	Redhill

Withdrawn 5/4/64

A poor old neglected 31870 at Reading South MPD on 23 April 1961, still three years from withdrawal.

31870 was widely travelled, and at times could be found in every corner of Kent as well as Cornwall. Like many it finished its days at Redhill where we find it parked 'out the back' about 1963. This is one that got a mechanical lubricator and also an ad hoc piping running from the steam take-off (from the boiler to the manifold in the cab) along the boiler more or less above the hand rail. It was possibly a steam feed for the mechanical lubricator atomiser. The said mechanical lubricator served the valves and pistons. Richard Vitler Collection.

31871

To traffic as A871 on 31/7/25
Renumbered 1871 4/9/31; 31871 11/6/48

Works

Ex Woolwich 12/6/25		
12/6/25-31/7/25**B**		
6/1/27-8/4/27**A**	39,595	
12/9/28-19/9/28**D**	44,973	
20/10/28-26/10/28**D**	47,265	
20/3/29**D**		
8/4/29-17/5/29**A**	57,670	
31/7/31-4/9/31**A**	61,461	
3/5/33-21/6/33**B**	43,745	Extension of mileage 5,000
11/1/34-1/3/34**C**	58,538	
23/11/34-22/1/35**A**	78,425	198 copper and 336 steel stays renewed 100 copper riveted over 48 nuts renewed [12 steel stays in back corners replaced by copper] Copper Tubeplate 8 studs fitted Firehole rivets hammered 173 new small tubes 'Tubes Ltd' Large tubes repaired steel with copper ends
8/11/35-30/11/35**D**	28,003	Brighton 4 roof stays renewed
13/12/36-20/2/37**C**	57,335	Bricklayers Arms Extension of mileage 5,000 12 new small tubes
11/1/38-22/2/38**A**	79,114	
6/9/38-12/9/38**C**	16,030	Class plate fitted
3/10/39-25/10/39**C**	40,621	Extension of mileage 5,000
9/6/41-2/7/41**A**	82,252	
10/9/42-28/11/42**C**		Stewarts Lane
1/6/45-4/7/45**A**	107,507	435 copper stays renewed and 175 riveted over Copper Tubeplate 74 studs fitted 2 fusible plugs Firehole rivets hammered Set new small tubes 'Tubes Ltd' Large tubes repaired steel with copper tubes
29/1/48-3/3/48**A**	83,914	
3/6/48-11/6/48**D**	3,598	
20/2/51-15/3/51**HI**	66,752	Copper stays riveted over "in fire area" Internal Tubeplate 4 laps caulked 2 fusible plugs Set new small tubes 'Howells' large tubes 3 repaired steel with copper ends
5/4/51**NC**	66,752	Eastleigh Weighing only
10/3/53-27/3/53**GO**	124,726	
15/11/54-2/12/54**LI-HI**	49,974	
7/11/56-24/11/56**GO**	106,696	269 copper stays renewed 23 holes bushed Internal Tubeplate new 2 fusible plugs barrel ring caulked, scaled 173 new small tubes 'Stewart and Lloyds' electrically welded Firehole 15 rivets caulked Foundation Ring 40 new rivets Set new large tubes
28/8/58-19/9/58**LI**	48,562	Blowdown valve gear and water treatment fitted complete CI (cast iron) firebars fitted copper stay renewed 450 copper stays riveted over Internal Tubeplate "14 lap studs fitted flanges caulked 46 flanges and 20 corner rivets caulked 2 fusible plugs" 3 mud door holes welded 173 new small tubes 'Tube products' electrical welded 3 new large tubes 18 expanded and rerulled
17/11/58-22/11/58**LC**	51,297	
1/3/61-25/3/61**GO**	126,795	AWS part fitted 'Overhead live wire notices' New type CI firebars Full frame conversion Manganese liners 260 copper and 621 steel stays renewed 340 copper riveted over 621 nuts renewed 159 holes bushed Internal Tubeplate new 2 fusible plugs Smokebox Tubeplate new Barrel scaled 173 new small tubes 'Tube Products' electrical welded Set new small tubes
6/4/62-9/4/62**NC**		

Tenders

No.3060	8/4/27
No.3029	17/5/29
No.3043	22/2/38
No.3006	25/3/61

Boilers

No.910	8/4/27
No.997	17/5/29
No.885	4/9/31
No.998	22/1/35
No.871	22/2/38
No.873	2/7/41
No.829	4/7/45
No.854	3/3/48
No.1167	27/3/53
No.895	24/11/56
No.969	25/3/61

Allocations

9/8/25	Bricklayers Arms
25/3/44	Exmouth Jct
31/5/48	Plymouth Friary
8/1/49	Exmouth Jct
12/11/49	Plymouth Friary
5/2/51	Fratton
8/10/51	Bricklayers Arms
14/6/59	Redhill

Withdrawn 7/12/63 Cut up at Eastleigh Works w/e 1/2/64

31871 runs a freight through Ashford on 18 August 1959. The train is coming eastwards up from Folkestone or Dover to Victoria or Holborn Viaduct (or a yard short thereof) via Tonbridge and Orpington/the Chislehurst loop. Part of Ashford Works visible in background, Hastings line going off right. D.C. Ovenden, ColourRail

31871 at Tonbridge on 8 July 1961, at the down platform; the train looks to be from Redhill or shunting back out to the carriage sidings. Less likely, it is a shunt move as there is no tail lamp. The headcode indicates Tonbridge to Brighton via Eridge so possibly it is coming in from the sidings. The stock is one of the Maunsell restriction 1 4-sets. D.C. Ovenden, ColourRail

31872

To traffic as A872 on 10/8/25
Renumbered 1872 20/8/32; 31872 12/7/49

Works

Ex-Woolwich 16/7/25

16/7/25-10/8/25**B**		
28/11/25-7/12/25**D**		
7/4/26-9/4/26**D**		
23/2/27-20/5/27**A**	41,027	
13/5/29-22/6/29**A**	59,928	
11/2/31		Bricklayers Arms 14 steel stays renewed
3/7/31-28/8/31**B**	50,771	Extension of mileage 10,000 1 steel stay and 1 nut renewed All small tubes expanded and rebeaded
23/5/32		Bricklayers Arms Renewal of 26 steel stays
14/7/32-20/8/32**A**	71,835	
10/3/34-7/4/34**C**		Bricklayers Arms Extension of mileage 10,000
13/9/34-1/11/34**C**	58,180	
13/8/35-20/9/35**A**	78,347	
8/4/36-6/5/36**C**	16,005	
11/2/37-19/3/37**C**	37,664	
10/5/37**D**		Bricklayers Arms 8 stays renewed
10/9/37**D**		Bricklayers Arms 4 stays renewed
7/12/37-18/1/38**C**	52,664	Bricklayers Arms
22/11/38-3/1/39**A**	72,999	188 copper and 129 nickel stays renewed 60 copper riveted over 84 nuts renewed [164 steel stays replaced by copper] 216 roof stays renewed Copper Tubeplate new Set new small tubes 'Chesterfield Tube Co' large tubes repaired steel with copper ends [5 roller expanders]
12/2/42-28/2/42		Brighton Extension of mileage 10,000
12/4/42-22/5/42**C**		Stewarts Lane Extension of mileage 10,000 Copper stays riveted over "in fire area" [Fracture between 2 stays R H side firebox drawn together] Small tubes second hand and pieced All large tubes expanded and referruled
23/8/43-22/9/43**A**	95,604	
17/6/46-13/7/46**A**	74,221	47 copper and 95 steel stays renewed 50 copper riveted over 180 nuts renewed Copper Tubeplate 20 studs fitted Firehole 11 new rivets Set new small tubes 'Talbot and Stead' Large tubes repaired steel with copper ends
12/11/47-17/12/47**C**		Salisbury
2/6/49-12/7/49**A**	77,545	
24/10/51-16/11/51**HI**	70,691	
23/10/52-14/11/52**HI**	96,457	
21/10/53-10/11/53		Bricklayers Arms
6/4/54-30/4/54**GO**	131,981	525 copper and 705 steel stays renewed 705 nuts renewed 444 holes bushed New Firebox Smokebox Tubeplate new Barrel scaled 173 new small tubes 'Howells' set new large tubes
12/7/55-4/8/55		Bricklayers Arms 173 small tubes repaired
18/1/56-4/2/56**LI**	50,741	62 copper stays riveted over 239 nuts renewed 2 fusible plugs Foundation Ring 24 copper rivets caulked 32 new small tubes 141 rebeaded 3 new large tubes 18 expanded and referruled
7/6/56-20/6/56**LC**	58,796	No Boiler work
13/8/57-31/8/57**LI-HI**	89,328	106 copper stays riveted over 175 nuts renewed "36 studs fitted flanges in fire area caulked 20 corner rivets caulked" 3 mud hole door holes welded 173 new small tubes 'Universal'
5/2/59-28/2/59**GO**	126,486	New type CI (cast iron) firebars Blowdown valve and water treatment complete 733 copper stays renewed 440 copper riveted over "72 lap studs fitted Tube and back plate flanges to weld 5 corner rivets caulked" 2 fusible plugs Smokebox Tubeplate levelled 1 mud door hole welded Barrel scaled 173 new small tubes 'Tube Products' electrical welded Firehole 15 new rivets
22/3/61-15/4/61**LI**	72,157	AWS part fitted 453 copper stays riveted over Internal Tubeplate 58 studs fitted seams caulked 2 fusible plugs 32 new small tubes 'Tube Products' electrical welded 141 rebeaded 3 new large tubes 18 expanded and referruled Firehole 15 rivets caulked
7/2/62-8/2/62		Bricklayers Arms

Tenders

No.3061	20/5/27

Boilers

No.911	20/5/27
No.988	22/6/29
No.892	20/8/32
No.976	20/9/35
No.1028	3/1/39
No.974	22/9/43
No.996	13/7/46
No.832	12/7/49
No.1081	30/4/54
No.1060	28/2/59

Allocations

6/9/25	Bricklayers Arms
25/3/44	Salisbury
27/6/51	Bricklayers Arms
14/6/59	Redhill

Withdrawn 1/6/63 Cut up at Eastleigh Works w/e 10/8/63

Left. 31872 trundles a couple of vans during a day out in the Garden of England before a return home to Bricklayers Arms, 9 July 1952. Tender still blank.

Below. In a pretty picture, 31872 leaves Betchworth in May 1963; it had been at Redhill since 1959.

31873

To traffic as A873 on 16/9/25
Renumbered 1873 7/4/33; 31873 14/5/48

Works
Ex Woolwich 14/7/25

14/7/25-16/9/25		
12/12/27-23/12/27**A**	59,845	
28/4/28-25/5/28**C**	9,810	
15/8/28-1/9/28**D**	16,517	
7/8/29-21/8/29**C**	41,093	
23/5/30-28/6/30**A**	75,390	
25/2/31-16/4/31**C**		Brighton
12/6/32		Bricklayers Arms Renewal of stays
16/9/32-12/10/32**B**	50,270	Extension of mileage 10,000
11/1/33		Bricklayers Arms Stays
4/3/33-7/4/33**A**	64,228	92 copper and 833 steel stays renewed 175 copper riveted over 2 roof nuts renewed Firehole rivets hammered Set new small tubes 'Howell and Co' Large tubes repaired steel with copper ends
11/4/35-18/5/35**C**	55,806	Extension of mileage 10,000 4 copper stays renewed 50 copper riveted over 147 nuts renewed
21/7/35-23/8/35**C**		Bricklayers Arms "148 small tubes renewed. Set of Superheaters renewed at B' Arms"
1/5/36-17/6/36**A**	75,104	
3/3/39-12/4/39**A**	67,413	Class plate fitted
23/10/41-4/2/42		Brighton
1/2/44-26/2/44**A**	109,808	382 copper and 431 steel stays renewed 228 roof stays renewed 457 holes bushed Copper Tubeplate new Barrel cleaned [Boiler repaired at Brighton] Set new small tubes 'Howell and Co' Large tubes repaired steel with copper ends
10/11/45-7/1/46**C**		Salisbury
31/8/46-19/9/46**C**	53,789	
5/4/48-14/5/48**A**	91,236	525 copper and 705 nickel plated stays renewed 191 holes bushed New Firebox Set new small tubes 'Tubes Ltd' Set new large tubes steel with copper ends
17/5/50-15/6/50**LI**	53,689	24 nuts renewed 32 new small tubes 'Howells' 141 rebeaded
23/6/52-11/7/52**LI**	110,515	50 copper stays riveted over 229 nuts renewed Internal Tubeplate laps and 30 rivets caulked 173 new small tubes 'Howells' 6 new large tubes 15 expanded and referulled
20/4/54-29/5/54**GO**	157,749	All copper stays renewed 14 holes bushed Internal Tubeplate new All tubes renewed
16/1/56-3/2/56**LI**	49,598	405 copper stays riveted over 2 fusible plugs 173 new small tubes 3 new large tubes 18 expanded and referulled
8/1/58-25/1/58**LI-HI**	100,530	11 copper stays renewed 448 copper riveted over "24 flanges and 20 corner rivets caulked flanges caulked and 36 studs fitted" 2 fusible plugs 173 new small tubes 'Stewart and Lloyds' electrically welded
16/9/58-19/9/58**NC**	121,192	Blowdown valve gear and water treatment fitted complete
31/7/59-12/9/59**GO**	145,459	ATC CI firebars 525 copper and 705 steel stays renewed 705 nuts renewed 109 holes bushed Internal Tubeplate new 2 fusible plugs Barrel scaled
26/1/60-10/2/60**return**	8,197	
18/10/61-19/10/61**NC**		Bricklayers Arms
18/12/62-19/1/63**LI**	73,375	Eastleigh 247 monel metal stays riveted over 247 nuts renewed 2 fusible plugs 30 new small tubes 'Stewart and Lloyds' 21 large tubes referulled

Tenders

No.3062	23/12/27
No.3028	12/4/39
No.3062	11/7/52

Boilers

No.912	23/12/27
No.976	28/6/30
No.985	7/4/33
No.1042	17/6/36
No.959	12/4/39
No.1044	26/2/44
No.998	14/5/48
No.865	29/5/54
No.975	12/9/59

Allocations

4/10/25	Bricklayers Arms
15/6/35	Ashford
2/11/35	Bricklayers Arms
10/11/38	Hither Green
30/1/39	Bricklayers Arms
25/3/44	Salisbury
27/6/51	Bricklayers Arms
30/6/62	Brighton
6/1/64	Redhill
18/1/65	Guildford

Withdrawn 23/1/66

31873, at Eastleigh with first BR lettering in a 'sunshine' version in 1948.

31873 at Hither Green MPD on 23 April 1956; small first emblem on tender. transporttreasury

31874

To traffic as A874 on 9/1925
Renumbered 1874, 31874 no dates

Works

29/4/44		390 copper stays renewed 100 copper riveted over Copper Tubeplate 117 studs fitted
firehole		13 new rivets Set new small tubes 'Howell and Co' Large tubes expanded and referruled
28/3/47		Set new small tubes 'Tubes Ltd' large tubes expanded and referruled
12/6/50		No Boiler work
3/4/52		268 nuts renewed 173 new small tubes 'Tubes Ltd' 6 large tubes repaired 18 second hand expanded and referruled Firehole 11 rivets caulked
31/7/53**GO**		136 copper and 501 monel metal stays renewed 82nuts renewed 305 holes bushed "Firehole plate laps welded" Barrel scaled 173 new small tubes 'Tubes Ltd' Firehole 10 new rivets Set new large tubes
18/2/55-10/3/55**LI-HI**	44,339	3 copper stays renewed 218 nuts renewed 2 fusible plugs 173 new small tubes 'Universal' Firehole 17 rivets caulked Set new large tubes
25/4/57-25/5/57**GO**	102,046	Front end conversion New type injectors fitted to Drg.A.10317 1,012 copper stays renewed 228 roof stays and 444 roof nuts renewed New Firebox 2 fusible plugs "Pitting on Barrel welded" Barrel scaled Firehole new rivets 173 new small tubes 'Universal' Set new large tubes
9/6/58-27/6/58**LC**	29,184	173 new small tubes 'Stewart and Lloyds' electrically welded 3 large tubes repaired 18 second hand expanded and referruled
20/5/59-6/6/59**LI-HI**	54,126	New type CI (cast iron) firebars Blowdown valve gear and water treatment 202 copper stays riveted over Internal Tubeplate 18 flange rivets caulked Firehole lap and flanges caulked 2 fusible plugs 173 new small tubes 'Stewart and Lloyds' electrically welded Firehole 15 rivets caulked Set new large tubes
3/10/61-28/10/61**GO**	115,465	AWS complete spark arrester 234 copper stays renewed 450 copper riveted over "Tubeplate flanges welded and 6 studs fitted Firehole plate and half side laps and 142 rivets caulked" 2 fusible plugs 2 mud door holes welded Barrel scaled 173 new small tubes 'Tube Products' electrically welded Set new large tubes Firehole 15 rivets caulked Foundation Ring 98 new rivets

Tenders
No.3063 no date
No.3011 no date

Boilers
No.936 29/4/44

No.976 in	12/6/50
No.1064	12/9/53
No.887	25/5/57
No.855	28/10/61

Allocations

4/10/25	Bricklayers Arms
10/11/38	Hither Green
30/1/39	Bricklayers Arms
26/2/44	Salisbury
7/10/44	Guildford
21/4/45	Eastleigh
28/12/47	Exmouth Jct
31/5/48	Plymouth Friary
4/9/48	Exmouth Jct
8/12/50	Salisbury
27/6/51	Hither Green
22/7/51	Bricklayers Arms
10/2/61	Exmouth Jct

Withdrawn 3/64 Engine preserved

If ever an illustration serves to indicate the wartime neglect of cleaning this is surely it, in the form of 1874 at Eastleigh early in 1947. There is a date recorded (28/3/47) for a *Set new small tubes 'Tubes Ltd' large tubes expanded and referruled* and presumably 1847 would have emerged from that looking a bit more respectable. How gratifying that it should end up preserved, the only N. It is quite a story and even more of a 'Phoenix from the Ashes' saga than most. Donate now to the Swanage Moguls Fund! John Eyers, South Western Circle.

31874 looking much brighter, in its second spell as an Exmouth Junction loco, probably not long after its General of 1961 when it also got AWS. It had new frames and a BR chimney from May 1957. ColourRail

31875

To traffic as A875 on 28/8/25
Renumbered 1875 30/12/33; 31875 27/5/49

Works

Ex Woolwich 14/7/25		
14/7/25-28/8/25		
26/1/28-4/4/28**A**	66,777	
11/4/28-28/4/28**D**		
9/8/28-16/8/28**D**	14,285	
28/2/29-16/3/29**C**	25,937	
16/1/31-21/2/31**A**	75,124	
9/6/32-14/7/32**D**	27,568	Extension of mileage 5,000
29/11/33-30/12/33**A**	59,172	109 copper and 801 steel stays renewed 150 copper riveted over [32 steel stays replaced by copper] Copper Tubeplate 15 studs fitted firehole rivets hammered Set new small tubes 'Tubes Ltd' Large tubes repaired steel with copper ends
20/12/35-31/1/36**B**	57,909	Extension of mileage 15,000 4 copper stays renewed 100 copper riveted over 73 nuts renewed Set new small tubes 'Talbot and Stead' Large tubes expanded and referulled
4/5/36-12/6/36**C**	62,010	Extension of mileage 5,000
22/7/37-3/9/37**A**	87,293	918 copper stays renewed 135 copper riveted over [All steel stays replaced by copper] 204 roof stays renewed 2 holes bushed Copper Tubeplate new Set new small tubes 'Talbot and Stead' set new large tubes steel with copper ends
10/5/37**D**		Bricklayers Arms 3 copper stays renewed [replacing steel]
12/6/40-13/7/40**A**	70,337	Class plate fitted
9/4/42-8/5/42**B**	44,616	Extension of mileage 10,000
29/12/43-26/1/44**A**	89,455	
23/6/45**D**	41,767	
20/9/45-19/10/45**C**		Bricklayers Arms
31/12/46-25/1/47**A**	79,933	
12/4/49-27/5/49**LI**	70,374	
29/8/50-22/9/50**GO**	102,459	
7/2/52-4/4/52**HI**	52,642	
2/10/53-24/10/53**HI**	94,303	
6/12/54-24/12/54**GO**	129,678	27 copper and 708 nickel plates stays renewed 708 nuts renewed "23 studs fitted in laps" Barrel scaled 173 new small tubes 'Talbot and Stead' Firehole 11 rivets caulked Set new large tubes
18/5/56-23/6/56	42,732	Bricklayers Arms 173 new small tubes 'Stewart and Lloyds' electrically welded
19/3/57-6/4/57**LI**	66,692	1 copper stays renewed 100 copper stays riveted over 219 nuts renewed 2 fusible plugs 32 new small tubes 'Universal' 141 rebeaded 3 new large tubes 18 expanded and referulled Firehole 15 rivets caulked Foundation Ring 12 corner rivets caulked
9/4/58-21/5/58	27,831	Bricklayers Arms 173 new small tubes Set new large tubes
28/8/58-13/9/58**LC**	103,852	
12/2/60-5/3/60**GO**	137,836	New type CI (cast iron) firebars Water treatment 720 copper stays renewed 228 copper riveted over "48 lap studs fitted Firehole lap welded Flanges caulked in fire area 20 flange and 20 corner rivets caulked" 2 fusible plugs Smokebox Tubeplate levelled Barrel scaled 173 new small tubes 'Stewart and Lloyds' electrically welded Set new large tubes Firehole 15 new rivets Foundation Ring 99 new rivets
27/2/62-24/3/62**LC**	59,055	AWS complete [less batteries] spark arrester 2 copper stays renewed 401 copper riveted over "Door lap and flanges caulked 44 flange rivets caulked" 2 fusible plugs 32 new small tubes 141 rebeaded 3 new large tubes 18 expanded and referulled Firehole 15 rivets caulked

Tenders

No.3016	4/4/28
No.3064	28/4/28
No.3014	27/5/49

Boilers

No.914	4/4/28
No.859	21/2/31
No.987	30/12/33
No.972	3/9/37
No.897	13/7/40
No.1010	26/1/44
No.971	25/1/47
No.844	22/9/50
No.963	24/12/54
No.1044	5/3/60

Allocations

6/9/25	Stewarts Lane
20/6/36	Bricklayers Arms
10/11/38	Hither Green
30/1/39	Bricklayers Arms
25/3/44	Eastleigh
21/4/45	Bricklayers Arms
20/4/46	Exmouth Jct
31/5/48	Plymouth Friary
4/9/48	Exmouth Jct
8/12/50	Salisbury
27/6/51	Hither Green
22/7/51	Bricklayers Arms
10/2/61	Exmouth Jct

Withdrawn 5/9/64. Sold to J. Cashmore, Newport 29/9/64

31875, another N eliminated in the 'wholesale dieselisation' of September 1964, at Okehampton station about June 1960. The two locos (the far one is a T9 4-4-0) are standing in the up platform, at the down end of the station. The T9 is probably between duties and acting as station pilot, a circumstance which was common around this time. The N is off a Plymouth-Exeter train (already taken forward) and is probably going to set back after the T9 has finished its work to take charge of the goods train standing in the military sidings.

31875 has a peculiar pale look to it at Okehampton shed; this condition could only result, presumably, from fine ash being shovelled off the cab, billowing in the wind and coating wet/oily surfaces. The loco carries the new WR Exmouth Junction 83D, dating from September 1963. A. Scarsbrook, Initial Photographics.

N1
31822

To traffic as 822 on 24/3/23
Renumbered 1822 24/10/31; 31822 11/3/49

Works

13/8/23-7/9/23**L**	13,192	
27/2/24-12/3/24**C**		
1/12/24-4/12/24**D**		
30/3/25-23/6/25**A**	47,826	
8/9/26**D**		
15/12/26-27/1/27**C**	31,711	
18/2/27**D**		
30/3/27-13/4/27**D**	33,679	
15/12/27-8/12/28**A**	47,015	
5/11/29-6/11/29**D**	21,936	
4/3/30-28/3/30**D**	27,188	
16/12/30-17/12/30**D**	44,088	
9/6/31-12/6/31**D**	50,770	
18/8/31-24/10/31**A**	54,127	307 copper stays renewed and 175 riveted over Set new small tubes 'Chesterfield Tube Co'
3/5/33**D**	38,949	
1/6/33-4/8/33**C**		Bricklayers Arms Extension of mileage 5,000 Stays hammered up
10/5/34-30/6/34**A**	58,167	
14/9/34-9/10/34**D**	5,514	
7/10/35-29/10/35**D**	32,423	
5/6/36-30/7/36**B**	48,731	
18/8/36-21/8/36**D**	50,336	Extension of mileage 15,000
12/1/37-15/3/37**C**	60,068	
5/10/37-11/11/37**A**	76,890	206 copper stays and 170 nuts renewed Copper Firehole 11 steel stays replaced by copper. Set new small tubes 'Chesterfield Tube Co'
3/8/39**D**		
14/9/39-4/10/39**C**	46,181	Class plate fitted Extension of mileage 15,000 350 copper stays riveted over 5 new small tubes all others expanded
27/3/40-18/4/40**C**	57,474	300 copper stays riveted over 146 new small tubes 'Howell and Co'
24/5/40-29/5/40**D**	60,124	
16/7/41-20/8/41**A**	84,091	
18/11/41-15/1/42**C**	3,705	
16/5/43-17/5/43**D**		Bricklayers Arms
17/9/43-27/10/43**C**	46,942	
25/1/44-1/4/44**C**	52,062	
17/10/44-16/11/44		Brighton Extension of mileage 30,000
22/5/46-15/6/46**A**	101,628	
30/5/47**D**		Hither Green
12/2/49-11/3/49**HI**	77,609	
10/1/51-21/2/51**GO**	84,949	
28/2/51-1/3/51**Defect**		
23/2/52**NC**	26,620	Hither Green
9/4/53-1/5/53**HI**		
18/1/55-11/2/55**GO**	107,092	553 copper stays renewed and 250 riveted over 173 new small tubes 'Howells' Firehole 15 rivets caulked
25/5/56-16/6/56**LI-HI**	38,713	389 copper stays riveted over 2 fusible plugs 173 new small tubes 'Stewart and Lloyds' electrically welded
5/12/57-3/1/58**HI**	84,863	557 copper stays riveted over 2 fusible plugs173 new small tubes 'Universal' 3 new large tubes 18 second hand
16/9/58-27/9/58**LC**	106,436	280 copper stays riveted over 173 new small tubes 'Tube Products' 11 second hand large tubes
19/1/59-30/1/59**NC-LC**	114,862	
23/2/60-19/3/60**GO**	137,814	New type CI firebars 705 monel metal stays and 705 nuts renewed New firebox 173 new small tubes 'Stewarts and Lloyds' electrically welded
14/3/62-7/4/62**LC-LI**	54,881	AWS complete [minus batteries] Crown cleaned scales descaled 173 new small tubes 'Tube Products'

Tenders
No.3100 from new
No.3047 8/12/28
No.3055 24/10/31

Boilers

No.848	23/6/25
No.936	24/10/31
No.961	30/6/34
No.990	11/11/37
No.1019	20/8/41
No.1000	15/6/46
No.989	21/2/51
No.893	11/2/55
No.1018	19/3/60

Allocations

3/19/23 Bricklayers Arms
3/11/34 New Cross Gate
28/12/35 Tonbridge
21/4/45 Bricklayers Arm
14/7/45 Hither Green
15/6/46 Tonbridge
21/2/48 St Leonards
5/8/50 Hither Green
14/6/59 Tonbridge
30/6/62 Stewarts Lane

Withdrawn 17/11/62 Sold 7/3/64

Left. The first N1, A822 taken off the N production line and made into a three cylinder N1, then converted to match the 'production' engines 876-880. As 31822 and a Tonbridge engine, it is still going strong near Ruckinge south of Tonbridge on 2 July 1961. Straight-sided 3,500 gallon tender just like many N class. D.C. Ovenden, ColourRail

Below. 31822 at Ashford on 14 June 1960. The smoke deflectors have a different shape because there was no curved drop at the front of the N1 running plate; the oblong handhold and grab iron were thus positioned somewhat differently. It was April 1962 before 31822 got AWS, after which it saw just seven months of further service. D.C. Ovenden, ColourRail

N1
31876

To traffic as A876 3/1930
Renumbered 1876, 31876, no dates

Works

10/8/32	14 steel stays riveted over and 14 nuts renewed 110 small tubes expanded and rebeaded
17/5/33	32 steel stays replaced by copper Set new small tubes 'Howell and Co'
12/4/34	82 new small tubes
4/12/36	34 steel stays replaced by copper All small tubes expanded and rebeaded
23/10/40	166 steel stays replaced by copper set , new small tubes "Talbot and Stead"; large tubes repaired, steel with copper ends
25/9/48	525 copper stays renewed New firebox Set new small tubes 'Howells and Co' Set new large tubes new steel with copper ends
15/2/49	Back fusible plug renewed
26/10/50	80 copper stays riveted over 260 nuts renewed 173 new small tubes 'Talbot and Stead' 21 new large tubes
15/5/52-5/6/52**HI**	150 nuts renewed Internal Tube 17 studs fitted in laps 173 new small tubes 'Tubes Ltd'
9/2/54-6/3/54**GO**	133,157
14/7/55-19/8/55**HI**	42,459
28/5/57-15/6/57**LI-HI**	94,443
30/10/57-16/11/57**return**	104,148
6/4/59-1/5/59**GO**	141,040 New type CI (cast iron) firebars
22/11/60-29/12/60**LI-HI**	43,316 AWS part fitted 154 copper stays riveted over 236 nuts renewed 173 new small tubes 'Tube Products' electrically welded
6/2/61-10/2/61**NC**	46,546 Casing back lhs fracture welded

Tender
No.3101 no date

Boilers
No.990 from new
No.993 17/5/33
No.1085 23/10/40
No.1028 25/9/48
No.995 14/7/55
No.992 22/11/60

Allocations
22/3/30 New Cross Gate
28/12/35 Bricklayers Arms
28/3/42 Tonbridge
21/4/45 Bricklayers Arms
14/7/45 Hither Green
15/6/46 Tonbridge
21/2/48 St Leonards
5/8/50 Hither Green
14/6/59 Tonbridge
30/6/62 Stewarts Lane

Withdrawn 11/62 Cut up at Eastleigh Works w/e 26/10/63
NB Limited records available for 31876; all Works visits to Ashford Works unless stated

31876 near St Mary Cray with a down Kent Coast service on 13 June 1959, the last Saturday of steam passenger working on the line before EMUs took over. The loco still had a couple of years at Tonbridge and was regularly back on the line on freight. The N1s (not 31822 though) had 4,000 gallon tenders which were straight sided but otherwise wholly unlike the similar-looking tenders on the Ns. Peter Groom.

31876 (it got AWS in 1960) at Tonbridge shed on 26 May 1963. All the N1s had been at Tonbridge and were transferred *en bloc* to Stewarts Lane in June 1962; similarly they were all withdrawn from there at the end of that year, rendering the class 'extinct' in one blow. 31876 had, however, made its way back to Tonbridge before then, only to fail; it stood on this spot intact for some time but now the rods are off ready for their owner to be towed to Eastleigh for scrapping, months after 'official' withdrawal from – Stewarts Lane. Peter Groom.

N1
31877

To traffic as A877 on 4/4/30
Renumbered 1877 25/3/33; 31877 4/6/49

Works

22/2/33-25/3/33**A**	63,341	274 nuts renewed Set new small tubes 'Howells and Co'
9/7/34**C**		New Cross Gate 30 nuts renewed 33 new small tubes
23/1/35-15/4/35**C**	44,566	Extension of mileage 5,000 393 steel stays renewed 86 nuts renewed 34 new small tubes 'Talbot and Stead'
21/10/35-4/12/35**C**	53,453	Brighton 20 copper stays riveted over 2 tube holes bushed 41 new small tubes
5/6/36-23/7/36**A**	63,587	New cylinders
16/3/37-5/5/37**C**	18,683	
5/1/39-8/2/39**C**	56,743	Class plate fitted Extension of mileage 10,000
24/7/39-23/8/39**C**	66,703	Bricklayers Arms
21/10/39-21/11/39**A**	69,790	
27/5/40-23/7/40**C**	12,544	
30/7/42-29/8/42**B**	61,441	Extension of mileage 15,000
2/6/44-22/7/44**A**	100,676	
8/6/45-28/7/45**C**	21,163	
24/12/46-25/1/47**B**	51,536	
3/5/49-4/6/49**A**	96,529	
4/7/50-25/7/50**HC**	29,140	
2/12/50-3/1/51		Hither Green
5/6/52-27/6/52**HI**	74,978	
5/9/52-26/9/52**Return**		
14/12/53-12/1/54**LC**	108,223	Bricklayers Arms
25/2/55-23/4/55**GO**	135,382	Reverser spring gear fitted
30/4/56-30/5/56**LC**	35,925	Hither Green
8/6/56-28/6/56**LC**	35,925	
8/5/57-25/5/57**LI-HI**	61,599	
28/4/58-10/5/58**LC**	90,215	
17/6/59-18/7/59**GO**	120,255	New type CI firebars 705 nuts renewed New Firebox 2 fusible plugs 173 new small tubes Stewart and Lloyds' electically welded
7/12/60-12/1/61**LC**	39,272	Set new small tubes 'Tube Products'
17/10/61-11/11/61**LI-HI**	62,405	AWS part fitted 55 copper stays riveted over 266 nuts renewed Firehole 15 rivets caulked

Tender
No.3102 from new

Boilers
No.993 from new
No.1025 25/3/33
No.1041 23/7/36
No.1073 21/11/39
No.1017 22/7/44
No.939 4/6/49
No.1073 24/3/55
No.1025 18/7/59

Allocations
19/4/30 New Cross Gate
28/12/35 Bricklayers Arms
28/3/42 Tonbridge
21/4/45 Bricklayers Arms
26/4/45 Hither Green
15/6/46 Tonbridge
21/2/48 St Leonards
14/6/59 Tonbridge
30/6/62 Stewarts Lane

Withdrawn 17/11/62 Cut up at Eastleigh Works w/e 24/8/63
All works visits to Ashford Works unless stated

31877 continuing its turn (see also page 40) at St Leonards MPD on 9 August 1956; the prominent casing along the running plate by the firebox was another difference compared to the Ns. Present both sides, it covered the brackets attached to the top of the frame and the side of the firebox. These bore the weight of the rear of the boiler and firebox, with allowance made for expansion. transporttreasury

31877 at Hither Green MPD on 6 June 1959; the front sandbox could hardly have been more prominent on the three cylinder moguls – reminiscent, as mentioned earlier, of an industrial saddle tank. R.C. Riley, transporttreasury

N1
31878

To traffic as A878 on 11/4/30
Renumbered 1878 13/1/34; 31878 6/1/49

Works

3/7/31-7/7/31**D**		Bricklayers Arms
14/11/32-14/1/33**C**	56,435	
6/12/33-13/1/34**A**	71,398	Copper Tube 30 studs fitted Set new small tubes 'Chesterfield Tube Co'
28/5/35-21/6/35**D**	35,517	620 copper stays riveted over
29/10/35-6/12/35**C**	53,453	Bricklayers Arms Copper Tube seams caulked
10/9/36-5/11/36**C**	61,094	5 tube holes bushed 132 new small tubes 'Tubes Ltd' other small tubes expanded and rebeaded
28/5/37-9/7/37**A**	73,541	349 steel stays and 531 copper renewed Copper Tube 12 studs fitted Set new small tubes, 'Howell and Co'
29/6/39-4/8/39**C**	46,656	Class plate fitted 300 copper stays riveted over 25 new small tubes 'Howell and Co'
5/1/40-24/1/40**D**	57,265	Bricklayers Arms
12/3/40-16/4/40**A**	59,696	
31/12/41-3/2/42**C**	46,116	Extension of mileage 10,000
20/10/43-24/11/43**A**	86,968	811 copper stays renewed and 304 riveted over Set new small tubes 'Talbot and Stead'
20/11/45-15/12/45**C**		Hither Green Retubed
6/2/47-15/4/47**A**	81,311	Copper Tube 101 studs fitted Set new small tubes 'Talbot and Stead'
25/11/48-6/1/49**B**	43,651	21 large tubes repaired steel with copper ends
31/7/50-15/9/50**HC**		New Firebox 173 new small tubes 'Talbot and Stead'
27/11/50-22/12/50**NC**	73,244	
5/5/52-23/5/52**HI**	108,768	2 fusible plugs 173 new small tubes 'Tubes Ltd'
19/6/53-13/7/53**LC**	138,434	350 copper stays riveted over 13 studs fitted in Tubeplate lap 173 new small tubes
3/11/54-25/11/54**GO**	177,101	355 steel stays and 355 nuts renewed 173 new small tubes 'Howells and Co'
7/4/56-5/5/56**LC**		Bricklayers Arms 173 new small tubes 'Stewart and Lloyds' electrically welded
22/8/56-31/8/56**LC**	51,865	No boiler work
27/8/57-21/9/57**GO**	81,776	173 new small tubes 'Tube Products'
13/2/59-7/3/59**LC**	41,430	522 copper stays riveted over 3 large tubes repaired
14/10/59-7/11/59**LI-HI**	62,130	New type CI (cast iron) firebars 589 copper stays riveted over 2 fusible plugs 32 new small tubes
16/6/60-29/6/60**NC-LC**	76,993	
2/12/60-7/1/61**LC-HC**	91,697	AWS part fitted 249 copper stays renewed and 270 riveted over 173 new small tubes 'Stewart and Lloyds'

Tender
No.3103 from new

Boilers
No.991 from new
No.940 13/1/34
No.993 9/7/37
No.1059 16/4/40
No.1038 24/11/43
No.1027 15/4/47
No.870 15/9/50
No.1032 25/11/54
No.1027 12/9/57

Allocations
19/4/30 New Cross Gate
13/7/35 Eastbourne
28/12/35 Bricklayers Arms
28/3/42 Tonbridge
21/4/45 Bricklayers Arms
26/4/45 Hither Green
14/6/47 Tonbridge
28/12/47 Hither Green
14/6/59 Tonbridge
30/6/62 Stewarts Lane

Withdrawn 17/11/62 Cut up at Eastleigh Works w/e 31/8/63
All works visits to Ashford Works unless stated

Top. 31878 with a short if heavy freight, at Vale Rise bridge, Tonbridge, 10 September 1959. RailOnline

Middle. 31878 snakes into the up platform at Paddock Wood on 10 June 1961. It would not necessarily be bound for London, and might terminate at Tonbridge, maybe shunt into the sidings, then form another service to London, or Redhill, or 'loco to shed' at Tonbridge. The stock is a Maunsell restriction 4 three set, PMV utility van then a BR Mk 1 3-set. B. Wadey transporttreasury

Below. 31878 at Ashford, coming in from either the Hastings line or the carriage sidings, possibly to form the next stopper to Tonbridge. BR Mk 1 3-set plus Maunsell restriction 1 stock, by the look of it, probably a 4-coach set.

N1
31879

To traffic as A879 on 17/4/30
Renumbered 1879 2/12/33; 31879 29/1/49

Works

1/12/32-7/1/33**B**	47,820	Extension of mileage 5,000
30/3/33**D**		New Cross Gate Stays renewed
7/7/33-28/7/33**D**	57,298	
27/10/33-2/12/33**A**	61,530	
1/5/35-24/5/35**C**	34,186	
30/4/36-14/5/36**D**		Brighton
5/6/36-13/7/36**B**	54,589	Extension of mileage 5,000
14/5/37-24/6/37**A**	77,551	
16/12/38-4/1/39**D**	45,077	Brighton
6/6/39-30/6/39**C**	58,326	Class plate fitted
13/11/39-12/12/39**B**	69,846	Extension of mileage 15,000
26/11/40-24/12/40**A**	95,355	100 copper stays riveted over 303 nuts renewed Set new small tubes 'Howells and Co'
18/9/41-22/10/41**C**	16,000	Brighton 74 nuts renewed 6 small tubes removed and hole plugged
17/4/43-19/5/43**C**	51,746	Extension of mileage 10,000 100 nuts renewed 143 small tubes repaired
25/6/43-25/8/43**D**	53,171	86 monel metal stays replaced by copper
19/9/44-20/3/45**A**	78,275	Brighton
5/7/47-31/7/47**C**		
22/9/47**D**	57,050	
13/12/48-29/1/49**A**	87,400	
12/10/50-3/11/50**HC**	43,592	
28/2/51-20/3/51		Hither Green
7/7/52-25/7/52**GO**	82,953	Set new small tubes 'Tubes Ltd'
1/1/54-25/1/54	41,077	Hither Green
1/10/54-23/10/54**HI**	59,507	New type injectors fitted 200 copper stays riveted over 108 nuts renewed 18 studs fitted in laps 32 new small tubes 141 rebeaded
3/10/55-28/10/55	87,785	Hither Green
2/12/55-9/12/55**NC**	88,446	Casing Back fracture in right side welded
15/8/56-8/9/56**GO**	110,440	
7/5/58-5/6/58**LC**	50,435	Hither Green
11/12/58-3/1/59**LI**	66,503	New type firebars
21/1/60-6/2/60**LC**	94,067	
10/11/60-4/1/61**LC-GO**	112,624	AWS part fitted New type CI firebars
10/4/62-5/5/62**LC**	36,090	

Tender
No.3104 from new

Boilers
No.992 from new
No.1000 2/12/33
No.894 24/6/37
No.1066 24/12/40
No.1073 20/3/45
No.1156 29/1/49
No.1036 25/7/52
No.991 8/9/56

Allocations
19/4/30 New Cross Gate
13/7/35 Eastbourne
28/12/35 Tonbridge
21/5/38 Stewarts Lane
15/6/40 Tonbridge
21/4/45 Bricklayers Arms
14/7/45 Hither Green
14/6/59 Tonbridge
30/6/62 Stewarts Lane

Withdrawn 17/11/62 Cut up at Eastleigh Works w/e 7/12/63
All works visits to Ashford Works unless stated

31879 at home at Hither Green in the 1950s; all the three cylinder moguls had single slidebars. Initial Photographics

31879 at Doleham, on 16 September 1961. Doleham Halt was actually between Ore and Winchelsea and opened in 1907 to be served by the new SECR railmotor service from Hastings to Rye. The set is a narrow bodied restriction 0 Hastings line set, one of 213-216, by this date formed of two brake thirds and a composite. By this time there were few restriction 0 sets remaining (probably just these) as the main Tonbridge to Hastings line service was by then in the hands of the diesel units. However, there were still a couple of loco hauled trains on the line, mostly overnight/early morning so the sets were also used between Hastings and Ashford. D.C. Ovenden, ColourRail

N1
31880

To traffic as A880 on 1/11/30
Renumbered 1880 22/7/33; 31880 29/9/48

Works

18/2/31		New Cross Gate Superheater tube renewed
14/6/33-22/7/33**A**	53,290	
4/4/35-16/5/35**C**	39,892	Extension of mileage 5,000
14/11/35-20/12/35**C**	51,343	Extension of mileage 10,000
12/8/36-9/10/36**B**	68,260	Brighton. Extension of mileage 5,000
16/8/37-22/9/37**A**	93,702	
18/8/39-21/9/39**B**	54,386	Class plate fitted Extension of mileage 15,000
1/11/40-4/11/40**D**	84,683	
4/3/41-4/4/41**A**	91,149	
10/12/42-13/1/43**C**	42,871	Extension of mileage 5,000
14/10/43-20/11/43**C**		Ashford shed
28/3/44-22/4/44**D**	70,694	
17/11/44-3/1/45**C**		Bricklayers Arms
23/3/45-28/4/45**A**	88,578	
23/12/45-16/1/46**C**		Nine Elms
21/10/47-9/12/47	66,433	Brighton Extension of mileage 5,000
10/9/48-29/9/48**D**	83,517	
15/7/49-2/9/49**A**	102,576	200 copper stays riveted over Internal Tube 34 rivets replaced by studs Set new small tubes 'Howells and Co'
4/12/51-4/1/52**HI**		47 studs fitted in Lap welded Set new small tubes 'Tubes Ltd'
18/3/54-10/4/54**GO**		109,170 1,012 copper stays and 444 roof nuts renewed Set new small tubes 'Howells and Co'
4/8/54-27/8/54**HC-LC**	9,396	No boiler work
19/8/55-2/9/55**LC**	35,273	No boiler work
17/9/55-17/10/55**LI**	35,618	Hither Green
2/11/55-19/11/55**NC-HC**	36,414	
25/4/57-18/5/57**LI-HI**	78,463	303 copper stays renewed and 213 riveted over 2 fusible plugs Set new small tubes 'Universal' 15 rivets in Firehole
11/11/58-22/11/58**LC** welded	118,149	400 copper stays riveted over 173 new small tubes 'Stewart and Lloyds' electrically
15/9/59-10/10/59**GO**	142,378	New type CI firebars 175 copper and 650 monel metal stays plus 650 nuts renewed 2 fusible plugs 173 new small tubes 'Tube Products' electically welded Foundation Ring 137 rivets
8/12/59-24/12/59**LC**	3,607	
24/5/61-24/6/61**LI**	47,829	150 copper stays riveted over 277 nuts renewed 2 fusible plugs 173 new small tubes electically welded 18 second hand large tubes

Tender
No.3105 from new

Boilers
No.994 from new
No.986 22/7/33
No.891 22/9/37
No.911 4/4/41
No.869 28/4/45
No.860 2/9/49
No.900 10/4/54
No.995 10/10/59

Allocations
29/11/30 New Cross Gate
13/7/35 Eastbourne
28/12/35 Tonbridge
21/5/38 Stewarts Lane
15/6/40 Tonbridge
21/4/45 Bricklayers Arms
14/7/45 Hither Green
14/6/59 Tonbridge
30/6/62 Stewarts Lane

Withdrawn 17/11/62 Cut up at Eastleigh Works w/e 16/11/63
All works visits to Ashford Works unless stated

31880 at Redhill shed on 4 August 1955. The N1s remained resolutely of the Eastern and Central lines, and were never based in The West. It was also the only N1 never to be equipped with AWS. Initial Photographics.

Endpiece

The Way Ahead. U Mogul 31637 at Southampton on 26 December 1956. The U and U1 2-6-0s, together with much about the preceding River tanks, are described in *The Book of the Southern Moguls Part Two U, U1 Classes* due end 2018. Paul Strong.